MapPoint's Standard Toolbar

Button	Name	Function
	New	Restores MapPoint to its default view (as shown in Figure 2-1) so that you can create a new map, set of driving directions, or whatever.
	Open	Click this button to open a MapPoint file stored on your computer.
	Save	The first time you click this button after a new map or route is generated, you will be prompted to name the file before it is saved. When you click this button while viewing a saved map, the current file is saved under the same filename.
	Print	This button lets you print a quick copy of the current map view using the default Print settings (one copy with normal resolution produced on your system's default printer).
	Page Setup	Click here to set the paper size and orientation as well as the margins.
	Cut	After selecting an element, you can click Cut to remove it and hold it in the Clipboard. The item can then be pasted into another application (like a Word document).
	Copy	Again, the selected item is put into the Clipboard for future use; however, this time the item is copied instead of cut, so the original stays in place.
	Paste	This button takes the selected item residing in your Clipboard and puts it into a place you select.
	Undo	Click this button to undo the last action you performed. The button is *grayed out* (unavailable) if the last action cannot be undone.
	Redo	This button reverses the action of the Undo command, and it too will gray out if the action can't be redone.
	Legend and Overview	Clicking this button toggles the Legend and Overview pane open and closed. It's open by default, but closing it can increase the amount of map territory visible on-screen.
	Territories	Clicking this button launches the Create Territories Wizard, or opens or closes the Territories Manager pane if you've already created territories on the map.
	Find Nearby Places	After you've selected a point on the map, click this button to see what's nearby. By default, MapPoint searches for places within one mile of the chosen location.
	Route Planner	One click opens the Route Planner pane from which you can begin planning your journey.
	Driving Directions	This button toggles the Directions pane open and closed. The pane is closed by default because it remains empty until driving directions are generated from the Route Planner.
	Link Data Wizard	If you want to link external data to a map, this is the perfect starting point. Click this button to specify to which file you want MapPoint to link. You'll learn more about linking to your data source in chapters 8, 9, and 10.
	Import Data Wizard	When you're ready to begin analyzing external data, click this button to tell MapPoint where to find the data you want to examine. We'll discuss the ins and outs of importing data in chapters 8, 9, and 10.
	Data Mapping Wizard	This is the tool you use to create those fancy Sized Pie Chart maps, Shaded Area maps, and Multiple Symbol Pushpin maps.

(continued)

MapPoint® For Dummies®

Cheat Sheet

MapPoint's Standard Toolbar *(continued)*

Button	Name	Function
	Export to Excel	After you've specified which map data you want to export, click this button to have the chosen records exported to an Excel worksheet.
	Show Information	This toggle button turns off and on the display of additional information about a selected place or pushpin.
	Search the Web	Select a place on the map and click this button to connect to the World Wide Web and open an MSN Search page displaying a set of links about the selected place.
	Drawing Toolbar	The Drawing toolbar is shown by default, but you may want to hide it to free up more display space on-screen. Click the Drawing Toolbar button to turn the element off and on.
	Location and Scale Toolbar	This gray bar above the map screen displays the location and distance scale of the currently displayed map. By clicking the Location and Scale Toolbar button, you can hide the scale that appears above your map pane by default. If the map's scale does not appear above the map pane, clicking the Location and Scale Toolbar button will display it.
	Help	Click here to access MapPoint 2002's Help topics. You can browse these files by Contents or Index, or by typing a question in the Answer Wizard.

When You Can't Use Undo/Redo

Some actions can't be reversed using the Undo/Redo commands. For the actions marked with an asterisk (*) here, you will also be unable to undo any action taken before that action. These actions include:

New*

Open*

Save

Exit*

Cut sets* (cutting individual objects can be reversed)

Delete sets* (deleting individual objects can be reversed)

Paste Link*

Link Data*

Update Linked Sets*

New data mapping of demographic data*

Match Records*

COM Add-ins (the underlying action may clear the Undo stack)

Show or hide the Territory Manager pane*

Create territory group*

Delete territory group*

Delete territory*

Import Data*

Map Style

Flat map or Globe at High Zoom Level

Show or Hide Places

Hungry Minds™

For Dummies: Bestselling Book Series for Beginners

MapPoint® FOR DUMMIES®

by BJ Holtgrewe and Jill T. Freeze

Hungry Minds™

Best-Selling Books • Digital Downloads • e-Books • Answer Networks • e-Newsletters • Branded Web Sites • e-Learning

New York, NY ◆ Cleveland, OH ◆ Indianapolis, IN

MapPoint® For Dummies®

Published by
Hungry Minds, Inc.
909 Third Avenue
New York, NY 10022
www.hungryminds.com
www.dummies.com

Copyright © 2002 Hungry Minds, Inc. All rights reserved. No part of this book, including interior design, cover design, and icons, may be reproduced or transmitted in any form, by any means (electronic, photocopying, recording, or otherwise) without the prior written permission of the publisher.

Library of Congress Control Number: 2001092926

ISBN: 0-7645-1623-X

Printed in the United States of America

10 9 8 7 6 5 4 3 2 1

1B/QX/QR/QS/IN

Distributed in the United States by Hungry Minds, Inc.

Distributed by CDG Books Canada Inc. for Canada; by Transworld Publishers Limited in the United Kingdom; by IDG Norge Books for Norway; by IDG Sweden Books for Sweden; by IDG Books Australia Publishing Corporation Pty. Ltd. for Australia and New Zealand; by TransQuest Publishers Pte Ltd. for Singapore, Malaysia, Thailand, Indonesia, and Hong Kong; by Gotop Information Inc. for Taiwan; by ICG Muse, Inc. for Japan; by Intersoft for South Africa; by Eyrolles for France; by International Thomson Publishing for Germany, Austria and Switzerland; by Distribuidora Cuspide for Argentina; by LR International for Brazil; by Galileo Libros for Chile; by Ediciones ZETA S.C.R. Ltda. for Peru; by WS Computer Publishing Corporation, Inc., for the Philippines; by Contemporanea de Ediciones for Venezuela; by Express Computer Distributors for the Caribbean and West Indies; by Micronesia Media Distributor, Inc. for Micronesia; by Chips Computadoras S.A. de C.V. for Mexico; by Editorial Norma de Panama S.A. for Panama; by American Bookshops for Finland.

For general information on Hungry Minds' products and services please contact our Customer Care Department within the U.S. at 800-762-2974, outside the U.S. at 317-572-3993 or fax 317-572-4002.

For sales inquiries and reseller information, including discounts, premium and bulk quantity sales, and foreign-language translations, please contact our Customer Care Department at 800-434-3422, fax 317-572-4002, or write to Hungry Minds, Inc., Attn: Customer Care Department, 10475 Crosspoint Boulevard, Indianapolis, IN 46256.

For information on licensing foreign or domestic rights, please contact our Sub-Rights Customer Care Department at 212-884-5000.

For information on using Hungry Minds' products and services in the classroom or for ordering examination copies, please contact our Educational Sales Department at 800-434-2086 or fax 317-572-4005.

For press review copies, author interviews, or other publicity information, please contact our Public Relations Department at 317-572-3168 or fax 317-572-4168.

For authorization to photocopy items for corporate, personal, or educational use, please contact Copyright Clearance Center, 222 Rosewood Drive, Danvers, MA 01923, or fax 978-750-4470.

Hungry Minds™ is a trademark of Hungry Minds, Inc.

About the Authors

BJ Holtgrewe is a Senior Product Manager/Technical Evangelist in the Microsoft Business Tools Division. He spends every waking hour spreading the gospel of Microsoft's MapPoint technology to customers, developers, software vendors, Microsoft Solution Providers, and almost anyone else who will listen — you will have lasting memories if you sit next to him on a long flight! As a member of Geography Business Unit, BJ helps shape the vision for Microsoft products that have geographic and location-aware functionality. Prior to his Technical Evangelist role he was a Product Planner for MapPoint. When he first joined the team he served as the Lead Program Manager in the Microsoft Map Building System team. BJ is currently immersed in Microsoft's .NET initiative and holds two patents in the area of location awareness. He is a speaker at numerous conferences and seminars. BJ also serves on the Editorial Advisory Board of *Geographic World* magazine. Before life at Microsoft, he was a project and design consultant and worked for software companies on the East Coast and in Europe. In his spare time he loves to travel the world (someone needs to check the accuracy of the maps!). He has an incurable appetite for European professional cycling and old printed maps. Even earlier in his history he was an avid skydiver instructor, internationally rated skydiving judge, and underwater search-and-recovery diver. You can reach BJ at bjholt@microsoft.com or check out his personal Web site at www.dataweave.com.

Jill T. Freeze is a freelance management consultant who has worked with such organizations as the John F. Kennedy Center for the Performing Arts, the National Endowment for the Arts, the Smithsonian Institute, and the White House. Having used computers extensively for more than a decade for work and play, Jill finally decided to put her experience to good use writing computer books. She has written ten well-received titles that have garnered rave reviews from readers and reviewers worldwide and have been translated into a number of languages. Recent books include *SAMS Teach Yourself Computer Basics in 24 Hours,* Third Edition (SAMS, 2001), *Savvy Online Shopping* (Microsoft Press, 2000), and *Peter Norton's Complete Guide to Microsoft Office 2000* (SAMS, 1999). You'll also find her articles in *MS OfficePRO* magazine. Jill is a top-rated beta tester for Microsoft who has won awards for her active participation in Internet Explorer, Office, MapPoint, and Windows beta programs. Her formal education includes a bachelor's degree, *magna cum laude*, from the University of Massachusetts at Amherst (in Arts Administration and Writing) and a master's degree from George Washington University (in Nonprofit Administration). For fun, Jill likes shopping, listening to music, playing with her four cats and Golden Retriever, writing fiction, quilting, reading a variety of fiction titles, volunteering at her children's school, watching NASCAR races, surfing the Net, playing her flute, and playing with her husband, Wayne (also a computer book author and columnist) and two children, Christopher and Samantha. Jill can be reached at JFreeze@JustPC.com, or you can visit her on the Web at www.JustPC.com.

Dedication

To the memory of Christine Rose DiTerlizzi, who left us in body but not spirit during the summer of 2001. She was always an inspiration in the way she lived and died. She embraced her path and taught others by example to work hard to accept theirs.

—BJ

To our beloved country, our leaders, the heroes and servicemen and women, and the many victims and survivors of September 11, 2001.... God Bless America!

—Jill

Author's Acknowledgments

BJ Holtgrewe: It turns out that authoring a book is the easy part. Having a quality support team at home, work, and in the form of a first-class co-author and publishing team is where the real work lies. Without the entire passionate team of program managers, developers, user assistance editors, and the dedicated management team of the Microsoft Geographic Business Unit, this book would not have been worth doing. I have the honor of working with and observing them in many long hours of designing, coding, and proofing. More important, I thank them for their energetic passion for making the MapPoint "World" a truly usable place by provided an innovative application and the essential high quality maps. The "app and map" makes writing a book on a complex topic both easier and enjoyable. Thanks for the ongoing support and direction provided by Michael Graff, John Betz, Rik Temmink, and Sandra Andrews. I also would have never been in the right place at the right time to write this book if Judith LaPlante had not taken a chance and invited me to join the MapPoint team.

Special thanks to Microsoft's Bets Greer for her expert technical review. Her in-depth domain knowledge and writing skills are apparent in the Help section of MapPoint and she was a security blanket when it came to making sure we got all the details correctly documented. Many thanks also to Greg Slayden for his technical review of Chapter 10.

The folks at Hungry Minds rock! I'm grateful to Senior Acquisitions Editor Steve Hayes for his guidance in molding the direction of the book. Great thanks must also go to Editor Susan Christophersen and the entire editing and production team at Hungry Minds. Breaking in this first-time author was most likely a real challenge and their professional approach kept me motivated even into the late nights. I learned that a quality software book is just like software and more than just capturing many random thoughts and hoping that someone downstream will fill in the blanks. The editor's guidance made this undertaking a driven mission. Mark Twain was wrong.

This book was 15 months in the planning and 10 crazy weeks of intense writing. When Jill Freeze and I first discussed by e-mail teaming together as co-authors, I quickly learned to trust my instincts and just knew that she would more than carry her load. I thank her for her ever-present drive, intelligence, and always positive and friendly approach. She dissects software with the skill of a surgeon and makes the complex seem simple.

It's interesting to note that this book was almost done completely by e-mail and with only a few "get on the same page" conference calls. The team was always "virtual" and I'm still not sure what they look like! Just goes to show that with the Hungry Minds team and Jill as partners, I can write the next creation from some remote island (as long as I have a DSL connection!).

And finally many thanks are due Trip, Max, and Lynne Anne for their patient support during the frightful "I'm late with more chapters!" time-sinks that kicked the boys off the Internet while we waited for the DSL line to finally arrive at the new house and demanded "Soccer Mom" support to go the extra mile when "Soccer Dad" was pulling his hair out.

Jill T. Freeze: First, I'd like to thank BJ for giving me the opportunity to work on this book with him. I've loved MapPoint since the very first beta of the very first version, so it was a privilege to be able to write this book with a true insider from Microsoft! And of course none of it would be possible without the great crew from Hungry Minds, our awesome technical editor (Bets Greer from Microsoft), and my agent, Laura Belt.

Finally, I'd like to thank the three people who mean the most to me — my husband, Wayne Freeze (who not only writes computer books, too, but has published many magazine articles as well — some of which are about MapPoint); my 8-year old son, Christopher James; and my 7-year old daughter, Samantha Ashley. Such loving and supportive families are a must when you spend 12 to 16 hours a day behind the keyboard, and I am one lucky person to have them!

Publisher's Acknowledgments

We're proud of this book; please send us your comments through our Hungry Minds Online Registration Form located at www.dummies.com.

Some of the people who helped bring this book to market include the following:

Acquisitions, Editorial, and Media Development

Project Editor: Susan Christophersen

Senior Acquisitions Editor: Steve Hayes

Copy Editors: Susan Christophersen, Kim Darosett

Technical Editor: Bets Greer

Editorial Manager: Constance Carlisle

Permissions Editor: Carmen Krikorian

Media Development Specialist: Megan Decraene

Media Development Manager: Laura VanWinkle

Media Development Supervisor: Richard Graves

Editorial Assistants: Amanda Foxworth, Jean Rogers

Production

Project Coordinator: Dale White

Layout and Graphics: Joyce Haughey, Jackie Nicholas, Betty Schulte, Jacque Schneider, Jeremey Unger, Mary J. Virgin

Proofreaders: Laura Albert, John Greenough, Andy Hollandbeck, TECHBOOKS Production Services

Indexer: TECHBOOKS Production Services

General and Administrative

Hungry Minds Technology Publishing Group: Richard Swadley, Senior Vice President and Publisher; Mary Bednarek, Vice President and Publisher, Networking; Joseph Wikert, Vice President and Publisher, Web Development Group; Mary C. Corder, Editorial Director, Dummies Technology; Andy Cummings, Publishing Director, Dummies Technology; Barry Pruett, Publishing Director, Visual/Graphic Design

Hungry Minds Manufacturing: Ivor Parker, Vice President, Manufacturing

Hungry Minds Marketing: John Helmus, Assistant Vice President, Director of Marketing

Hungry Minds Production for Branded Press: Debbie Stailey, Production Director

Hungry Minds Sales: Michael Violano, Vice President, International Sales and Sub Rights

Contents at a Glance

Cartoons at a Glance

By Rich Tennant

page 37

page 317

page 7

page 205

page 99

page 237

Cartoon Information:
Fax: 978-546-7747
E-Mail: richtennant@the5thwave.com
World Wide Web: www.the5thwave.com

Table of Contents

· ·

Introduction

- -

*T*he creation and use of maps have helped humankind advance through the ages. In modern times, governments and businesses have discovered the power of business mapping.

Unfortunately the traditional modern-day approach to the problem usually requires the expense of a high-end Graphic Information System (GIS), the purchase and/or the construction of semi-accurate spatial datasets (very large digital representations of roads, political and administrative boundaries, bodies of water and places, and so on) and high-powered computers to store the gigabytes of spatial data. Then to top it all off, these organizations need to hire Ph.D. cartographers who know how to make this whole thing work.

Of course, that was until you happened upon a copy of MapPoint. Microsoft MapPoint is your ticket to a journey of everyday business mapping just as gas station maps were the key to your cross-country family vacations.

With MapPoint maps, you can gain valuable geographic insight in the following ways:

- Illustrate business information with the added location-based insight.
- Identify business trends with the insight provided by seeing them on a map.
- Effectively communicate information and trends geographically.
- Turn plain, locationless pie charts into geographic gems.
- Take those thousands of rows and columns of data and gain insight that only a map can provide.

About This Book

We want this book to be useful for the novice as well as the intermediate user who spends his or her days working at a desk or on a laptop just trying to get real things done. We also explain the technical aspects of MapPoint to make sure that the techies and (GIS) users can not only gain insight into the application but also quickly come up to speed on the MapPoint object model and the new ActiveX control.

We hope you enjoy this book as much as we enjoyed writing it, and we would love to hear about your passions and experiences with successful, everyday business mapping.

How This Book Is Organized

Although it might be very tempting to dive right in (or should we say drive right in), getting a view of MapPoint from a 50,000 feet level will help you build a foundation from which you can get the most out of the business maps.

Part 1: Introducing MapPoint

Think of the early sections of this book as a Geography 101 refresher course that also shows you the basics of how MapPoint works. In this part, you find out why MapPoint is the most underrated member of the Microsoft Office family. You also discover the new features in the version and gain insight in how to navigate and understand the various parts that makeup the MapPoint workspace.

Part II: Test Driving MapPoint

In this part, you find out how to start using MapPoint. You see how to find locations and mark them with a Pushpin, as well as how to find points of interest (POIs), build a set of driving directions, and generate an entire route that MapPoint will plan in terms of minimizing your driving time spent and keeping fuel costs down.

Part III: Presenting and Analyzing Information with MapPoint

In this part, you find out how to customize a map's appearance and to extract certain parts that you can share with others. This part deals with printing and distributing your maps via e-mail and publishing your maps on the Web. You'll also see just how easy it is to incorporate these maps into PowerPoint presentations, Publisher newsletters and brochures, and the like. Further, this part helps you use MapPoint to make sense of seemingly random numbers in Excel and Access files and shed a whole new light on data you may have been collecting for years.

Part IV: Using MapPoint with Other Products

In this part, you find out how to take advantage of the tight integration of MapPoint with other Office 2000 and Office XP applications. You get an explanation as how to use a Global Positioning System (GPS) device connected to your laptop so that you can track your movement across the map. You also get the scoop on Pocket Streets, the mapping companion of MapPoint that works on the Pocket PC.

Part V: Programming MapPoint

This part provides the programmers in the audience with the jump start you need for extending the functionality on MapPoint through the new extended object model. These chapters present Visual Basic code samples demonstrating how to create COM Add-ins to extend MapPoint functionality and projects that demonstrate how to use the MapPoint ActiveX Control to extend your own mission-critical applications. After reading these sections, you will truly gain control of the world!

Note: Although nonprogrammers can gain insight into how MapPoint can be extended, the chapters in Part V are directed to the reader who has a basic understanding of Visual Basic programming

You can find the code for all the projects presented in these chapters on CD1 in the code samples folder.

Part VI: The Part of Tens

In this final section, you find out about techniques that will help you tweek and exploit MapPoint features to increase the value of your efforts in ways that just did not fit well in the earlier sections of this book. You also gain some insight into the many types of business uses that can benefit from the power of MapPoint.

Who Should Read This Book?

If you don't know what a Geographic Information System is, don't fret. We wrote this book to be used by beginners and intermediate users alike. Business mapping may seem to be difficult and complicated, but this book is dedicated to proving that it isn't.

You don't need to be a cartographer or statistician to use this book. But if you are a cartographer, you can still benefit from this book in that MapPoint is not your father's GIS. It's much easier to use.

Foolish Assumptions

To use this book, we assume that you know a few things about your computer and your Microsoft Office applications. You also need to have a working knowledge of Visual Basic programming, but only if you want to use the code samples in Part V.

To get the most out of *MapPoint For Dummies,* we presume that you:

✔ Have Microsoft MapPoint, Microsoft Access, and/or Excel 97/2000/2002 on your Windows 98/Me/NT/2000 or XP computer (it's okay if you have the complete Office suite; in fact, we explore some neat tricks and Smart Tag features that make MapPoint work together with Microsoft Word 2002 and Excel 2002.) It's also okay if you don't already have MapPoint! We provide a 60-day evaluation copy on the CDs at the back of this book.

✔ Know the basics of using Microsoft Office applications (most importantly, Access and Excel).

✔ Have a basic working knowledge of Visual Basic 6.0 programming to make use both of the programming power provided by MapPoint and to use the projects and code presented in the Part V.

Conventions Used in This Book

Understanding some conventions used throughout the book will make life easier. When we tell you to *select* something, it means to highlight an item by clicking it. This applies to menu items, items in list boxes, and places on a map or in the map legend. To *click* an item, you press and release the left mouse button on a specific location, button, or other item on the screen. *Right-click* refers to clicking with the right mouse button. To *double-click* means to click the left mouse button twice in rapid succession.

Sometimes we refer to key combinations, which means that you hold down one key while pressing another. We indicate these key combinations with a plus sign, like so:

Ctrl+Z

which means to hold down the Ctrl key while pressing the Z key. In MapPoint, this restores the map to its previous state, just before you made the last change to it.

A sequence of menu commands appears with an arrow showing the progression of commands. So, for example, the sequence

File⇨Open

means that you first click File and then Open.

Icons Used in This Book

The icons that appear in the margins of this book are meant to draw your attention to text that we want you to pay special attention to for various reasons. The icons we use are the following:

This icon indicates a new feature in this version of MapPoint.

Remember icons are designed as gentle reminders pointing you in a direction that will get you to success more quickly.

In a few places in this book, we mark a few special points worth noting with this icon.

The Tip Icon indicates information and insight that will save you time and energy as you see how to get MapPoint to do what you want it to do.

If you are a true believer in the power of Dummies books, you will stop and read slowly as you pass the warning icons. Think of them as road signs that can guide you in the dark down a curvy dark road and can keep you out of the ditch. You could go fast and just ignore them, and you could also close your eyes and drive your car 100 mph on a mountain road!

We marked all the code samples with this icon to point you in the direction of CD1 and the code samples folder. You can type them in from scratch or you can copy them over to your hard drive and save the time of having to prove that you know how to type.

Part I
Introducing
MapPoint

The 5th Wave   By Rich Tennant

©RICHTENNANT

"Oh, Scarecrow! Without MapPoint on your laptop, how will we find anything in Oz?"

In this part . . .

*L*earning the ropes of a new software program can be tough enough without adding the confusion of what the program can really do for you, which button does what, and so on. In this part of the book, we attempt to wipe away that confusion for good so that you can dive in and put MapPoint to work for you.

After reading these chapters, your head will be filled with ideas of how to use MapPoint on the job and at home. As an added bonus, you may even be able to wow your boss with all kinds of resource-saving tips. And if you are the boss, we guarantee that you'll find ways to look at your business in a whole new light.

Chapter 1

Presenting Microsoft MapPoint

· ·

· ·

At first glance, you may confuse MapPoint with the slew of trip-planning software lining store shelves. Although it's true that MapPoint can do most everything these programs can do and better, it goes far beyond that. Where Microsoft Excel turns columns and rows of numbers into meaningful charts and graphs, MapPoint turns raw data into graphically significant maps from which you can gain some pretty amazing insights.

Whether you want to wow your board of directors at an upcoming meeting, plan for the expansion of your company, or analyze your business's sales, MapPoint can help you in ways you may have never even imagined.

You may want to take a few moments to install and play with the trial version of MapPoint 2002 included with this book. After you've spent some time getting to know MapPoint and reading this book, we think you'll see why MapPoint 2002 may very well be the best Microsoft Office application you probably haven't been using.

What's the Point of Using MapPoint?

We're the first to admit that MapPoint can do all kinds of neat stuff, but unless that neat stuff has some value to you . . . well, who cares, right? The following scenarios illustrate a few of the ways that you may be able to use MapPoint in your personal and professional lives:

✔ As your company's tech support guru, you're summoned to an important client's office to handle a major crisis. Of course you haven't been to the client's office before, and he's steaming mad. This is no time to pull out your dog-eared atlas or take a leisurely drive through town in search of his office; you need to get there yesterday! Let MapPoint save the day.

✔ Before attending a power lunch at an out-of-the-way ethnic restaurant, you need to pick up your business partner at the airport. You can find the most time-efficient way to accomplish the task with MapPoint.

✔ Your company has decided to launch a nationwide sales force to place its products. MapPoint can help you set up territories for the reps.

✔ Business is booming, and it's clearly time to expand, but where? Feed your customer database into MapPoint and let it tell you where the biggest demand is.

✔ You're a realtor for an executive placement service and need to find a home for a client. This client also wants to be in a specific school district for her children. Present her with a MapPoint printout of available properties near the school.

✔ As the coordinator of your company's annual conference, you've hired a limo to pick up a few of the high-profile speakers (who are, incidentally, all staying at different hotels). No problem; MapPoint will show you — and the driver — how to get the job done.

✔ You want to open a new apparel store in that building you own downtown, but you're wondering whether it should carry inexpensive clothes for senior citizens or trendy fashions for socialites. Let MapPoint's demographic data help you find the best answer.

✔ You've decided to take the family along on your latest business trip, but secretly dread the inevitable "Are we there yet?" whines from the kids. With a MapPoint itinerary, the kids will always know exactly where you are. And best of all, if you take MapPoint on the road with you on a laptop or handheld computer, you can even search out the closest Burger King for those yummy ham, egg, and cheese breakfast croissants!

MapPoint facilitates more-educated business decision-making by enabling you to plot the demographics of your customers, sales trends, and the like. You can even map your information along with data from your competitors to gain powerful insight into what works and what doesn't.

Additionally, optimized route planning and scheduling help you optimize staff time and improve customer service at the same time.

But other applications can do what MapPoint does, can't they?

If you find yourself reading the scenarios in the "What's the Point of Using MapPoint?" section and saying, "Yeah, but I can already do that with [fill in the blank]," then you should know a few more things about what makes MapPoint unique.

People frequently ask how MapPoint differs from Microsoft Streets & Trips. Although both tools produce driving directions, optimized routes, and such, they're targeted at two very different types of users. Street & Trips (with its retail price of just under $45) is intended to help you get where you need to be quickly and easily. This holds true whether you're planning a family trip or the weekly route for your chimney sweep business. But routing and trip planning is all that Streets & Trips does. For some users, that may be all they want or need.

If you want to be able to take your customer data and analyze it for strategic planning or targeted advertising campaigns, then MapPoint is the tool for you. Likewise, if you want to compare your business performance to the demographic makeup of a certain area, only MapPoint can help you. Even with a price tag of $250, it's a bargain compared to the cost of hiring a professional analyst! Furthermore,

MapPoint is designed to work closely with Microsoft Office 2000 and Office XP, so incorporating your findings into a Word document, PowerPoint presentation, or Web page, or e-mailing them to a colleague is a breeze.

And if you've worked with Microsoft Excel 2000, you may wonder what makes MapPoint's data maps different from those you can build in Excel 2000. Two things stand out — MapPoint's ability to analyze data down to the street level, and the availability of demographic data in MapPoint. You see, Excel 2000 can chart data by state only, end of story. Although that may be sufficient for some tasks, it can't help you find out where in the city your customers are coming from. Likewise, Excel can't tap into a host of demographic data to lead you to a predominantly female neighborhood for your new women-only health club. MapPoint can. The capability to perform sophisticated data analysis is where MapPoint really shines.

Finally, you can integrate MapPoint into your own programs. This makes it possible to create customized maps and/or MapPoint-enabled programs specifically targeted at your needs or users.

Making data more meaningful

In some ways, MapPoint may be one of those tools you don't even realize you need yet. Try this quick experiment: Take a look at Figure 1-1. What does it tell you? It's a perfectly good spreadsheet full of numbers, but it takes a good while to make any sense of those numbers.

Figure 1-1:
Although
spread-
sheets
certainly
have their
place,
making
sense of
geographic
al
information
presented in
this format
may be
harder.

	A	B	C	D	E	F	G	H	I	J
1	State	Total Sales	Clothing	Footwear						
2	SD	588,000	230,000	358,000						
3	MN	600,000	500,000	100,000						
4	IA	320,000	1,000	319,000						
5	NE	800,000	400,000	400,000						
6	CA	5,000	2,000	3,000						
7	MA	1,000	500	500						
8	WY	25,000	15,000	10,000						
9	MT	182,000	140,000	42,000						

Microsoft Excel - salesbystate.xls

File Edit View Insert Format Tools Data Window Help Acrobat

Arial 10 B I U

A10

Sheet1 Sheet2 Sheet3

Ready NUM

Now look at the MapPoint map in Figure 1-2, generated by using the same set of numbers found in the spreadsheet. In this figure, you can easily see that maybe it's time for the Iowa store to scale back its clothing inventory and focus solely on footwear — a conclusion that's a bit more difficult and time-consuming to reach by staring at a sheet of numbers. How can you tell? Because MapPoint's legend clearly spells out what's what.

At the top of the legend for the sized pie chart map shown in Figure 1-2, you can see three circles that correspond to a state's annual sales performance: the bigger the circle, the bigger the sales compared to the other states. Below this legend, you see color-coded "pie slices" that correspond to the types of merchandise these stores sell in relation to one another. Of course, the types of legend elements that appear will vary depending on the type of data map you create, but no matter what, all your mapped elements will be labeled for easy viewing and interpretation. Furthermore, MapPoint provides screen tips (little gray boxes that display the details of the selected element) for every map element when you run your mouse pointer over the top of it.

The sized pie chart map shown in Figure 1-2 is just one of the new types of data maps available in MapPoint 2002.

The Data Map takes information from the spreadsheet and puts a new spin on it, making it an invaluable tool for marketing and business development professionals.

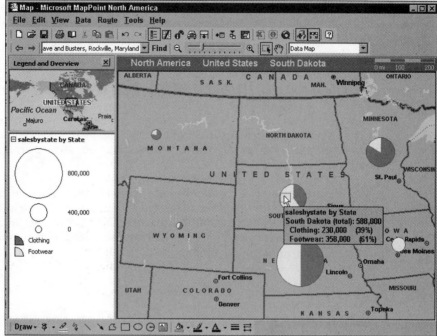

Figure 1-2:
A screen tip
gives you
the full
breakdown
when you
mouse over
a chart.

Plotting your location on a map

Show your customers and clients exactly where you're located by generating a customized map. Mark your location and then resize the map for use in direct mailings and ads, and on your Web site.

Keep in mind that in addition to Road Maps intended to be navigational aids, MapPoint can also build Terrain and Political Maps, among others, as described in Chapter 2.

Creating virtual Pushpins

You've probably seen sales or membership offices with maps tacked up on the walls. The maps are dotted with all kinds of pushpins or stickers to indicate successful sales or the physical locations of the organization's members. Well, MapPoint helps you create sets of virtual Pushpins, thus enabling you to convert those cumbersome wall-mounted maps to paper documents, PowerPoint presentations, the Web, and more.

MapPoint 2002 lets you use multiple Pushpin symbols in a single Pushpin set. You can read more about this in Chapter 4. You can also design your very own Pushpin symbol to create a truly customized Pushpin map.

Mapping demographic data

Does your business cater to higher-income families? Are you providing a service to seniors, but need to know where they can be best served? By tapping into MapPoint's demographic data, you can find your answers quickly and easily.

With business-related demographic information provided by Claritas, Inc. (for the United States) and CompuSearch (for Canada), you can find out the age, education level, income, household size, and more about the population in the selected area. In addition, you can purchase MapPoint-compatible specialized data (traffic counts for intersections, shopping center locations, consumer demand, and so on) from a variety of sources.

Evaluating potential business locations

Say you're scouting out a new location for your business. It may help to check out the competition or supporting businesses and points of interest (POIs). (Points of interest include restaurants, hotels, museums, and other places that may be of interest, as discussed in Chapter 3.) The third location of your local pizza chain may do extraordinarily well in a location near the zoo or art museum, but not if it's within two blocks of a national pizza chain.

By marking the location you want to research and telling MapPoint to display the appropriate points of interest, you can get a sense of how viable the prospective site is (see Figure 1-3).

Marking your sales territories

Need to set some boundaries for your sales force? Use MapPoint's Create Territories Wizard to do the job. If each salesperson has his or her client addresses saved in an Excel worksheet or database, you can use that information to automatically chart the territories. Conversely, you can set territories manually by drawing them on the map.

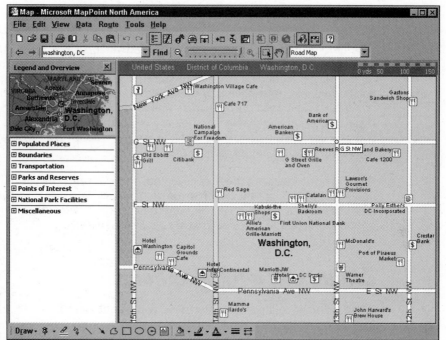

Figure 1-3:
Ahhh . . . no
shortage of
eating
places in
this town!
By zooming
in to the
location you
wish
research,
you can find
a host of
details.

The ability to define territories in MapPoint is a brand-new feature in
MapPoint 2002.

Getting driving directions

If you spend a lot of time on the road, MapPoint's driving directions and route
planning capabilities could very well save you some headaches. Whether
you're venturing into new sections of your hometown or to uncharted territory, you can get there with minimum hassle. Just plug in an address for your
starting point and one for your destination, and you're good to go! MapPoint
produces a step-by-step set of driving directions that you can share with
others via e-mail or by printing them. (To learn more about this feature,
please see Chapter 5.)

What's more, you can print out the directions in a variety of formats to meet
just about any conceivable need. Chapter 7 gives you the lowdown on the
various printout types available to you in MapPoint 2002.

Planning the best route

Whether you can plot your entire route in advance, or you need to add emergency stops on the fly, you'll appreciate MapPoint's flexible, easy-to-use Route Planner. Schedule stops at predetermined times, or have MapPoint calculate the most time-efficient route. Additionally, MapPoint can estimate how much fuel you'll need for the trip as well as the trip's overall cost. Some of these options are available whether you're planning a simple point-to-point trip or a dozen-stop corporate route. Learn more about the world of routing with MapPoint in Chapter 5.

Routing printouts are a piece of cake, too. You can print the entire route highlighted on a map, or you can create strip maps with driving directions that look similar to a Triple A TripTik. And these are just two of the printing options available to you; see Chapter 7 for more details.

Zoning out with MapPoint

When it comes to a person's alertness, zoning out can be a bad thing, but it's just the opposite with MapPoint. Do you want your account reps located within a half hour's drive of their clients? Do you own a small sub shop and want to restrict your delivery service to within a 10-minute driving radius of the restaurant?

Defining drivetime zones is available for the first time in MapPoint 2002. Drivetime Zones are covered in greater detail in Chapter 5.

Using MapPoint's drivetime zones, you can effortlessly see how far you can travel from any location in a specified amount of time. Simply choose your starting point on the map, tell MapPoint the maximum driving time for the zone, and then specify whether you want the zone area drawn behind roads or shaded in a solid color.

Monitoring your position with GPS support

MapPoint's Global Positioning System (GPS) support makes it possible to monitor your progress every step of the way. With a GPS receiver properly installed and configured on your computer, you can monitor your exact location on a MapPoint map. MapPoint checks for your location every 15 seconds and then displays it on the map so you can clearly see your progress on your journey.

You can find more information on GPS support in Chapter 12.

Taking MapPoint on the road

Taking MapPoint on the road with you may be nice, but balancing a laptop on the passenger seat can be a precarious proposition at best. And have you ever tried to look into a laptop screen in the sunshine? Forget it; you can't see a thing!

Luckily, affordable Windows CE–based palm-sized handhelds and Pocket PCs have entered the market. Because MapPoint supports Pocket Streets (a MapPoint-compatible mapping tool designed for Microsoft Windows CE-based handheld devices and PC companions), you can easily export MapPoint maps and routes to a PC handheld and take it on the road.

Read more about taking MapPoint on the road using Pocket Streets in Chapter 13.

Presenting the New and Improved MapPoint

MapPoint has been around since 1999, and with each new version, it has fulfilled more and more of the needs of its intended users. The release of MapPoint 2002 brought the first significant national media attention, as articles and reviews appeared on CNET, in *PC Magazine*, and in *MS OfficePRO*. Even newsgroups devoted to MapPoint started to swell in size. The public at large is on the brink of discovering MapPoint, but you're among the first to truly see what this application can do for you. Congratulations!

Of course, we realize that a few of you may have tinkered with MapPoint 2001 a bit as well. Unlike the designers of other applications whose 2002 releases were primarily incremental (restricted to bug fixes, stability issues, and perhaps a couple of useless new features), the MapPoint team went to great effort to expand the capability of the product as well. Here are some of the new features and capabilities in MapPoint 2002:

- ✔ **Territories:** Whether you want to define territories manually by drawing on a map, or you have existing data defining territories, this feature can help you get the job done.

- ✔ **Drivetime zones (DTZ):** Discover how far you can drive from a defined point in a specified amount of time.

- ✔ **Custom symbols:** Instead of being limited by MapPoint's standard Pushpin symbols, you can create your own Pushpin symbols based on your company logo or other significant symbol.

- **MapPoint Office COM add-in:** Effortlessly access MapPoint from within your favorite Office apps with this new feature.

- **Flat map view:** Do you need to see data from multiple countries at once? If so, you'll appreciate the new flat map view available at higher zoom levels.

And here are a few of the improvements in MapPoint 2002:

- **More map types:** Display more information than ever before thanks to a host of new map types including Sized Pie Chart maps, Multiple Symbol maps, and so on.

- **Extended programmability:** You can now automate most MapPoint tasks thanks to extended programmability.

- **Save as Web page enhancements:** Now when you save a map as a Web page, you can opt to change the size of a map, include hyperlinks, create a thumbnail sketch of the map, and so on.

- **Pushpin improvements:** Use a variety of Pushpin symbols to represent different types of points on the map, display multiple lines of information including hyperlinks in the Pushpin balloon, and more.

- **MapPoint tutorial:** Use the provided sample data and step-by-step instructions to discover MapPoint. Of course who needs the tutorial when you've got this book!

Want to upgrade to MapPoint 2002 from a previous version? Do you own a copy of Office XP and want to try MapPoint for the first time? Microsoft gives you a bit of incentive to do so — a $50 rebate. Check inside your MapPoint 2002 box for this valuable offer. To qualify for the rebate, you need a proof of purchase from both Office XP and MapPoint 2002 as well as a clearly marked sales receipt from your purchase of MapPoint 2002.

If you have a previous version of MapPoint installed on your computer, you won't be able to open files generated in MapPoint 2002 unless you upgrade. In MapPoint 2002, however, you can open files and templates created in MapPoint 2000 and 2001, as well as those created in Streets & Trips 2000 and 2001.

A Word about Compatibility

To install MapPoint 2002 (including the trial version included on one of this book's CDs), you need to be running Windows 98 or later on your computer. Windows NT users need Version 4.0 with Service Pack 6 or later to get the program up and running.

And before you get all excited about MapPoint's ability to import and export data, we should set the record straight. Although you're not likely to face compatibility issues, we need to put them out just the same.

To import MapPoint data into Microsoft Office, you need the 97 version or later of Word, Excel, Access, Outlook, Publisher, FrontPage, or PowerPoint. You also need the 97 versions of Excel, Access, or Outlook to import the data into MapPoint.

Finally, if you're using Microsoft SQL Server, you need to make sure you're working with Version 6.5 or newer in order to use it with MapPoint 2002.

Putting Europe at Your Fingertips

More and more corporations are multinational in scope these days, meaning that coverage limited to the United States and Canada may not cut it for you. If you need to access detailed information about Europe, you're in luck. Enter MapPoint 2002 Europe.

The European edition is available in five languages (English, French, German, Italian, and Spanish) and includes street-level maps of Great Britain, France, Germany, Spain, Italy, Netherlands, Denmark, Belgium, Luxemburg, Austria, and Switzerland, as well as detailed demographic information.

Chapter 2

Exploring the MapPoint Universe

As the old cliché goes, you've gotta walk before you can run. The same holds true for getting to know a new computer program. You've got to know the lay of the land before you can take full advantage of the more advanced features. After all, you probably wouldn't venture out into the middle of a huge forest without some kind of navigational aid, would you? Well maybe you would, but the odds of getting back in a timely manner may not be too good.

But seriously, a thorough understanding of MapPoint 2002's menus, toolbars, and workspace goes a long way in shortening the learning curve, which means less time poking around and trying to find things and more time for the good stuff!

What's Where in the MapPoint Window

Like every other computer program out there, MapPoint 2002 has a menu bar, toolbars, and a workspace. Figure 2-1 shows you exactly what you see when you launch MapPoint 2002.

The workspace elements in Figure 2-1 are what appear by default. You're introduced to a host of other task panes throughout the course of the book.

Navigation toolbar

Standard toolbar

Menu bar

Map window

Location and Scale toolbar

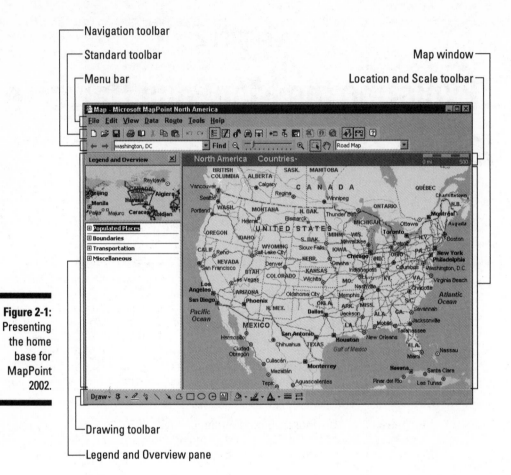

Figure 2-1:
Presenting
the home
base for
MapPoint
2002.

Drawing toolbar

Legend and Overview pane

Looking at the menu bar

MapPoint 2002's menu bar may look like menu bars you've seen before, but it unlocks a whole new set of commands. Here are some of the goodies you find under each menu item:

✔ **File:** In addition to the usual Open and Save commands, you can use this menu to save a map as a Web page or manage existing Web pages, e-mail a map to a friend or colleague, or export a map for use with Pocket Streets. (You can read about using Pocket Streets to take MapPoint on the road with you in Chapter 13.)

✔ **Edit:** You can find all the standard Copy, Cut, Paste, Delete, Redo, Undo, and Find commands here. In addition, you can choose from a couple of MapPoint-specific commands: Copy Map (which copies only the currently displayed map) and Copy Directions (which copies only the text of driving directions).

✔ **View:** Use this menu item to zoom in and out of a map (see "Zooming into place," later in this chapter), change the style of map viewed, and select whether or not certain panes or toolbars are displayed on-screen. You can even change the size of the font used on the map with this menu.

✔ **Data:** This is where you go to begin dabbling with territories and data analysis functions. (Chapters 8, 9, and 10 give you a crash course on these functions using MapPoint 2002.) You start here to import or link to external data sources, export data to Excel, set data and pushpin properties, and so on.

✔ **Route:** The Route menu lets you call the Route Planner into action, add stops to an existing route, optimize the course of a multi-stop route, and generate a set of driving directions. You also access this menu to update road construction information and tell MapPoint about areas you'd like to avoid when creating a route or set of driving directions. We explore these features in depth in Chapter 5.

✔ **Tools:** Start here to create drivetime zones (see Chapter 5 for details), measure distances on the map, find nearby places, set up GPS (global positioning system) support, and set general MapPoint options (such as unit of measurement and driving direction itinerary attributes).

✔ **Help:** If you find yourself in a real bind and even this book can't help you, consult the Help menu. From here, you can search the Help files, check the Web for guidance, or even register your copy of MapPoint.

Rather than use the menus to access some of MapPoint's more advanced features, you may want to check for a corresponding toolbar button. Microsoft's MapPoint team made sure that many of the more specialized tasks were converted to buttons on the Standard and Navigation toolbars so that they could be called into action with a single mouse click.

Nothing's standard about this toolbar

It may be called the Standard toolbar, but nothing could be further from the truth. Clicking a single button on this toolbar enables you to access many of MapPoint's best and most frequently used features. The bulleted list that follows shows you which button does what on the Standard toolbar.

For a graphical guide to the various buttons on this toolbar, please see the Cheat Sheet included at the front of this book. You can pull the sheet out and keep it by your computer for quick reference.

✔ **New:** Restores MapPoint to its default view (as shown in Figure 2-1) so that you can create a new map, set of driving directions, or whatever.

✔ **Open:** Click this button to open a MapPoint file stored on your computer.

✔ **Save:** The first time you click this button after a new map or route is generated, you will be prompted to name the file before it is saved. When you click this button while viewing a saved map, the current file is saved under the same filename.

✔ **Print:** This button lets you print a quick copy of the current map view using the default Print settings (one copy with normal resolution produced on your system's default printer).

✔ **Page Setup:** Click here to set the paper size and orientation as well as the margins.

✔ **Cut:** After selecting an element, you can click Cut to remove it and hold it in the Clipboard. The item can then be pasted into another application (such as a Word document).

✔ **Copy:** Again, the selected item is put into the Clipboard for future use; however, this time the item is copied instead of cut, so the original stays in place.

✔ **Paste:** This button takes the selected item residing in your Clipboard and puts it into a place you select.

✔ **Undo:** Click this button to undo the last action you performed. The button is *grayed out* (unavailable) if the last action cannot be undone.

✔ **Redo:** This button reverses the action of the Undo command, and it too will gray out if the action can't be redone.

✔ **Legend and Overview:** Clicking this button opens and closes the Legend and Overview pane. It's open by default, but closing it can increase the amount of map territory visible on-screen.

✔ **Territories:** Clicking this button launches the Create Territories Wizard, or opens or closes the Territories Manager pane if you've already created territories on the map.

✔ **Find Nearby Places:** After you've selected a point on the map, click this button to see what's nearby. By default, MapPoint searches for places within one mile of the chosen location.

✔ **Route Planner:** One click opens the Route Planner pane from which you can begin planning your journey.

✔ **Driving Directions:** This button toggles the Directions pane open and closed. The pane is closed by default because it remains empty until driving directions are generated from the Route Planner.

✔ **Link Data Wizard:** If you want to link external data to a map, this is the perfect starting point. Click this button to specify to which file you want MapPoint to link. You can find out more about data linking in Chapters 8, 9, and 10.

✔ **Import Data Wizard:** When you're ready to begin analyzing external data, click this button to tell MapPoint where to find the data you want to examine. To see how to work with imported data in MapPoint, refer to Chapters 8, 9, and 10.

✔ **Data Mapping Wizard:** This is the tool you use to create those fancy Sized Pie Chart maps, Shaded Area maps, and Multiple Symbol Pushpin maps.

✔ **Export to Excel:** After you've specified which map data you want to export, click this button to have the chosen records exported to an Excel worksheet.

✔ **Show Information:** This toggle button turns off and on the display of additional information about a selected place or pushpin.

✔ **Search the Web:** Select a place on the map and click this button to connect to the World Wide Web and open an MSN Search page displaying a set of links about the selected place.

✔ **Drawing Toolbar:** The Drawing toolbar is shown by default, but you may want to hide it to free up more display space on-screen. Click the Drawing Toolbar button to turn the element off and on.

✔ **Location and Scale Toolbar:** This gray bar above the map screen displays the location and distance scale of the currently displayed map. By clicking the Location and Scale Toolbar button, you can add or remove the scale from above your map pane. The scale, which appears by default, can be hidden by clicking the Location and Scale Toolbar button a second time.

✔ **Help:** Click here to access MapPoint 2002's Help topics. You can browse these files by Contents or Index, or by typing a question in the Answer Wizard.

Modifying the MapPoint Workspace

One of the great things about today's computer programs is that you can customize them to your liking. You can relocate toolbars, hide them altogether, resize the task panes, and even enlarge the font on-screen to ease eyestrain.

No matter what your personal preferences are, you can have MapPoint your way with a little bit of tweaking.

Hiding a toolbar

If you never use MapPoint's Drawing tool, don't let it clutter up your work-space. To hide it (or any other toolbar that doesn't meet your needs), all you need to do is right-click the toolbar to open a shortcut menu. Simply click the name of the toolbar you want to hide to remove its check mark.

Alternatively, you can access the View menu, select Toolbars, and click the name of the toolbar you want to view or hide.

Calling the toolbar back into action is as simple as repeating the steps in the preceding paragraph. Clicking the name of the hidden toolbar places a check mark next to its name and brings it back into view on-screen.

Relocating a toolbar

By default, all MapPoint toolbars are docked into position. You can tell that a toolbar is docked (or attached to the edge of the program window) when you see a vertical gray Move handle at the left end of the toolbar. Turn any tool-bar into a floating toolbar (one that is placed anywhere inside the program's workspace) by clicking its Move handle and dragging the toolbar into the desired position. Instead of a Move handle, floating toolbars have a blue title bar at the top, which you can click and drag to move the toolbar as needed.

To dock a floating toolbar, click its title bar and drag the toolbar to the top or bottom edge of the screen or up against another toolbar. The title bar then disappears and is replaced with the Move handle.

Resizing a task pane

Need to see more of the area on-screen without changing the zoom level? Want to squish the Legend and Overview pane a bit to cut down on wasted space? You can resize MapPoint panes with ease. Just point to the split bar between the panes you want to resize, and when the mouse pointer turns into a bar with two arrows, click and drag the panes into position.

Changing the font size

Whether you have trouble seeing MapPoint's small type, or you want to make the labels extra large for an upcoming PowerPoint presentation, you'll find making the necessary adjustments a breeze.

With the map you want to modify on-screen, choose View⇨Map Font. A menu shoots out with five choices: Largest, Larger, Medium, Smaller (the default), and Smallest. Click your selection, and within seconds, MapPoint redraws the map to your specifications.

Note that large fonts can easily clutter a map, making it more difficult to accurately define various streets, roads, and places. Large fonts also reduce the amount of information that can be viewed on-screen (for example, legend names may appear only partially). Unless the larger print is needed for accessibility reasons, you'd be wise to think carefully before applying the largest font setting.

MapPoint supports large fonts for users who may have trouble reading smaller type.

Reversing an action

With so much mapping and data analysis power at your fingertips, it's only natural that you may change your mind about an action you may have taken on a map. MapPoint 2002 gives you Undo and Redo buttons to help you back up a step or two in your work. The Undo button reverses the last change you made to your map, whereas the Redo button essentially reverses the Undo.

There are some exceptions to the kinds of actions that can be reversed however, as listed in Table 2-1.

Table 2-1	Irreversible actions
Action	*Actions before this cannot be undone either*
New	X
Open	X
Save	
Exit	X
Cut sets	X (Cutting individual objects can be reversed.)
Delete sets	X (Deleting individual objects can be reversed.)
Paste link	X
Link data	X
Update linked sets	X

(continued)

Table 2-1 *(continued)*

Action	Actions before this cannot be undone either
New data mapping of demographic data	X
Match records	X
COM add-ins (The underlying action may clear the Undo stack, however.)	
Show/hide Territory Manager pane	X
Create territory group	X
Delete territory group	X
Delete territory	X
Import data	X
Map style	
Flat map or globe at high zoom level	
Show/hide places	

Clearing the map

We all make mistakes. After all, we're only human. If you need to clear the map to start over again, click the New button at the far left end of the Standard toolbar. In cases where you've edited the map in some manner, you will be prompted to save the current map. If you want to do so, click Yes, name the map, and then click Save. If getting a clean slate is all you really want to do, click No and continue working.

Navigating a MapPoint Map

If getting around in real life were as simple as it is in MapPoint, then we'd *really* have something! Click and drag, and you've sailed from one coast to the other. Double-click to enter the state of your choice . . . oh, the possibilities.

Navigating a MapPoint map typically involves zooming in on or out to a location, and/or panning to refine your view.

Zooming into place

Zooming refers to the altitude you are from a location — you *zoom in* to get closer to a spot, and *zoom out* to display a larger area on-screen. MapPoint 2002 gives you several ways to zoom into the desired position.

Jumping to a country or state

As you zoom in on a map, buttons appear on the Location and Scale toolbar. These buttons may be named after a continent, country, state, or city. You can jump to an area after which a button is named by simply clicking the button.

If multiple countries or states appear in your map pane, an arrow appears to the right of the word *Countries* or *States* in the gray Location and Scale toolbar (see Figure 2-2). Clicking the arrow button opens a drop-down menu of countries or states appearing on-screen. To jump to one of the countries or states on the list, simply click its name. The surrounding countries or states gray out, leaving the chosen location "lit" for easy viewing.

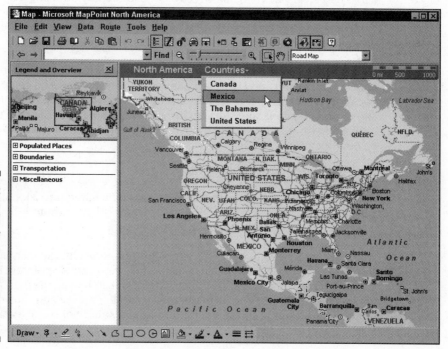

Figure 2-2:
Jump to the desired location by clicking the location name on the Location and Scale toolbar.

Moving in and out of position

On MapPoint's Navigation toolbar, you see two buttons shaped like magnifying glasses. One has a minus (–) sign inside of it, and the other has a plus (+) sign. As you might expect, clicking the button with the minus sign moves you further away from the center point, making a broader area visible on-screen. Clicking the button with the plus sign on it does the reverse — it zooms you in closer to the point centered in the map pane.

Do you own one of those neat wheel mice? If so, here's a cool zooming shortcut for you. With the mouse pointer inside the map pane, roll the mouse wheel away from you to zoom in on a spot, or toward you to zoom out.

Sliding into view with the Zoom Slider

Wouldn't it be neat to be able to visualize your maps from a variety of elevations? It may not be the most useful piece of information out there, but you have to admit it's interesting nonetheless.

With a paper map or atlas, you would find performing such a task impossible. Not so with MapPoint. In between the two magnifying glass buttons, you see a notched lever-like thing known as a Zoom Slider. By mousing over its lever, you see how many miles worth of territory are displayed in the map pane. You can then click and drag the lever to the left to increase the amount of ground covered on-screen, or to the right to take a closer look.

As you zoom in and out of various locations, you'll notice that the overview map in the Legend and Overview pane changes with you. The general area you're browsing in appears on the overview map (at the top of the Legend and Overview pane), and the specific area that appears in the map pane is outlined in bright blue on the overview map to help you maintain perspective on your location.

Drawing conclusions

Zooming is great and all, but controlling exactly what you're zooming in on can be challenging. With MapPoint, you can draw a box around the area you'd like to view, and zoom in on that alone.

To do this, you need to click the Select button (shown in the margin) on the Navigation toolbar. After clicking that button, your mouse pointer takes on the same arrow-in-a-box appearance when you run it over the map pane. Click in the upper-left corner of the area you'd like to see and then drag the mouse pointer down and to the right to form a square of sorts, as shown in Figure 2-3.

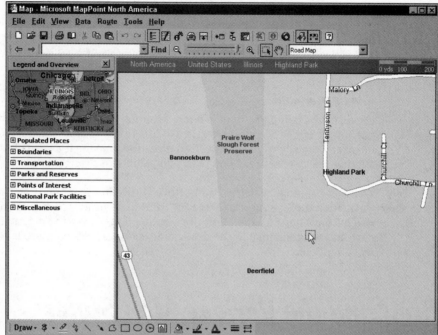

If you're satisfied with the area you selected, click inside the box to zoom in on the location. If you're not, simply click outside the box to make it disappear and then draw the box again.

Moving around the map

If you've ever spent time trying to hang a painting on the wall, then you understand the frustration of needing to move a little bit more one way or another. It's a fact of life — you're always going to need to make a few adjustments in order to get exactly what you want. Luckily, it's easy to make adjustments in MapPoint.

Taking steps in the right direction

When you move your mouse pointer to an edge of the map pane, it takes on the appearance of a big fat white arrow that points in the direction of the boundary you're touching. For example, if you move the mouse pointer over to the right edge of the window, the arrow points to the right, indicating that if you clicked your left mouse button at that moment, the map's view would shift to the right.

Using this technique, you can navigate the map in eight directions — to the right, to the left, up, down, diagonally to the upper left, diagonally to the upper right, diagonally to the lower left, and diagonally to the lower right. You can click the mouse button as many times as needed to find the desired view, or hold the mouse button down for continuous movement.

Panning for gold

Okay, maybe panning a map is not as exciting as panning for gold, but knowing how to pan in MapPoint is still a valuable skill. Panning enables you to move ever so slightly in the desired direction, making it a wise choice for shifting the view of areas you're looking at in close range.

 To begin panning, click the Pan button (shown in the margin) on the Navigation toolbar. After clicking this button, your mouse pointer mirrors the Pan button's hand shape. With the mouse pointer over the map pane, simply click and drag the map in the desired direction. That's all there is to panning with MapPoint!

Browsing the Various Map Styles

When it comes to maps, one size does not fit all. You may want to include a highly detailed Road Map on your company's Web site so potential customers can find you, but an uncluttered Data Map may be the only way your board of directors will be able to see your point at the annual meeting. MapPoint 2002 provides five styles of maps to meet a variety of needs. You can select the desired style using the Map Style drop-down box located on the Navigation toolbar. And don't be afraid to experiment a bit before you decide on a style to see which one meets your needs best.

Road Map

As the default map style in MapPoint 2002, the Road Map style contains detailed information about roads, highways, towns, and cities (see Figure 2-4). This style of map is best suited for displaying driving directions and illustrating your company's physical location.

 Here's a bit of trivia that may blow your mind: MapPoint 2002 contains 6.4 million miles of routable streets and roads in North America alone. And the European edition contains 4.8 million kilometers of streets and roads, and, well, that's a lot of real estate to work with!

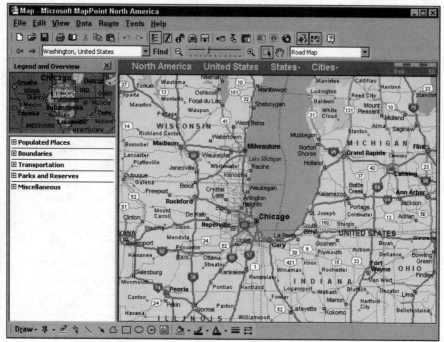

Figure 2-4:
Road Maps
give you
the most
detailed
view of a
specific
location.

Road and Data Map

MapPoint uses the Road and Data Map style like the one shown in Figure 2-5 as the default for displaying mapped data. This style of map offers the best of both worlds — street-level detail and a less cluttered, uniformly colored background for easy visibility so that your data not only is accurate but also shows up well.

A Road and Data Map should be your first choice if you intend to present data tracked to the street address level. If your data only goes to the town, city, or state level, however, a simple Data Map may suffice.

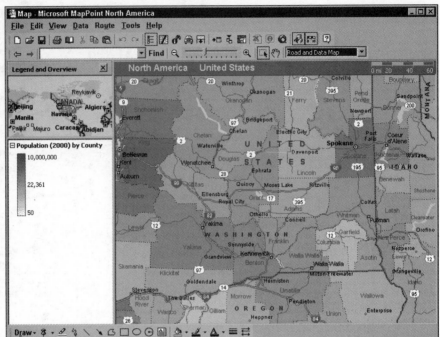

Figure 2-5:
The Road
and Data
Map
combines
the
accuracy of
a street-
level map
with the
clarity of the
Data Map.

Data Map

Do you have a lot of city, town, or state level data that you want to present in the cleanest manner possible? The Data Map style may do the trick (see Figure 2-6). With a minimum of labeling and clutter, it leaves the view wide open to communicate your point.

This style of map lends itself particularly well to inclusion in a PowerPoint presentation or in a printout for a grant application, feasibility study, or similar document. The labeling is sparse yet it exists enough for the viewer to get the gist of your data analysis.

Terrain Map

If the geographical terrain of the area in question makes a difference to the viewer of your map, then a Terrain Map is the way to go. As you can see in Figure 2-7, a Terrain Map displays the elevation of an area along with the usual roads, highways, cities, and towns.

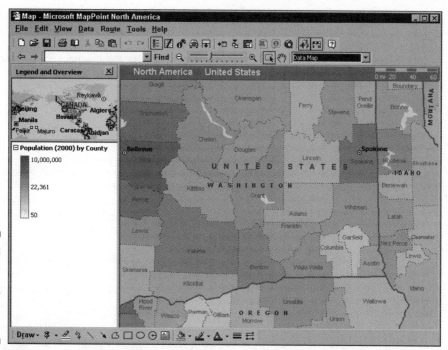

Figure 2-6:
When
clarity is a
priority, try
the Data
Map style.

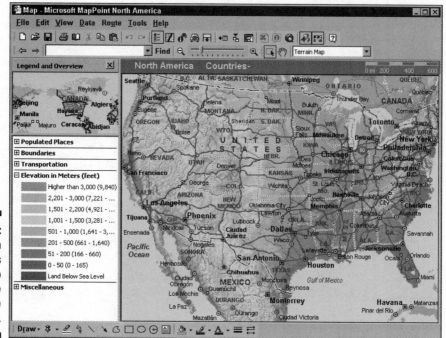

Figure 2-7:
Terrain
Maps
literally help
you see the
lay of the
land.

Realtors can use Terrain Maps to help familiarize clients with the geographical makeup of large parcels of land, and resort managers may wish to use them to demonstrate the existence of terrain conducive to skiing, mountain hiking, and so on. At lower elevations, additional colors are used to mark bodies of water, parks, and the like.

Political Map

Certain situations may require taking an area's political boundaries into account. Perhaps you're dealing with exporting or importing goods, national security, or a similar potentially sensitive situation. MapPoint's Political Map style (see Figure 2-8) lets you see exactly where the power lies. Political boundaries are clearly defined, and the different political areas are color-coded, leaving no question as to who's in charge where.

The colors themselves don't mean anything specific; they simply denote a change in political jurisdiction (for example, Mexico may be shades of orange and the U.S. shades of pink). The colors used may vary depending on your map view.

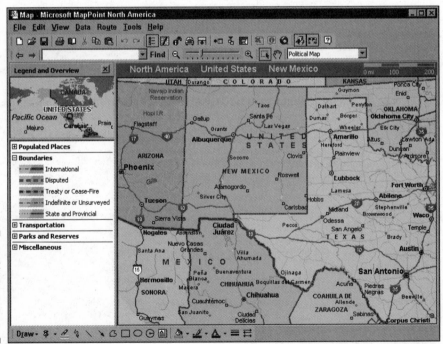

Figure 2-8: You can't escape politics even in MapPoint!

Part II
Test Driving MapPoint

The 5th Wave   By Rich Tennant

©RICHTENNANT.COM

See? I told you MapPoint could find the La Brea tar pits.

In this part . . .

Have you ever taken a new car for a test drive? You take it for a spin around the block, press a few buttons to see how all the controls work. . .you know the drill. Well, consider these next few chapters your test drive of MapPoint. Instead of just reading about what the program can do, you'll actually start to do things with it.

In addition to finding out how to find locations and mark them with a Pushpin, you discover how to find points of interest (POIs), build a set of driving directions, and even generate an entire route that is optimized to minimize time spent on the road as well as fuel costs. These chapters could keep you playing with MapPoint for hours!

Chapter 3

Interpreting a MapPoint Map

O n a MapPoint map, is a national forest a POI (point of interest), or does it show up on the Parks and Reserves legend? There's no point wasting your time trying to figure out what all these specially shaded areas mean when it can be spelled out for you plain and simple. By the way, national forests are *not* considered points of interest; they appear on the Parks and Reserves legend instead.

And to make interpreting map shadings and legends even trickier, certain legends appear only if you're zoomed down to a relatively low level (see Chapter 2 for more on zooming in MapPoint). This makes sense from a logistics standpoint — after all, it's not easy to spot a Dairy Queen from several miles away! But it can complicate things when you see roads but not some of the other landmarks you might expect. Oh yeah, and you might see different legends for a Political map than you would for Data maps.

In this chapter, we focus on helping you make sense of what you see on a MapPoint map.

Working with MapPoint's Legends

If it weren't for legends, maps would be little more than random collections of squiggly lines. Thanks to legends, you can distinguish streets from toll roads, towns from major cities, and so on. And when it comes to Data maps, a legend gives the shaded areas or pie chart slices real meaning.

In MapPoint, the legends appear in the Legend and Overview pane on the left side of the screen. (If the Legend and Overview pane is not currently visible on-screen, choose View➪Legend and Overview to open it.) Each legend category is labeled and comes with a plus (+) sign to the left of it. When you click this plus sign, the chosen legend expands to display pertinent map features. When you click a minus (–) sign, the chosen legend section collapses again.

People with limited vision or those who are simply uncomfortable using a mouse for such precise work may find double-clicking the legend name a bit easier to handle. When double-clicked once, the legend category expands. When double-clicked again, the category collapses.

Keep in mind that map-feature symbols may vary in appearance depending on how closely you're viewing an area. For example, at high-altitude viewing, an interstate highway looks like a single red line. Upon zooming in, however, the Transportation legend reveals two thick, red, parallel lines that represent an interstate highway.

Populated Places

Knowing the approximate population of a city or town is of utmost importance whether you're just passing through or contemplating the location for the newest branch of your bank.

Figure 3-1 shows you how MapPoint marks places with various populations.

Figure 3-1:
The
Populated
Places
legend.

Boundaries

The Boundaries legend tells you where one state, province, or county begins and another one ends. This is vital information not only for navigation but also for high-level data analysis.

You'll also find special map features to mark cease-fire or treaty zones as well as unsurveyed, indefinite, or disputed boundaries. Consult Figure 3-2 to see how MapPoint labels various types of boundaries.

Figure 3-2:
The
Boundaries
legend.

Transportation

MapPoint's Transportation legend is arguably the most important of the bunch. It helps you distinguish between toll roads, railroad tracks, interstate highways, tunnels, and other road types. You also find markings for other modes of transportation including ferries, airports, heliports, subway and bus stops, and so on.

This information helps businesses choose prime locations near major intersections, and helps realtors steer families away from homes in potentially dangerous areas near highways and railroad tracks. You can even spot nearby gas stations using this legend's symbols. Likewise, detailed markings from the Transportation legend can help you visualize a recently generated route so you know what kind of traffic to expect.

Don't forget that the appearance of these symbols may change slightly depending how close — or how far — you are from the surface of the map.

Understandably, this is the largest legend category of the bunch. Figure 3-3 pretty much proves it by pointing out many of the possible map features in the Transportation category. On your screen, scroll down the scroll bar to the right of this legend to see the rest of the features.

Figure 3-3:
The
Transporta-
tion legend.

Parks and Reserves

Many businesses can benefit from being located near a state park or golf course. For them, the heavy traffic means big business. The Parks and Reserves legend can also help lead realtors to premium real estate locations near country clubs and local parks, or it can help businesses in search of reasonably priced land steer clear of higher-priced golf-course locations. And hey, this legend can even help you track down a little fun when you're ready to take a break!

Figure 3-4 presents the map features that appear on the Parks and Reserves legend.

Figure 3-4:
The Parks
and
Reserves
legend.

Parks and Reserves
National Park or Reserve
National or State Forest
Other Park
Indigenous Reserve
Military Reserve
Cemetery
Golf Course
Small Park

Points of Interest (POIs)

Although the Transportation legend may win the nod for being the most important, the Points of Interest legend is perhaps the most useful (and certainly the most fun). To see this legend, however, you need to zoom in on a populated area, as described in Chapter 2.

MapPoint 2002's Points of Interest legend includes such fun items as aquariums, zoos, restaurants, marinas, shopping, museums, cinemas, and convention centers. You can even find some more practical sites here, too: ATMs and banks, hospitals, police stations, post offices, and so on.

Okay, but how is all this information useful? The presence of such a wide variety of POIs is an analyst's dream. You can scout out the competition, look for a location that isn't already served by a business like yours, and find a spot that's likely to be frequented by your types of customers or clients.

For travelers, knowing where the nearest hospital, police station, rest area, and bank is can really save the day, especially when you're in a totally unfamiliar environment.

Or what if you're trying to wine and dine new clients? Locate that highly rated steakhouse near their hotel, and use the information contained in MapPoint to call and make a reservation.

Even if you personally don't need this kind of information in your work, we guarantee you'll at least have a lot of fun playing with it! Figure 3-5 displays some of the points of interest that you see marked on MapPoint maps. Scroll down the scroll bar on your screen next to this legend to see more of its features.

Figure 3-5:
Click the
Zoom tool
on the
Standard
toolbar and
then click
an area on a
map to
reveal its
points of
interest.

National Park Facilities

Are you a tour coordinator who books trips and hikes through national parks? Is your company planning to build a fancy themed hotel near a certain national park? If either of these scenarios rings even close to true, you may find this legend quite interesting.

You can find not only the national parks themselves in MapPoint but also the location of the facilities there. Figure 3-6 shows you some of the facilities you can locate by using MapPoint; scroll down the scroll bar on your screen to see more.

Figure 3-6:
The
National
Park
Facilities
legend.

Miscellaneous

Even MapPoint needs a catchall category for various symbols that don't fit neatly into other categories! If the presence of a body of water or a special landmark is critical to your research, then this is the legend for you. Along with identifying bodies of water, items on this legend include waterfalls, casinos, volcanoes, and other unique place types. The symbols for these items appear in Figure 3-7.

Figure 3-7:
The
Miscella-
neous
legend.

Showing and Hiding POIs on the Map

Being able to see all the points of interest on a map is handy, but they can crowd your view, potentially obstructing the visibility of crucial mapped data. Even if you aren't mapping data, you may just want to generate a clean map on which only your business appears. You wouldn't want to lead your customers straight to the competition, would you?

But before we show you how to hide points of interest, it's important to remind you that you can hide only POIs (the items listed in Figure 3-5, earlier in this chapter); items appearing on the rest of the legends remain in sight at all times.

Now back to business. To hide points of interest, you need to follow these steps:

1. **Choose View**➪**Show or Hide Places.**

   The Restaurants tab of the Show or Hide Places dialog box opens.

2. **Click the Uncheck All button on the bottom-right side of the dialog box.**

   MapPoint removes the check marks next to all restaurant types listed.

3. **Click the Places tab and then click the Uncheck All button.**

   This deselects all the categories of places to show on-screen.

4. **Click OK to save your changes.**

   The Show or Hide Places dialog box closes, leaving a perfectly clean map in its wake.

If, at some point, you change you mind and want to see all the points of interest on the map, simply repeat the preceding steps, only this time click the Check All button instead of the Uncheck All button in Steps 2 and 3.

Determining Which POIs Are Displayed

If you're doing marketing research or putting together a feasibility study, you may find it helpful to have only certain POIs appear on the map. When trying to raise capital for building a Ledo's Pizza in your town, you may want to produce a map with all the other local pizza places displayed on it. Doing so gives you the opportunity to prove two things: Your town doesn't have enough pizza shops, and the location you've chosen would serve folks who have to drive a considerable distance to get to a pizza shop.

MapPoint gives you complete control over which POIs appear on your maps, so go ahead — be selective!

To choose the POIs you want to appear on your map, you need to do the following:

1. **Choose View⇨Show or Hide Places.**

   The Show or Hide Places dialog box, shown in Figure 3-8, opens.

Figure 3-8: MapPoint selects all POIs by default.

2. **If you want only a few items displayed on your map, click the Uncheck All button on both tabs.**

   This step removes all previously selected items and makes choosing the handful of POIs you really want much easier.

3. **Next, work your way through both tabs and select the check boxes for the POIs you want included on your map.**

   Clicking the check box to the left of the POI puts a check mark in place and tells MapPoint to include it on the current map.

4. **After you've checked all desired POIs, click OK.**

   The dialog box disappears, and the map appears with only your selected POIs displayed.

Gathering More Information About a POI

Want to know more about a place you see on the map? Maybe you need the street address for a direct-mail campaign, or, perhaps, you need to call to make a reservation to wine and dine a prospective client. Whatever your reason for wanting to know more, you'll be glad to know that MapPoint can deliver.

Just the facts, ma'am

Finding the mailing address and phone number for a particular point of interest is as easy as double-clicking its respective symbol on the map. (Alternatively, you can click a point and select View⇨Show Information from MapPoint's menu bar.) After double-clicking a place, an information balloon like the one shown in Figure 3-9 appears. In it, you see the mailing address and phone number.

A little more info, please

For some points of interest, you may want to find out a little more than the basic information. Perhaps you'd like to see a corporate Web page for the selected restaurant to check out its plans for expansion. Or maybe you want to see what works of art reside in the chosen museum.

 MapPoint 2002 makes it a cinch to gather more data about a point of interest. Just click the POI's symbol to select it and then click the Search the Web button on the Standard toolbar. An Internet Explorer window opens to an MSN Search page of results based on the selected place.

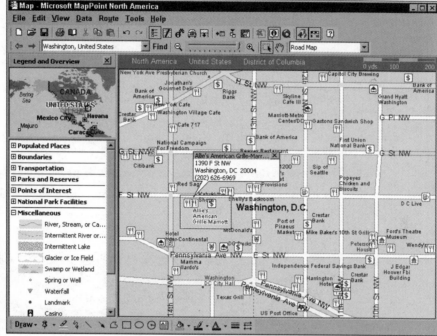

Figure 3-9:
Gather
basic
contact
information
about a
place with
minimal
effort.

Measuring the Distance between Points

You've done tons of research to scout out the best location for your new business venture, but now you want to look at the distance between points. How far is that electronics superstore from the prospective site for your mom and pop computer store? Is that new location so close to the marina that traffic will overwhelm your buyers-to-be?

You don't need to program a route to get that kind of information out of MapPoint; instead, use the handy-dandy Measure Distance tool.

Freeform measurement for accuracy

Typically, you'll want to measure the distance that a person would have to walk or drive to get from one point to another. To get this kind of accuracy, you need to use MapPoint's freeform Measure Distance tool.

To use the tool, follow these steps:

1. Position the map pane so that both points are visible.

2. **Choose Tools⇨Measure Distance.**

   Your mouse pointer turns into a large plus (+) sign of sorts.

3. **Place the mouse pointer on the starting point of the journey, using the center of the plus sign as a guide.**

4. **Click and hold down the left mouse button and then drag the pointer (which looks like a pencil) to its destination.**

   MapPoint draws a thick black line on-screen to let you know where you've been, and all the while, a running total of the mileage is displayed near your mouse pointer (see Figure 3-10).

5. **When you're done measuring, double-click or press the Esc key.**

   This restores your mouse pointer to its default state so you can continue working in MapPoint.

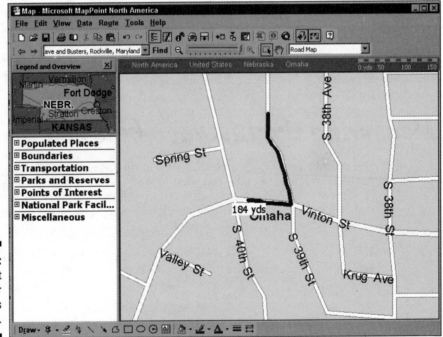

Figure 3-10:
MapPoint
marks your
path with its
virtual pen.

Getting a guesstimate of the distance

Until you get the hang of it, trying to do freeform distance measuring can be a bit tricky. If you don't need an exact measurement or merely need to get an idea of the distance between two points, then you may want to consider performing a point-to-point measurement instead. Just follow these steps:

1. **Choose Tools⇨Measure Distance.**

2. **Align the mouse pointer's plus (+) sign with the starting point and then click it.**

   The measuring tool is anchored to the location you chose.

3. **Drag the mouse pointer to the desired spot and then click it.**

   As you move the mouse, a straight line extends from your mouse pointer back to the starting point. This sets the mouse pointer in the new location so you can drag it in a second straight line.

4. **Repeat Step 3 as many times as it takes to chart the desired path.**

   MapPoint keeps a running total of the distance "traveled" and displays it near the mouse pointer.

5. **Double-click or press the Esc key to stop measuring and see the final result.**

Chapter 4

Locating Places on the Map

....

In This Chapter

▶ Conducting address searches
▶ Plotting an intersection on the map
▶ Finding latitude and longitude coordinates
▶ Displaying nearby places
▶ Working with Pushpins

....

Maybe you're wondering if that fancy new house on Lakeshore Drive you saw advertised in the paper is really by a lake's shore, or if the address is a bit of a deception. Or, perhaps, you need to send one of your account reps out to pick up a colleague whose truck has broken down, and all you have is an intersection of street names to go by. For either of these types of tasks, you could spend precious time squinting over a map, or you could run a MapPoint search within seconds. And while you're plotting the routes for your sales reps, for example, you can display all the Holiday Inns along the way so they can take advantage of your prearranged corporate discount.

Finding certain kinds of places (such as a specific street address or a major landmark) on the map is pretty straightforward, but getting down to specifics such as finding a specific intersection, determining which restaurants are within a mile of a location, or mapping a location based on latitude and longitude can pose some unique challenges.

Finding an Address on the Map

An address alone can mean very little. Take 3000 Connecticut Avenue, NW, Washington, DC. The collection of numbers and letters tell you little more than the fact that the address is somewhere in the northwestern part of Washington, DC. But if you plot the address on a map, it becomes immediately apparent that the address is located right across the street from the world-class National Zoological Park, as well as close to a host of unique restaurants and taverns.

Troubleshooting MapPoint address searches

The North American edition of MapPoint 2002 contains street-level maps of the entire United States plus all major urban areas in Canada. (You can also find some street-level maps of major cities in Mexico; however, MapPoint can't map street addresses for that particular area.) That's a lot of data, so it's no surprise that you may encounter a glitch once in awhile when requesting an address. It won't happen often, mind you, but when it does, we want you to be armed with the information you need to deal with the situation.

If MapPoint happens to draw a blank with the information you provided, here are some suggestions for troubleshooting:

✔ When requesting the location of an address, make sure that you have not used the following elements in the Street Address field: post office box numbers, rural route numbers, suite or apartment numbers, or fractions contained in an address (for example, a duplex where the mailing address of the second residence could be expressed as *222½ Main Street* should be entered as *222 Main Street*).

✔ Is the search moving a bit slower than you expected? Add the zip or postal code if you have it. This information speeds up MapPoint's search time considerably.

✔ Did you use the Find a Location box on the Navigation toolbar instead of the Find dialog box? If so, you may want to switch to the Find dialog box (choose Edit⇨Find) to make it perfectly clear that you're seeking an address, not a place.

✔ If, by some odd circumstance, the street name includes an ampersand (&), replace the ampersand with the word *and*. MapPoint uses ampersands for its intersection searches only.

✔ Does the street name you entered have an abbreviation associated with it (for example, St. Paul, Marcus Bros.)? If so, try spelling out the abbreviation (Saint Paul, Marcus Brothers). That may be enough to help MapPoint locate the address on the map.

✔ Don't know the exact spelling of the street name? Never fear; make an educated guess, and let MapPoint present you with a list of possibilities from which to choose.

To perform an address search, just follow these steps:

1. **With MapPoint up and running, choose Edit⇨Find from the menu bar.**

   The Address tab of the Find dialog box appears, as shown in Figure 4-1. This dialog box lets you enter additional information about the address you're trying to find and presents an assortment of options if multiple addresses were found based on your search.

2. **Enter the desired street address, city, and ZIP code (if known) in the appropriate text boxes. Select the state (if known) from the State drop-down menu.**

3. **Click the Find button.**

   Within seconds, MapPoint presents a list of possible matches for the requested address.

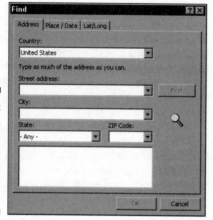

4. Click the correct address and then click OK.

MapPoint clearly marks the address with a Pushpin (see Figure 4-2). Also, a special My Pushpins legend now appears at the top of the legend section of the Legend and Overview pane. You can save your changes to the map (including your new Pushpin) by clicking Save and naming the map.

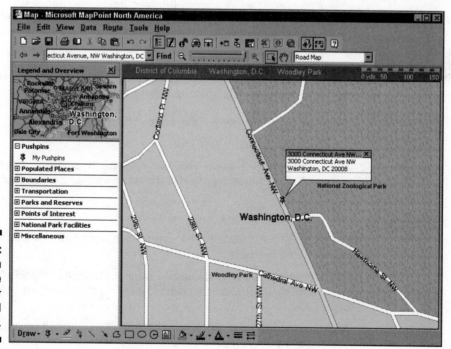

Figure 4-2:
A Pushpin
marks the
spot of your
selected
address.

TIP

Looking for a shortcut? You may be able to enter the full address directly into the Find a Location text box on the Navigation toolbar. (It's the textbox immediately to the right of the Back/Forward arrow buttons.) This eliminates executing the menu sequence presented in Step 1 of the preceding section, but it's not quite as accurate as using the Address tab of the Find dialog box because it's not obvious whether MapPoint is supposed to search for a place (say, Mount Rushmore or Deep Creek Lake in Maryland) or an address (such as 1 Microsoft Way, Redmond, Washington).

If MapPoint suspects that you are trying to find a place such as a certain lake or landmark, it may center the map pane on the closest match and then open the Place/Data tab of the Find dialog box to present you with a list of possible matches. Click the name of the desired place and then click the OK button to center the map on the chosen location.

If the entered data is believed to be a street address instead, you'll see the Address tab of the Find dialog box (refer to Figure 4-2). Just fill in the appropriate text boxes as described in the previous section; then click OK.

Locating an Intersection on the Map

Using MapPoint, you can locate any intersection in the United States or urban areas in Canada. Because street numbers aren't always as visible on buildings as we'd like, plotting an intersection is a great way to track someone down on the road. It's also a helpful way to get your bearings in a new area.

Finding an intersection on a map is a bit different than locating an address. You need to follow these steps to see where a specific intersection is located:

1. **From the MapPoint menu bar, choose Edit⇨Find.**

   The Address tab of the Find dialog box appears.

2. **In the Street Address text box, enter the name of the intersection you want to find, separating the street names with an ampersand (&).**

   The Street Address box may read something like 41st & Louise, 10th & Minnesota Avenue, or something similar.

3. **Enter the city and state in the appropriate text boxes to make the search more focused.**

4. **After entering all the appropriate information, click the Find button to make sure that the desired address has been properly located; then click OK.**

   The intersection appears centered on the map, marked with a Pushpin. You can save the map along with the intersection Pushpin by clicking the Save button and then naming the map.

But you've got it all wrong!

Okay, you've searched for your company's building using MapPoint and do a double take at the resulting Pushpin because it's not where you think it should be. It doesn't happen often, but when it does, it can be downright baffling.

Microsoft's MapPoint team takes great pride in the accuracy of its street-level data (which is obtained from a variety of outside data vendors), but they acknowledge that nothing is perfect, and things can indeed change due to new construction, recently completed roadwork, and the like. As a result, Microsoft has incorporated a Map Feedback feature in MapPoint that enables users to report map errors and inconsistencies, which Microsoft can in turn pass on to the appropriate data vendor for future updates.

To report such an error or inconsistency, launch MapPoint and then center the spot that is inaccurately placed on-screen. Next, click Tools⇨ Send Map Feedback on the Standard toolbar. This command launches MapPoint's Feedback Wizard, in which you'll work your way through a series of steps to help the Microsoft MapPoint team and their data vendors pinpoint the problem or omission. In the meantime, you can create your own Pushpin for the desired location by following the directions in the section titled "Creating Pushpins," which can be found later in this chapter.

Searching for Places Using MapPoint

Perhaps you're looking for a specific place, but don't have the address. Maybe you're coordinating your company's annual conference in the Baltimore area and want to hold a social event at the National Aquarium. Or maybe you need to map local Shell gas stations so your sales force can gas up on their rounds.

Whatever the case, you should know that it's just as easy to find a specific store, restaurant, tourist attraction, or interstate highway exit as it is to find a certain street address. In fact, in many ways it's even easier because the absence of a street address makes using the convenient Find a Location text box an asset rather than a liability.

To begin tracking down a specific place in MapPoint, follow these steps:

1. **In MapPoint's Find a Location box on the Navigation toolbar, enter the name of the place followed by a comma and the city name, and another comma and a state or province name, and then press Enter.**

   For example, to find Mount Rushmore, you enter **Mount Rushmore, South Dakota** in the text box. You can even enter something like **Ledo's Pizza, Laurel, Maryland**, and MapPoint will attempt to locate it for you. MapPoint searches for the desired location and then either centers it on the map and creates a Pushpin for it (in which case, this was a simple one-step maneuver), or presents you with a list of possibilities from which to choose.

Obviously with interstate highway exits and certain tourist attractions, you may not know the city. That's fine, but at least give MapPoint a state or province to work with. That narrows the search field considerably.

2. **If MapPoint gave you a number of options from which to choose, click the most appropriate one and then click OK.**

   The Find dialog box closes, and the chosen point appears centered on the map and marked with a Pushpin.

3. **To save the point for future reference, click Save and name the file.**

Still not finding what you want? If the place name contains an abbreviation, try spelling it out (Fort Meade instead of Ft. Meade). Or if the place name could possibly be construed as a street address (as in the Massachusetts Avenue Gallery), open the Find dialog box (choose Edit➪Find) and enter the place name on the Place/Data tab. This reinforces the fact that you're looking for a place by its name rather than by its address.

Charting a Position Based on Latitude and Longitude Coordinates

Whether you're working with a GPS (Global Positioning System) device, tracking the weather, or boating, you may find yourself needing to verify a location by using the latitude and longitude coordinates.

Before you begin however, note that MapPoint maps are based on information from the WGS 84 (World Geodetic System 1984). If your device or maps are based on a different set of data, you can expect to see some variances in position between the two sources.

You can search for coordinates in straight decimal format, or in DMS (degrees, minutes, seconds) format by following these steps:

1. **Choose Edit➪Find From the MapPoint menu bar.**

   The Find dialog box appears (refer to Figure 4-1). The Address tab is displayed by default.

2. **Click the Lat/Long tab (shown in Figure 4-3).**

3. **Enter the latitude and longitude coordinates in the boxes provided and then click OK.**

   MapPoint centers the location on the map and marks it with a Pushpin.

What if you want to go the reverse direction and find the latitude and longitude of a certain point? No problem; just use MapPoint's Location Sensor.

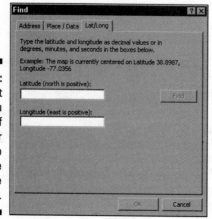

Figure 4-3:
MapPoint
gives you
a brief
reminder
of how to
enter the
coordinate
values.

To determine the coordinates of a desired location, simply display it on the map and then choose Tools⇨Location Sensor. A little Location Sensor box appears in the bottom-right corner of the map window (see Figure 4-4). Your mouse pointer then turns into a virtual location sensor — run it over a location, and you'll see the corresponding latitude and longitude coordinates in the Location Sensor window.

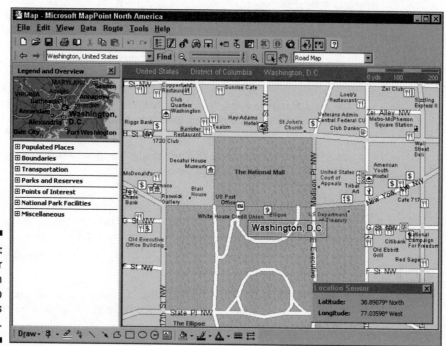

Figure 4-4:
Mouse over
any point on
the map to
see its
coordinates.

The lowdown on latitude and longitude

Okay, who among us can explain what latitude and longitude coordinates are, and how they're derived? Good for you! As for the rest of us mere mortals, here's a quick rundown.

Latitude measures how far north or south of the equator a given point is. The equator sits at 0 degrees. The North Pole is 90 degrees north (or +90), and the South Pole is, well, 90 degrees south (or –90); therefore, the latitude is

expressed as a decimal value between –90 and +90.

The longitude, on the other hand, refers to a point's relative location east or west of the prime meridian, which runs through Greenwich, England. In the case of longitude, eastern points carry the positive value, and western points carry the negative value. The values range from –180 degrees (far west) to +180 (far east).

Determining What's Near a Specific Location

One of the neat things about MapPoint is that it can help find certain bits of information quickly and easily. For example, say you want to find out what's nearby a new office location you're scoping out for your company. Paper maps give you few clues, and even plotting a site's location in MapPoint with the points of interest showing can leave you wondering just how far away the things you see really are.

To determine what's nearby a certain point, you need to do the following:

1. **Create a Pushpin for a certain point that you want to analyze on the map, as described at various points in this chapter (you have multiple methods to choose from).**

2. **Next, right-click the point's Pushpin and choose Find Nearby Places from the resulting shortcut menu.**

   The point is re-centered on the map, and a circle is drawn around it to reflect the tool's default search radius of one mile (see Figure 4-5). The Find Nearby Places pane also appears on the left side of the screen, replacing the familiar Legend and Overview pane.

   If you want to change the search radius, check out the "Widening the search" section, later in this chapter.

3. **In the Find Nearby Places pane, click a plus (+) sign to see the names of the places and well as the distance from those places to your original search point.**

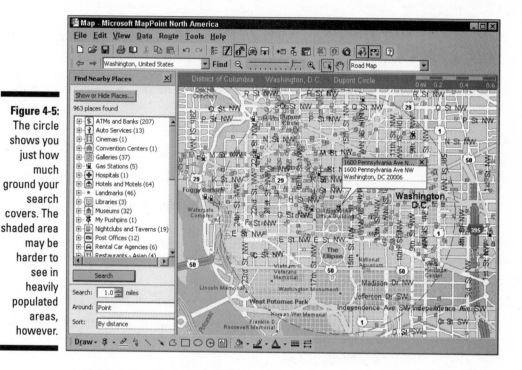

Figure 4-5:
The circle
shows you
just how
much
ground your
search
covers. The
shaded area
may be
harder to
see in
heavily
populated
areas,
however.

The Find Nearby Places pane lists the types of places MapPoint found within the one-mile radius.

4. Double-click the name of a place of interest to select its icon on the map and show the information balloon.

The information balloon provides the mailing address and phone number of the chosen place.

5. Click the Close (X) button to close the Find Nearby Places pane.

You can bring back the Legend and Overview Pane by clicking the Legend and Overview button on the Standard toolbar.

You can also have MapPoint find places near a route as well. To do this, create or open a route (you find out how to do this in Chapter 5), and then choose Tools⇨Find Nearby Places. From the Around drop-down box, select the Entire Route option. The entire route is highlighted, and all places within one mile of it are listed in the Find Nearby Places pane. You can also have MapPoint limit the search to a specific stretch of your trip by clicking a line in the Directions pane, and then choosing Tools⇨Find Nearby Places.

Hiding unwanted places

If you're trying to assess the potential competition in the area of your proposed steak house, then you'll probably only want to see other steak houses, not libraries, schools, hotels, and so on. Irrelevant places would only fog your analysis.

Fortunately, MapPoint enables you to easily pick and choose which nearby places are displayed. All you have to do is follow these simple steps to narrow the field:

1. **Either do a Find Nearby Places search by following the steps in the preceding section, or choose Tools⇨Find Nearby Places on the menu bar.**

   The Find Nearby Places pane replaces the Legend and Overview pane, and your map takes on the appearance of the one in Figure 4-5.

2. **Click the Show or Hide Places button.**

   The Restaurant tab of the Show or Hide Places dialog box appears.

3. **Because all types of restaurants are displayed by default, you need to deselect the check boxes of those you want to hide. Do the same for the Places tab.**

   If you want to hide all but one or two items, you may find it helpful to click the Uncheck All button on each tab. That way you only need to click the few items you want to see.

4. **Click OK to dismiss the dialog box and refresh the map.**

You can repeat these same steps to toggle chosen place types off or on. That way you can see what you want to, when you want to.

Widening the search

In a large city, a one-mile radius may turn up dozens of restaurants, for example, but in rural areas, you may have to expand your area several miles to even uncover a single town cafe. MapPoint gives you the flexibility to broaden your search for nearby places if needed or desired.

With the Find Nearby Places pane open, all you need to do is double-click inside the Search box, enter the desired number of miles, and then press Enter. The circle surrounding the selected point changes in size to reflect the number of miles entered. And remember, you can express the number of miles in decimal points as well.

Working with Pushpins

For decades, Pushpin-filled maps have donned the walls of many a sales office, proudly marking the spots of successful sales or clients. With the advent of MapPoint, however, the world of Pushpins has changed forever. And best of all, these Pushpins can't prick your fingers!

In addition to simply marking a spot, you can do any of the following with a MapPoint Pushpin:

✔ Assign a text-filled balloon to each Pushpin, making it possible to see the Pushpin's contact details — name, address, phone number, and so on. The information is displayed when you double-click a Pushpin.

✔ Include a hyperlink to the client's corporate Web site or to an individual e-mail address in a Pushpin's text balloon.

✔ Color-code Pushpins, as well as change their appearance altogether, or even design your own Pushpin symbols.

✔ Use the data attached to Pushpins to run complex data analysis with MapPoint charts or export the data into Excel to run calculations.

✔ Use account information in Excel, Outlook, Access, Publisher, or SQL Server to create a set of Pushpins with minimal effort.

Creating Pushpins

MapPoint enables you to create Pushpins several different ways. When you search for an address or place, a Pushpin is automatically generated for you. Or if you want to "draw" your Pushpins by hand, you can do so by using MapPoint's Drawing toolbar. Simply click the Create a Pushpin button near the left end of the Drawing toolbar; then click the desired location of your Pushpin on the map. The Pushpin appears on-screen with an empty Pushpin balloon, as shown in Figure 4-6.

You can also generate Pushpins from data residing in other Microsoft applications. We show you how in Chapter 8.

Editing the Pushpin balloon text

The gray bar at the top of the Pushpin balloon holds the title of the Pushpin — the name of the business, place, or person. You can modify any Pushpin's name, whether the Pushpin was created manually or generated by MapPoint following a search. To do so, simply click inside the gray bar and delete or enter text as desired. The title can contain up to 128 characters, but we suggest you use significantly fewer — say 29 or fewer if possible — so that the entire title is viewable in the standard Pushpin balloon.

You can also add information such as the street address, mailing address, phone number, or primary contact person's name to the Pushpin balloon by clicking inside the white portion of the balloon and keying that information in. Press Enter after each line of text to expand the balloon's size automatically. If the information exists in another Windows application, you can cut and paste it into the balloon.

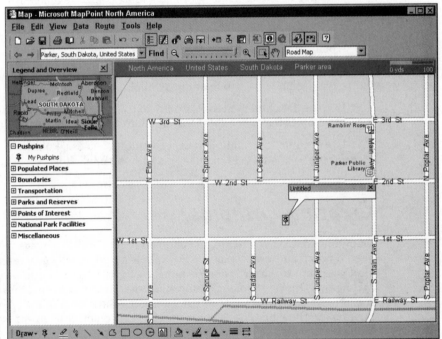

Figure 4-6:
Your
Pushpin
is waiting.

Adding hyperlinks to Pushpin balloons

Say that you want to be able to click a Pushpin and jump to the related company's Web site, or, better yet, have MapPoint fire off a pre-addressed e-mail message to the Pushpin's designated contact. MapPoint enables you to do both of these tasks and more. Here's the lowdown on adding different types of links to a Pushpin balloon:

✔ **A Web site link:** Including a link to a Web site is as easy as typing the URL (for example, **www.mydomain.com**). After you enter **www** followed a dot and the first letter of the domain name, the text becomes blue in color, and it's underlined, confirming its status as a hyperlink. If the Web site doesn't have the standard *www* prefix, you need to enter **http://** before the site's address.

We suggest that you test a link before you distribute the map to make sure everything's in working order. Typos can easily sneak in when you're working late at night; it happens to the best of us. Save yourself some grief by double-checking the links.

✔ **An e-mail address link:** To link to an e-mail address, simply enter **mailto:** followed by the desired e-mail address. Do not include a space between the colon and the e-mail address or the link will not work properly. When the resulting blue underlined text is clicked, your e-mail program launches a pre-addressed new message window for you to enter whatever message you want to send.

✔ **A link to a personal file or a file residing on a shared network:** This is a great way to leap from a Pushpin balloon to say an Excel file of sales statistics, or a Word document outlining the organization's purpose or goals. To form this link, enter **file:** followed by the full path/address of the file to which you'd like to link.

If you're not one hundred percent sure what the full path to the file is, open the file and then choose File⇨Properties from the menu bar. On the General tab of the Properties dialog box, you see the word *Location.* Next to this word is the path name you need. Just follow the path name with the document name and applicable file extension, and you're good to go!

Again, the text takes on the blue underlined hyperlink appearance. Click the link to open the specified file (assuming you have the application that created the linked document installed on your computer).

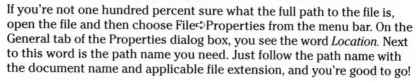

Did you get an error message when you tested the file link? Windows 2000 and Windows XP users may notice that the majority of their documents are stored in subdirectories of a Documents and Settings directory. The spaces in this (or any other) directory can spell big trouble for MapPoint's automatic link creator. After you press the spacebar on your keyboard, MapPoint stops recognizing the text as part of the link. So what can you do short of moving all the necessary files to a new directory? Here's an easy workaround, and it doesn't require you to reorganize your whole hard drive either! Instead of hitting the spacebar, simply enter **%20** between words. For example, the Documents and Settings directory would read `Documents%20and%20Settings`. Ta-da; it works now!

Manipulating Pushpins

You can manipulate MapPoint Pushpins many additional ways. Table 4-1 gives you a rundown of some of the most common modifications.

Table 4-1	Modifying MapPoint Pushpins
To Do This . . .	*. . . You Need to Do This*
Open a Pushpin balloon	Double-click the Pushpin whose balloon you want to open, or select the Pushpin on the map and click the Show Information button on the Standard toolbar.
Reposition a Pushpin balloon	Right-click on the open balloon, and then choose the desired Orientation from the shortcut menu. You can choose from Upper Right, Lower Right, Upper Left, or Lower Left.
Close a Pushpin balloon	Click the Close (X) button in the upper-right corner, or, with the Pushpin selected, click the Show Information button on the Standard toolbar.
Highlight a Pushpin on the map	Click the Pushpin you want to highlight and then choose Tools⇨Highlight. The Pushpin is circled in a bright yellow color, similar to that of a highlighter marker.
Delete a Pushpin	Click the Pushpin you want to delete and then press the Delete key. Keep in mind that you cannot delete Pushpins that are part of a linked set.
Move a Pushpin to a new location	Click and drag the Pushpin into position on the map.
Rename a Pushpin	Click inside its gray title bar, edit the name, and then save the map to make the change permanent.
Search for a Pushpin by name	With the map containing the Pushpin open, enter the desired Pushpin's name in the Find a Location box on the Navigation toolbar and then click the Find button.
View a single Pushpin within an overlapped group	Click the overlapped group of Pushpins to see a list of available Pushpins. After you've clicked the one you want to see, click OK. That Pushpin appears on top in plain view.

MapPoint didn't behave the way you expected it to? There may be a reason for that. If you link a set of Pushpins to data down the road, you may not be able to edit the Pushpin text or delete a Pushpin in the manner described in Table 4-1. It should also be noted that you can only delete Pushpins you define, not points of interest labeled by MapPoint. To remove POIs from view, you have to choose View⇨Show or Hide Places, deselect the categories you want to hide, and then click OK.

Changing the look of your Pushpins

If you don't like the subdued look of the default Pushpins, don't worry; MapPoint gives you more than 256 alternate choices. And the choices you make go far beyond mere aesthetics. For example, you can use the number Pushpins to map out a walking tour of your town, and then create a Word document displaying both the numbered map points and the narrative of each place's significance. Or you can plot commercial accounts with red Pushpins and individual clients with green Pushpins. The possibilities are endless.

Selecting a different Pushpin from the get-go

If you plan to use the Drawing toolbar to create a Pushpin, you can alter the Pushpin's appearance before creating it. Instead of clicking the Create Pushpin button, simply click the down arrow next to the Create Pushpin button. Doing so opens the sizable collection of Pushpin symbols from which you can choose (see Figure 4-7). Just click a specific Pushpin symbol to select it for the Pushpin you're about to create.

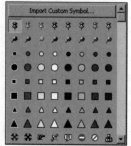

Figure 4-7: You can choose any of the Pushpin symbols in this collection.

Modifying an existing Pushpin's appearance

Need to change the look of an existing Pushpin? Want to assign different Pushpin symbols to various kinds of locations? You can change your MapPoint Pushpins one at a time by right-clicking on the Pushpin and choosing Properties from the shortcut menu. The Pushpin Properties dialog box, shown in Figure 4-8, appears. Use the Symbol down arrow button to access your collection of Pushpin symbols, and click the one you want to use. After you've made your selection, click OK to dismiss the dialog box. Within seconds, your newly chosen Pushpin symbol appears on-screen.

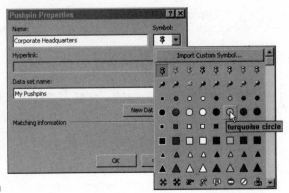

Figure 4-8:
A symbol
change is
just a mouse
click away.

Changing all the Pushpins at once

Perhaps the default Pushpins are just a bit too drab for that PowerPoint presentation you're cooking up. Changing them all at once is a snap when you
follow these easy steps:

1. **In the Legend and Overview pane, right-click on the name of the
   Pushpin set you want to modify, and then choose Properties from the
   shortcut menu. (The default name of a Pushpin set is *My Pushpins*.)**

   The My Pushpins Properties dialog box opens. It's basically identical to
   the dialog in Figure 4-8, except that it contains a summary of how many
   Pushpins are included in the selected set, how many (if any) addresses
   were not matched to a Pushpin, and how many addresses in the set were
   not assigned a Pushpin. You should note that this information is really
   only of significance when you've imported data to be turned into
   MapPoint to be converted to Pushpins, as you can see in Chapter 8.

   The exact name of the dialog box depends on the name of the selected
   Pushpin set. For example, if the Pushpin set is called MapPoint Fans
   Pushpins, the dialog box is called MapPoint Fans Pushpins Properties.

2. **From the Symbol drop-down box, click the desired Pushpin design.**

   This may sound a bit hokey at first, but consider the intent of the
   mapped Pushpins before selecting a Pushpin style. For example, the
   audience at the back of an auditorium may not be able to discern the
   intricate Pushpin design used in your PowerPoint presentation.
   Something big, bold, and colorful may be far more effective. Or if you're
   planning to include the Pushpins on a corporate Web page, you may
   want to choose a Pushpin color that complements the Web page, rather
   than detracts from it.

3. **Finally, click OK to apply the new style and close the dialog box.**

   Within seconds, all the Pushpins carry the newly chosen symbol.

Creating Pushpin Sets

So what exactly is a Pushpin set? Well, if you've ever placed a Pushpin on a map, then you've already created a Pushpin set. The creation of a single Pushpin on a map creates a Pushpin set called "My Pushpins" by default. (You can rename the Pushpin set anytime you want by following the directions in the section called "Renaming a Pushpin set," later in this chapter.) Typically, importing data from Excel, Outlook, Access, or a similar application can create Pushpin sets, but you can make them from scratch, too.

To create a new set of Pushpins from scratch, do the following:

1. **Place the first Pushpin on the map and then right-click it and choose the Properties option from the shortcut menu.**

   The Pushpin Properties dialog box appears (refer to Figure 4-8).

2. **Next, click the New Data Set button.**

   A tiny New Data Set dialog box appears with a single text box, waiting for you to select a name for the new data set.

3. **Enter the name of the data set to be created and then click OK.**

   The New Data Set dialog box closes, leaving only the Pushpin Properties dialog box, which now displays the newly chosen name in the Data Set Name box.

4. **Click OK to dismiss the last dialog box.**

Moving a Pushpin from one data set to another

If you need to move a Pushpin from one data set to another, you'll be happy to know it's a pretty simple task. Simply right-click on the Pushpin you want to relocate, choose Properties from the shortcut menu, and then choose the new location for the Pushpin from the Data Set Name drop-down box. Click OK to close the dialog box, and you're all done! Be sure to save your map after the change, though, to make sure everything's where you want it the next time around.

Renaming a Pushpin set

For whatever reason, you may find it necessary to rename a Pushpin set. After all, the default name, *My Pushpins,* certainly doesn't gain points for originality!

To rename a Pushpin set, right-click on its current name in the Legend and Overview pane, and choose Properties from the shortcut menu. Click inside the Name text box and then enter the desired name for the data set. Click OK to dismiss the dialog box and save the name change; it's as simple as that! You'll probably also want to go ahead and save the map at this point as a little insurance policy.

Deleting a Pushpin set

Want to kill an entire set of Pushpins in a single step? Just click the Pushpin set name in the Legend and Overview pane and then press Delete. MapPoint then prompts you to confirm the deletion. Keep in mind that after you click OK, the Pushpins are gone for good.

Designing Your Own Pushpin Symbols

Wouldn't it be neat to mark the locations of all your company's stores or offices with Pushpins that resemble the company's logo? Or maybe you have an in-house artist who wants to design a special Pushpin that coordinates well with your corporate Web site.

No matter what your personal situation is, you may appreciate the fact that you're not limited by the 256 Pushpins Microsoft provides from which you can choose.

But before you or a member of your staff jumps into the task of designing a custom Pushpin, you need to be aware of a few ground rules you'll have to abide by in order for the Pushpin to work effectively with MapPoint. These ground rules include the following:

✔ You can use any of the following file types for your Pushpin: uncompressed Windows bitmap (`.bmp`) files, Windows icon resource (`.ico`) files, or Windows cursor (`.cur`) files.

✔ The image size cannot not exceed 128 x 128 pixels.

✔ As for color depth, you can choose from 2, 16, or 24 bit, or 256 colors.

✔ Because MapPoint uses a large number of different colors at different times in the map-rendering process, you should design a Pushpin symbol based on MapPoint's custom symbols color palette. That way you won't experience unusual color shifts when your Pushpin is used on various types of maps.

 ✔ The upper left pixel color will be used to represent the optional transparent color value discussed in the "Tweaking the Pushpin's background," later in this chapter. You can make any pixel in the image this color, including those in the middle of the image, and they will disappear when transparency is activated.

Perhaps the easiest way to begin designing a Pushpin symbol is to build your own .bmp files in a program such as Microsoft Paint or Adobe Photoshop.

You can also do a search on the Internet for images and find freeware samples. Just to make life even easier, we have included a collection of sample .BMP files on one of the book's CDs, which you can use directly with MapPoint. You can also open them in Microsoft Paint and change them as desired.

Importing the custom Pushpin symbol

After designing a custom symbol, you need to import it into MapPoint in order to make it available. Follow these steps to import your newly designed Pushpin into MapPoint:

1. **On MapPoint's Drawing toolbar, click the down arrow next to the Create Pushpin button.**

   This opens the collection of Pushpins currently available in MapPoint.

2. **Click the Import Custom Symbol button.**

   A standard Open dialog box appears.

3. **Work your way to the directory in which the customized file is stored, and then double-click the filename when you locate it.**

   The customized symbol is available for use in MapPoint from this point forward.

Tweaking the Pushpin's background

You may want to modify your custom Pushpin's background transparency, depending on the intended output format of your map. The default transparent background is the most aesthetically pleasing by far, but perhaps a solid background would accentuate the Pushpins more for slide presentations and such.

If you want to experiment with this setting a bit, here's how to do it: On the Drawing toolbar, click the down arrow next to the Create Pushpin button. Next, right-click on the customized Pushpin you want to experiment with. To give the Pushpin a solid background, click the Transparency option to remove the check mark. Because the option is like a toggle switch, simply do the reverse to restore the transparency to the Pushpin's background.

Chapter 5

Basic Driver's Ed: Route Planning

· ·

In This Chapter

▶ Generating point-to-point driving directions

▶ Interpreting your itinerary

▶ Setting road type preferences

▶ Building and optimizing a route

▶ Updating road construction information

▶ Tweaking drive day times

▶ Managing fuel consumption and costs

▶ Working with drivetime zones

· ·

*W*hat would you say if we told you that you'd never have to pull over and ask for directions again? With MapPoint, you can effortlessly find the best way to get from one location to another. You even have the flexibility to define whether that "best way" is the shortest or quickest route, or simply the route that favors your preferred roads.

If you think those features are neat, you'll really love MapPoint's ability to take a handful of stops and turn them into an optimized route. No more zigzagging and aimless wandering around town to deploy account representatives, deliver pizzas, take the baseball team home, whatever.

Generating Point-to-Point Driving Directions

As a young driver in training, you need to cruise around the parking lot a bit before you can hit the highway. (Don't worry; we won't force you to practice parallel parking!) Just follow these steps to create a detailed set of point-to-point driving directions:

1. **Click MapPoint's Route Planner button (the little car button you see here in the margin) to begin planning your trip.**

   The Route Planner pane appears on the left side of the screen.

2. **Enter the starting point of your trip in the Type Place or Address text box at the top of the Route Planner (see Figure 5-1) and then click the Add to Route button.**

   For example, enter **Space Needle, Seattle, Washington** or **3000 Connecticut Avenue, NW, Washington, D.C.** If MapPoint finds a single match for your entry, the point will be added to your route. If no direct match or more than one match is found, the Address tab of the Find dialog box, shown in Figure 5-2, appears.

3. **Click OK if the address/location displayed is correct.**

   If the address shown is incorrect, simply edit the applicable field(s) and then click the Find button on the right side of the dialog box to have MapPoint search its database for the edited address.

   After you click OK, the address you entered appears as stop number one on your route.

4. **Repeat Steps 2 and 3, this time supplying the address of your desired destination.**

   This address becomes the second stop on your route.

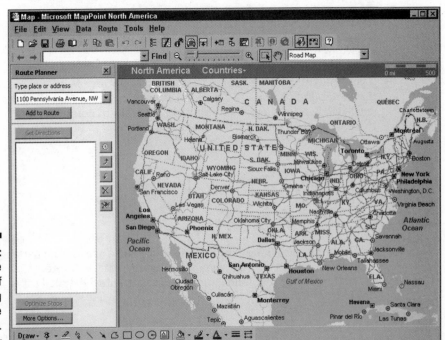

Figure 5-1:
Enter the
address of
your starting
point in the
text box.

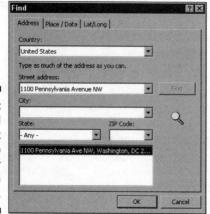

Figure 5-2:
The Find
dialog box
comes into
play for
route
planning.

5. Click the Get Directions button.

MapPoint computes the quickest route and then displays step-by-step driving directions, as shown in Figure 5-3. This customized itinerary is displayed in a special pane referred to as the *Directions pane*.

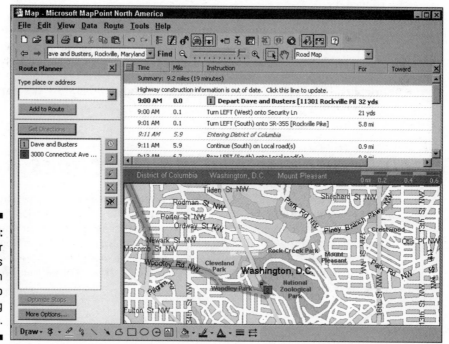

Figure 5-3:
Your
itinerary is
presented in
step-by-step
driving
directions.

Avoiding certain areas

What happens if you need to plan a route in your city and some of the roadways are closed because of a big parade? You can tell MapPoint to avoid a certain area by using the Drawing toolbar.

 Just click the Zoom button (shown in the margin) to zoom in close to the area you want to avoid (as described in Chapter 2), click the Rectangle button on the Drawing toolbar, and then point and click the mouse pointer in the upper-left corner of the area you want to avoid. Slowly drag

the pointer down and to the right until all of the area you want to avoid is included inside the rectangle. Release the mouse button, right-click the border of the box, and then choose Avoid Area from the shortcut menu.

The area you selected is highlighted in yellow, letting you know which area MapPoint plans to avoid. Define your trip or route as usual. When you create the itinerary, you'll notice that the area you selected was avoided just as you requested.

 To save the directions and corresponding map for future use, simply click the Save button (shown in the margin) on the Standard toolbar and name the file. Later on, you can choose File➪Open to retrieve the directions and map on demand.

After you enter an address or place name into the Route Planner, MapPoint remembers that information indefinitely (unless, of course, you ever reinstall MapPoint). So the next time you plan a trip or route containing a previously used address or place name, you can simply click the arrow button at the right end of the Type Place or Address text box, and choose the desired entry from the list.

Deciphering the Driving Directions

After you've produced a set of driving directions, the Directions pane contains an abbreviated summary of your trip — the trip's total mileage and an estimate of how long it will take to get to your destination, assuming you followed MapPoint's default 9:00 a.m. to 5:00 p.m. driving day (you find out how to change this setting in "Setting your average driving day," later in this chapter). This summary is followed by step-by-step driving directions (refer to Figure 5-3).

The driving directions contain five columns of information:

- ✔ **Time:** This column displays the approximate time you'll need to execute the accompanying step. By default, MapPoint assumes all travel starts at 9:00 a.m. and ends at 5:00 p.m. We show you how to change those settings in the section titled "Modifying the Default 9-to-5 Driving Day," later in this chapter.

- ✔ **Mile:** This column lists a running total of the number of miles driven to this point.

- ✔ **Instruction:** Here is where you find detailed directions such as "Turn right onto Montgomery Road" or "Merge onto I-95."

- ✔ **For:** This column tells you how many miles you will travel before executing the next direction.

- ✔ **Toward:** Think of this column as providing additional qualifying information for the instruction given. It may display a specific exit name, or give you alternate names for the road or highway mentioned.

Just underneath the Directions pane on the map, you see a bright green line highlighting your proposed travel route. A green box with a 1 in the middle marks your starting point, and a red box with a 2 in the middle marks your destination. On longer trips (those longer than eight hours in duration), you see blue boxes with a moon in them to designate suggested overnight stops.

Setting Route and Road-Type Preferences

MapPoint generates driving directions based on the quickest route available. But what if you want the shortest route instead? Or what if you'd like to avoid high-speed interstates or toll roads altogether? You can do all of those things with a few simple mouse clicks. MapPoint can also produce an itinerary that truly reflects your personal preferences.

Finding the shortest route

 If the high cost of fuel is foremost on your mind, you may want to create an itinerary that reflects the shortest distance to travel rather than the quickest way to get there. To set this preference, you need to open the route you wish to work with (click File⇨Open), click the Route Planner button (shown in the margin) to open the Route Planner pane, and then follow these steps:

1. Enter your starting point and travel destination information.

Follow Steps 1 through 4 in the "Generating Point-to-Point Driving Directions" section, earlier in this chapter.

2. Click the More Options button at the bottom of the Route Planner pane.

The More Route Options dialog box opens.

3. Click the Segments tab (shown in Figure 5-4).

Figure 5-4:
The Segments tab is where you tell MapPoint what kind of a journey you want to take.

4. Click the Shortest button.

Make sure that you click the button *labeled* "Shortest," not the tiniest button in the dialog box!

5. Click OK to apply your change and then click the Get Directions button in the Route Planner.

MapPoint creates a new itinerary based on the requested change.

While writing this chapter, we ran a little experiment to see just how much of a difference one would see in the shortest versus the quickest route. We defined a starting point just north of Washington, D.C., and a destination in rural southeastern South Dakota. Using the quickest route, the trip would take 20 hours and 36 minutes and would cover 1,302.1 miles. That's a long trip no matter how you slice it!

Now if we opted for the shortest distance, we could shave 50 miles off the journey, but the driving time would increase three hours thanks to the alternate routing to lower-speed roads. The decreased mileage and slower, more fuel-efficient travel speed of the shortest route can definitely save you some dough, but in today's highly competitive business world, the extra three hours may be too high of a price to pay. Only you can tell which option would be in your best interest.

Setting preferences for various types of roads

Digging up change for toll roads can be a major pain, especially if you're in a hurry and have no clue what you're going to have to cough up at the booth. Some people swear by the smooth roads and fine rest facilities located on America's toll roads, but others bristle at the thought of having to pay just to travel on a road. MapPoint can customize your route to include more — or fewer — toll roads.

And if you loathe driving on high-speed interstates, MapPoint can help you out there, too! Of course, all this preference setting can have its drawbacks in the form of increased mileage and/or travel time, but these factors may not matter to you.

You'll be pleased to know that you can define preference levels for four types of roads: interstates and limited access roads, other highways, arterial roads, and toll roads. And we're not talking basic "I like them"/"I don't like them" options, either. The preferences range within a seven-point continuum for each item on a scale of strongly disliking to strongly liking.

To begin defining preference levels for various types of roads, simply do the following:

1. **Open or generate a route.**

   To generate a route, refer to the steps in the section "Generating Point-to-Point Driving Directions," earlier in this chapter.

   You need to have an active route on-screen in order to adjust road preference options.

2. **Click the More Options button at the bottom of the Route Planner pane on the left side of the screen.**

   The More Route Options dialog box opens.

3. **Click the Segments tab (refer to Figure 5-4) and then click the name of the desired route segment if more than one option appears.**

4. **Click the Preferred Roads button.**

   You need to click this button in order to gain access to the Preferred Road Types button.

5. Click the Preferred Road Types button.

Now you can begin working with the continua in the Preferred Roads dialog box, as shown in Figure 5-5.

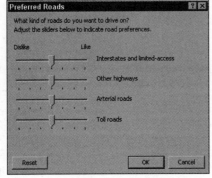

6. To make an adjustment, click and drag one of the little lever-like sliders in the desired direction and then release the mouse button to lock it into place.

7. Repeat Step 6 until you've configured all the road types to your liking.

8. Click OK to save your settings and then click OK again to close the More Route Options dialog box.

9. Click the Get Directions button to refresh the driving directions based on the new options.

A new itinerary appears in the Directions pane.

Adding Stops to a Route

Say that you've made your plans for the day and a client emergency comes up. With MapPoint, adding a last-minute stop is a lot simpler than you may think.

If you know about the stop before you enter the starting point and destination into MapPoint's Route Planner, the task of adding yet another stop is pretty easy. Simply begin planning your trip as described in "Generating Point-to-Point Driving Directions," earlier in this chapter, but before you enter the final stop, type in the middle stop's address and then click the Add to

Route button. This new address becomes stop number two on your journey. Add the information for your destination point and then click the Get Directions button to generate driving directions for the three-stop trip.

Adding an unanticipated stop to an existing route isn't terribly difficult, either. Just follow these steps:

1. **Clicking File⇨Open and navigate to the desired file to open the file containing the route you want to modify.**

2. **Enter the place name or address of the additional stop into the Route Planner and then click the Add to Route button.**

   This step makes the new stop the destination.

3. **To reorganize the stops listed in the Route Planner, click the name of the entry you need to move in the list of stops (it should be on the bottom of the list); then, click the Move Up button, as shown in Figure 5-6.**

4. **Click the Get Directions button to generate a new itinerary that includes the unanticipated pit stop.**

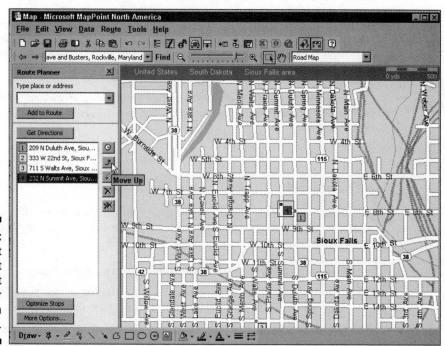

Figure 5-6: MapPoint makes it easy to put all of your stops in order.

Want to create a route based on one of your Pushpin sets (or even a select few Pushpins in a set)? No problem, thanks to MapPoint's Drawing tools. Find out just how easy it is to do in Chapter 6.

Let's Get Route-y! Creating a Fixed or Optimized Route

Whether you need an account representative to make multiple stops in a certain order, or you want to optimize a number of stops to ensure your sales team hits the biggest number of stops in the least amount of time possible, MapPoint is up to the task.

MapPoint has basically two kinds of routes: fixed and optimized. A *fixed route* is where you specify the order of the stops. This type of route would be useful for an account rep who may need to meet with people at each stop at a specific time.

An *optimized route,* on the other hand, would benefit a package delivery service, for example, where timing the arrival is less important than getting all the items to their destinations in the least amount of time. An optimized route simply means that MapPoint determines which order you should visit the stops to reach them in the least amount of time while consuming the least amount of fuel.

Optimized routes are almost always more efficient from an economic standpoint because your staff can accomplish more in less time and conserve fuel in the process.

Mapping a fixed route

In the following steps, you generate a fixed route of stops. In this case, *fixed* means you enter the stops in the order you need to make them. Here's a brief rundown:

1. **Click the Route Planner button to open the Route Planner.**

2. **Enter the address of the desired starting point in the Type Place or Address text box and then click the Add to Route button.**

3. **Enter the address or place name of your first (or next, in the case of subsequent stops) stop and then click the Add to Route button.**

4. **Keep repeating Step 3 until you've entered all your stops in the desired order.**

Everybody makes mistakes. If you get a couple of stops reversed or find that something's out of order in your list of stops, simply click the stop you need to move and then click the Move Up or Move Down button on the right side of the Route Planner. No harm done!

5. **After entering the information for the final stop, click the Get Directions button and watch MapPoint work its magic.**

Keep in mind that the final stop may be the same as the starting point for a delivery person, account rep, or salesperson. In that case, you want to right-click the first stop on your route and choose Add as End from the shortcut menu. That makes your starting point the end point of your route as well.

Optimizing a route

When you have more than one intermediate stop to make, MapPoint gives you the option of optimizing that route (or making it more time and fuel efficient). The starting point (designated by a green box with the number 1 inside of it) remains fixed during optimization, as does the end point (the address with a red box beside it). Addresses or places marked with a yellow box, however, are fair game for rearranging.

To optimize a route, simply follow Steps 1 through 4 for a fixed route in the preceding section, but this time you don't have to obsess over the order in which you enter the stops. After entering all the stops, click the Optimize Stops button near the bottom of the Route Planner and then click the Get Directions button to have MapPoint generate the optimized set of driving directions. MapPoint takes whatever data you provide it and produces an optimized route covering all the stops.

Keep two things in mind with regard to optimized routes. One is you need to have at least four stops in your route for the Optimize Stops button to become active. Second, if you've outlined a long, involved route, MapPoint may take a fair chunk of time to calculate the best route. We're not talking an enormous amount of time here, but it could be long enough to become noticeable for more complex jobs.

Avoiding Potholes and Other Road-Construction Headaches

It may not be this way where you live, but in the good ol' Midwest, snowy winters are followed not by spring, but by something not so affectionately known as "pothole season." The ice, salt, and chemicals do their number on the roads, leaving tons of dented wheel rims and other minor automobile damage in their wake. Sooner or later, construction crews get around to repairing some of the worst holes. In a few cases though, entire stretches of roads need resurfacing, snarling traffic beyond recognition. These repairs may make driving life smoother down the road, but they can be your worst nightmare if you are in a rush to get to an important meeting, or are running dangerously low on gas.

Although we can't guarantee you'll miss *every* construction-related traffic jam, we can sure help you eliminate some major headaches. Of course, as you might imagine, construction data changes regularly, so you need to update it periodically for best results.

At the beginning of each calendar month, the text driving directions include the following entry: Highway construction information is out of date. Click this line to update. You are asked whether you want to download new data from the Web. Choose Yes and, if you have an active Internet connection, the download will take place automatically.

To download the latest construction information, you need to establish a connection to the Internet and then follow these simple steps:

1. **Choose Route⇨Update Construction Information from the menu bar.**

   A dialog box pops up, asking whether you want to download fresh data from the Web.

2. **Click the Yes button.**

   MapPoint establishes a connection to a predefined Web site and begins downloading the necessary files.

Now, if you open a saved route, MapPoint will recalculate the driving directions and alert you to outdated construction data on the second line of the Directions pane. You'll see the text referred to in the previous Note about out-of-date information. Likewise, if you define a route with old construction information housed on your computer, the same message will appear. Simply click the line of text as directed to bring everything up-to-date.

By default, MapPoint displays construction information on your itinerary, as shown in Figure 5-7. If you decide that you'd rather hide this information, you can easily do so by choosing Route⇨More Options, clicking the Profile tab, and deselecting the Display Highway Construction on Route check box. After you click OK to apply the change, it remains in effect until you explicitly change it.

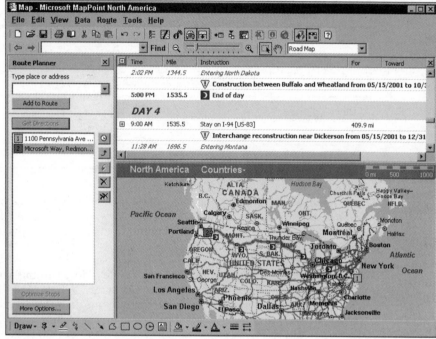

Figure 5-7:
Construction warnings displayed with your itinerary give you a heads-up to potential delays.

How Slowly Can You Go? Setting Average Driving Speeds

Do you have a bit of a lead foot when it comes to highway driving, or are you the kind of driver who scoots along the shoulder's edge tentatively? Although we certainly don't condone speeding (not only is it unsafe, but it can also get you into a whole lot of trouble), it should be noted that different states have different speed limits for various types of roads. For example, in the Baltimore/Washington, DC area, interstate speeds are still posted at 55 miles per hour in the more congested areas, but they quickly jump up to 65 miles per hour as you exit the cities proper. This variance in speed limits not only affects the duration of your trip, but also has an impact on gas mileage and related fuel costs.

To get the most accurate routes possible, you should look at MapPoint's driving speed settings to see if they accurately reflect the posted speeds in your area and/or the kind of driving you do. You may also want to adjust your speeds to reflect the actual travel speed given the time of day you intend to travel. For example, a road's posted speed may be 30 miles per hour, but rush-hour reality may be closer to 15 or 20 miles per hour. Table 5-1 shows the driving speed defaults Microsoft uses in MapPoint.

Table 5-1	Default Driving Speeds by Road Type
Road Type	*Default Speed*
Interstate highways	65 mph
Limited-access highways	60 mph
Other highways	50 mph
Arterial roads	35 mph
Streets	20 mph

In the table, we show 20 mph as the default for the Street setting, but a bug makes new installations of the program display and use 31 as the default. You can fix this by clicking Reset and saving the change in the standard MapPoint template.

You can adjust these settings by choosing Route⇨More Options and then clicking the Driving Speeds tab, as shown in Figure 5-8. Enter the desired speed for each road type or click the arrow buttons provided to make the desired changes. Clicking OK saves your settings and dismisses the dialog box. If you want to return to the default values listed in Table 5-1, just click the Reset button on the Driving Speeds tab.

Figure 5-8:
Adjust
MapPoint's
default
speeds to
reflect
speed limits
in your area.

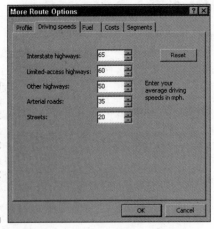

Modifying the Default 9-to-5 Driving Day

Okay, raise your hand if you really work between the hours of 9:00 and 5:00. Uh-huh, we thought so. Maybe Dolly Parton worked 9 to 5 in that old movie, but few of us do anymore. Whether it's because of flextime, shifts, or the need to work long hours to meet demand, the 9 to 5 workday has become almost as extinct as the average dinosaur.

Or what if you're on vacation and are willing to drive long hours to get to your destination quicker? No matter what your particular situation is, odds are you'll at least want to modify a route's start time.

MapPoint enables you to modify your travel time to your heart's content. And doing so ensures that your itinerary reflects the trip's actual duration as you intend to drive it. You can modify travel time in two basic ways:

- ✓ **Modify the average driving day.** This setting enables you to hit the road and stop driving whenever you want to. Adjust it to reflect your company's 7:30 a.m. to 6:00 p.m. daily delivery hours, or to head out on vacation at 6:00 a.m. and drive until midnight each day to reduce the number of hotel stays needed.

- ✓ **Set destination arrival time.** If you need to arrive at a conference, a wedding, or other special event by a specific time, you may want to let MapPoint tell you what time to leave. (For best results on long, eight-hour-plus trips, you'll want to customize your average daily driving day first and then schedule the arrival time for your destination.)

Setting your average driving day

Package delivery services start their day at what seems to be the crack of dawn, whereas Chinese food delivery may extend well into the night. Whether you're using MapPoint for work or leisure, you'll undoubtedly find the need to adjust the average driving day from time to time.

If you typically use MapPoint for shorter, local runs only, you may need to reset only the Start driving time because your trip will most likely be completed before the scheduled End driving time.

To change the driving day settings, follow these steps:

1. **Choose Route⇨More Options on the menu bar.**

   The Profile tab of the More Options dialog box appears, as shown in Figure 5-9.

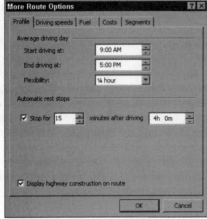

Figure 5-9:
You can
even give
yourself a
little wiggle
room when
it comes to
the start and
end of your
driving day
by setting
the
Flexibility
option.

2. **Modify the Start and End times any way you like.**

   Enter the desired times or use the arrow buttons to move the displays to the desired times.

   You can build some flexibility into your itinerary by using the Flexibility option's arrow buttons to specify how much deviation in time you're willing to accept in your route's scheduling.

   No flexibility is the minimum, and the amount can be as large as two hours. The default value is ¼ hour (or 15 minutes).

3. **Click OK to save your settings and close the dialog box.**

   You can now continue working in MapPoint.

When modifying a time in MapPoint, you needn't re-key the whole thing. Simply click the element (hour, minutes, or AM/PM) you want to change and then enter the new hour, minutes, and so on.

Getting to your destination on time

If you need to embark on a long journey with a specific arrival time, it can be difficult to predict when you need to leave in order to get to your destination on time. By scheduling the arrival time (along with setting the driving day times and scheduling rest stops), you turn the big decision over to MapPoint.

To have MapPoint calculate the required departure time for you, simply follow these steps:

1. **Click the Route Planner button to open the Route Planner.**

2. **Enter the starting and ending points of your trip along with any other stops you may need to make along the way.**

   For more information, see the section "Adding Stops to a Route," earlier in this chapter.

3. **Click the destination address or place name in the Route Planner to select it.**

4. **Click the Schedule Stop button (shown in the margin — it's the top button along the right side of the pane).**

   This opens the Schedule Stop dialog box, as shown in Figure 5-10.

Figure 5-10:
Let
MapPoint
help you
decide
when you
should
depart on
your
journey.

5. **Select the Arrive At check box to access the text box containing the arrival time.**

6. **Enter the required arrival time and then click OK to close the dialog box.**

7. **Click the Get Directions button to generate a new route based on your requirements.**

Scheduling the arrival time works great for shorter trips with no gas or rest stops required, but if you're going cross country, you need to factor in gas and food/rest stops and maybe even an overnight stay or two. Be realistic in setting your speeds and rest stops, too, or your MapPoint-generated departure time will be as good as useless.

Screeching to a Halt: Taking a Look at Different Types of Stops

As far as MapPoint is concerned, you can make three kinds of stops: scheduled breaks, touch-and-go stops, and specific stops you need to make on your route for a predefined amount of time. Each type of stop requires a slightly different method of setup, which we cover in the following sections.

Whew, I need a break: Rest stops

Scheduled break stops are appropriate in the following situations: to "force" yourself to get out and stretch once in awhile, to pad the itinerary for fuel stops, and to build meal time and restroom breaks into your itinerary's timeframe.

These scheduled breaks are for non-specific stops at a specific time. In other words, you may want to stretch your legs every four hours, but you don't have a specific place in mind at which to stop. You may just start keeping your eyes open for a good place to stop as the four-hour mark approaches.

To embed such a stop in your itinerary, follow these steps:

1. **Click File⇨Open or click the Open button to open a saved route; alternatively, create a new route.**

   Refer to "Adding Stops to a Route," earlier in this chapter, for more on creating a route.

   We recommend that you start in this manner because the type and length of the scheduled break will differ depending on the trip's length and purpose.

2. **Click the More Options button at the bottom of the Route Planner.**

   The Profile tab, shown back in Figure 5-9, appears by default.

3. **Select the Automatic Rest Stops check box.**

4. **Set the length of time desired for each rest stop in the first text box by using the arrow buttons or your keyboard.**

5. **Determine the frequency with which you'd like these stops to occur.**

   This is where you say, for example, "After three hours of driving, I'd like to stop."

6. **Click OK to save your selections and close the dialog box.**

7. **Regenerate your driving directions by clicking the Get Directions button.**

If you need to set multiple options for your trip or route, you don't have to regenerate the driving directions after setting each option. Instead, set all your options (driving speeds, rest stops, flexibility, and so on) and then click the Get Directions button.

Ready or not, here I am: Touch-and-go stops

Touch-and-go stops at a specific, predetermined location don't pad wait time into the itinerary, so they're best reserved for picking up passengers or parcels that are awaiting your arrival, or for making quick drop-offs.

To add these types of stops, just follow the steps in the "Adding Stops to a Route" section. You simply keep adding stops to your route; no further specialized steps are necessary.

We can't stress this enough: If there's even a remote chance that a stop will take more than a minute or two, you should probably invest the extra effort into scheduling the stop's duration. If you don't, the route that was supposed to end at 5:00 p.m. could end up taking an hour or more longer than anticipated. You find out how to define a stop's duration in the next section.

Hey, it's my job to stop! Scheduled stops

Many companies have employees who need to make the rounds on a regular basis. A home health care provider may need to visit a group of patients to perform blood tests on a daily basis, a snack food distributor may need to drop off a fresh load of potato chips to certain stores twice a week, a small-town bus driver may want to publish a bus schedule containing times of departure and arrival from major points of interest, and so on. A person or a company may want to call on MapPoint for routing advice for a number of reasons.

When you start digging in to some of the scheduled stop options, you'll be amazed at how flexible and powerful MapPoint really is. You can specify when the stop needs to be made, how much time you need for the stop, as well as when you want to leave the selected stop. All these options can be used together or separately to generate a route that works for your company, business, or trip.

You need to follow these steps in order to begin defining scheduled stop options:

1. **Click File⇨Open or click the Open button to open a saved route; or, create a new route.**

   See the "Adding Stops to a Route" section, earlier in this chapter, for more on creating a route.

2. **With the Route Planner open and the desired route displayed, double-click the stop you want to define a schedule for.**

   The Schedule Stop dialog box opens (refer to Figure 5-10).

3. **Select the first check box if you want to specify how long MapPoint should allow for the selected stop.**

   Choose any number of hours, minutes, or both for the stop, or you can use the second drop-down box to specify the number of nights allowed for the stop instead.

   Please note that the start and end points obviously do not have every option available to them. For example, you can't set the departure time for the final stop because, well, it's the final stop!

4. **Select the second check box if you want to set the time at which you need to arrive at the selected stop.**

   Enter the desired time or use the buttons provided to select the desired time. This option is great for those who need to make scheduled appointments by a certain time (that medical professional we mentioned earlier, for example).

5. **Select the Depart At option if you want to specify when you want to hit the road again.** Enter the desired time or use the buttons provided to select the desired time.

6. **After you've set all the desired options, click OK to save your settings, click the Get Directions button, and then continue working in MapPoint.**

Drag-and-drop stops

As you generate your route and discover what's nearby, you may see a landmark or two worth exploring along the way. Here's a wonderfully easy way to add these stops to your route.

After you've generated a route, click the green highlighted area in the map pane. This selects the route and changes the color of its highlight to a bright blue. At that point, your mouse pointer appears in the shape of a flag. Click the route and drag your mouse to the spot you wish to add to your itinerary. When you release the mouse button, MapPoint rebuilds your itinerary, incorporating the new stop.

You can do this drag-and-drop routing as much as you want, and the beauty of it is that you can schedule the new stops just as easily as you can schedule other stops on your route!

Fooling Around with Fuel Settings

Back in the summer of 2001, it was feared that gas prices would hit (or exceed) $3 per gallon! For companies or individuals who make their living on (or simply have fun on) the road, such news can be devastating if it's not planned or provided for.

Knowing the exact cost of a route or stop can help businesses set their prices accordingly and can help individuals make sure they have enough dough on hand to complete that cross-country vacation. MapPoint can even tell you when to stop and gas up, and best of all, these numbers are customized for your particular needs, whether you're driving a tiny car or an 18-wheel rig.

"Gas-timating" the cost of fuel for your trip or route

To estimate the cost of a route, follow these steps:

1. **Choose Route⇨More Options and then click the Fuel tab.**

   The Fuel tab of the More Route Options dialog box appears, as shown in Figure 5-11.

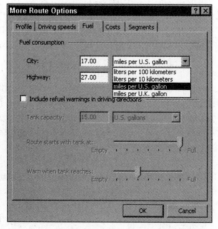

Figure 5-11:
Use the drop-down box to access fuel measurements.

2. **In the City and Highway text boxes, enter the city and highway mileage of the vehicle you'll be using for the route or trip.**

   Be sure to use the drop-down box provided to select the proper unit of measurement for your fuel (Miles per U.S. gallon is the default value).

   Simply enter the estimated numbers and then click the OK button.

3. **Click the Costs tab.**

4. **Enter the cost per unit of fuel in the Fuel Price text box; then, use the drop-down box to select the appropriate unit of measurement.**

   MapPoint uses this data along with the rate of fuel consumption to calculate the cost of fuel for your trip or route.

   If your journey takes you through a number of locations (say, a cross-country trip from Washington state to Florida), you may want to use the average fuel cost for the entire trip to generate a better cost estimate. Keep in mind that fuel costs in major cities or in tourist areas may be higher than they are at your local pumps.

5. **Click OK to save your settings and close the dialog box.**

   The cost of fuel for your trip or route is listed in the summary at the bottom of your driving directions.

If you have a long trip ahead of you, read on to find out how you can instruct MapPoint to include low-fuel warnings in your itinerary.

Time to fill 'er up: Setting low-fuel warnings

The miles can just slip by on long trips if you're surrounded by gorgeous scenery and bopping along to some cool tunes on the radio. But nothing can ruin your day more than running out of gas. MapPoint can help minimize the odds of this happening by placing low-fuel warnings in your itinerary.

If you're really organized, you can actually use this information to schedule fuel stops on the itinerary before you leave. You can do this by generating a set of driving directions, right-clicking the green highlighted route in the map pane, and selecting What's Nearby from the shortcut menu. You can then work with the Find Nearby Places pane as described in Chapter 4 to find gas stations at critical points and add them to your itinerary.

Follow these easy steps to incorporate the warnings into your itinerary:

1. **Choose Route⇨More Options and then click the Fuel tab.**

   The Fuel tab of the More Route Options dialog box appears (refer to Figure 5-11).

2. **Select the Include Refuel Warnings in Driving Directions check box.**

   Selecting this check box activates additional options and settings you need to configure (see Figure 5-12).

3. **Enter the tank capacity of your vehicle and then use the drop-down box to select a non-U.S. unit of tank capacity measurement.**

4. **Click and drag the Route Starts with Tank At lever into the position that best describes the vehicle's fuel status.**

   You need to tell MapPoint whether you'll be starting the route with a full tank of fuel, a half tank, or whatever.

5. **Click and drag the lever into the desired position to specify when you want MapPoint to warn you to refuel.**

   This setting, too, is expressed in terms of the fuel tank's status. Whether you want to be warned when you reach a half a tank of fuel, or you want to live dangerously and push it to a quarter tank, is up to you.

   At the risk of stating the obvious, not all roads are heavily traveled. If you're traveling I-90 from Sioux Falls, South Dakota, toward Mount Rushmore, you'd better give yourself plenty of warning to refuel. Gas stations aren't easy to come by in that area. If Baltimore to Orlando via I-95 is the route of choice, that's a slightly different story. Not only will you encounter many major metropolitan areas en route, but you'll also find a generous assortment of rest stops, truck stops, and small towns with gas stations. You can push your luck a bit more in those types of situations.

6. **Click OK to save your settings and close the dialog box.**

   The next time you check an itinerary, you should see one-line refuel warnings sprinkled throughout the driving directions. (Of course, the warnings won't appear on shorter routes where you don't run the risk of running out of gas.)

Figure 5-12:
Take control
over how
much
refueling
leeway
MapPoint
gives you.

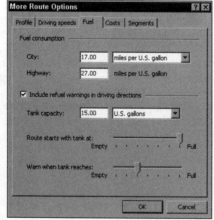

Setting Drivetime Zones

You may be wondering what in the world drivetime zones are. Basically, they are zones that are centered around a specific point on the map. They identify what distances you can drive from that point in a specified amount of time.

Say that you manage a small Chinese restaurant and want to define a delivery area where the driving time is no more than ten minutes away. No problem. Or, perhaps you run a shuttle service out of an airport and want to set fees based on the destination's proximity to the airport. Again, no problem; MapPoint lets you define multiple drivetime zones, too.

Creating a drivetime zone

To begin defining a drivetime zone, follow these steps:

1. **Set or open a Pushpin to use as your center point, as described in Chapter 4.**

2. **Choose Tools⇨Create Drivetime Zone from the menu bar.**

   The Create Drivetime Zone dialog box opens.

3. **Enter the desired number of minutes or use the arrow buttons in the Minutes box to define how far the Drivetime Zone should extend out from your central point.**

4. **Select the Draw Drivetime Zone Behind Roads check box if you want to be able to view specific roads in the zone.**

5. **Select the Fill Drivetime Zone with Solid Color check box if you want to view the area in general.**

6. **Click OK.**

   MapPoint begins building your drivetime zone. Within moments, you see a map similar to the one shown in Figure 5-13.

Although MapPoint lets you define drivetime zones up to 999 minutes in length (16, closing in on 17, hours worth of driving), you should note that such a job is going to take awhile to run. MapPoint must perform a lot of calculations in order to derive a long drivetime zone, so consider this a friendly warning. Lengthy drivetime zones won't just pop up on-screen, but the delay shouldn't be so significant that you need to run the job overnight.

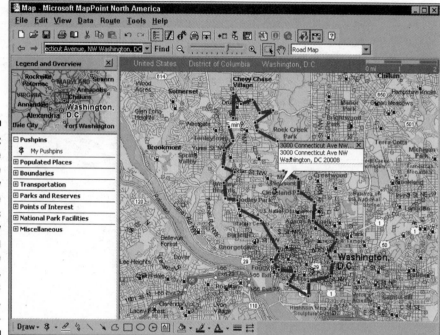

Figure 5-13:
Of course
the
accuracy
of these
results
may vary
depending
on the
weather,
traffic
volume,
and such.

And if you doubt for an instant that drivetime zones are thorough, consider Figure 5-14. (We've filled in the drivetime zone in a solid color to emphasize our point.) Amidst the shaded-in drivetime zone, you see parts of the map that aren't shaded in. Why? Because, perhaps, there isn't an interstate exit close to that spot, meaning you'd have to endure congested in-town traffic to get to the bare spot, making it physically impossible to reach that area in the allocated time.

Building multiple drivetime zones

Believe it or not, all you have to do to create multiple drivetime zones based on a single point is keep repeating the steps in the preceding section. Just make sure you click the Pushpin before executing each round of steps. That way you'll be certain that each drivetime zone is set on an identical center point.

When mapping multiple drivetime zones, start with the longest and work your way to the shortest. That way, all drivetime zones will be visible without having to tweak them with the Drawing toolbar.

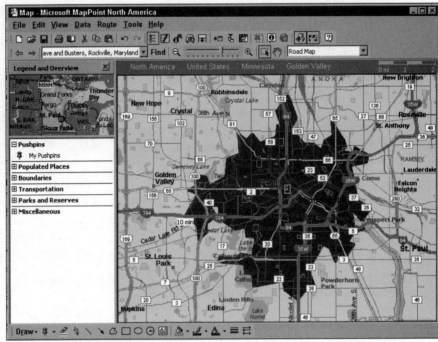

Figure 5-14:
Just
because a
destination
looks as
though it's
close
doesn't
mean that
you'll be
able to
make it
there
quickly.

To emphasize the differences in the various drivetime zones, you may want to change the fill color or border color of each zone. We show you how to do that in the next section.

Modifying the appearance of your drivetime zones

You have a variety of options at your disposal to make your drivetime zone map look just right. You can show or hide the labels, change colors, modify the border width, or even adjust the shape of the drivetime zone's borders.

As you go about making these modifications, however, keep in mind the intended purpose of your map. Your actions will vary radically depending on whether the map will be printed and distributed, or simply used for informational purposes in-house.

Showing or hiding drivetime zone labels

Take a moment to look back at Figure 5-14. Notice the little label to the left side of the drivetime zone that says 10 min? That label is a tremendous resource when you want to remind yourself what the various borders or areas mean. But if you need to publish a rate chart for your prospective clients, all that may matter is where one rate begins and another ends; whether that dividing line is 10 minutes or 15 is almost irrelevant to clients as long as they know where their destination falls.

These minute mark labels appear by default. If you want to remove them from view, simply right-click the drivetime zone's border or colored area, and choose Hide Size from the shortcut menu. To show hidden labels, right-click the drivetime zone's border or inside its colored area; this time, however, select the Show Size option.

 When clicking a drivetime zone that's drawn behind roads, try to click a point as far away from any roadways as possible. Clicking near a road could "trick" MapPoint into functioning as though you're trying to select a place on the map rather than the drivetime zone itself.

Selecting a different border width

When you want to use bordered drivetime zones in a presentation, you want to select a border thickness that's wide enough to be seen, but not so wide that it obstructs your view of the various zones. Luckily, border thickness is a quick adjustment, so you can try a few different widths on for size before settling on one.

By default, MapPoint's drivetime zone borders are 5 points wide. You can make them as thin as 1 point, or as thick as 14 points. To adjust the drivetime zone border width, click the border of the zone you want to modify and then click the Line Style button on the Drawing toolbar. Double-click the desired line width to close the menu and have MapPoint redraw the zone.

Coloring in the lines

Don't like the bright blue lines MapPoint draws by default? No sweat; change their color by clicking the border you want to recolor and then clicking the Line Color arrow button. This opens a palette of 40 predefined color choices from which you can choose. To pick one, just click it. The Line Color palette then closes, and the drivetime zone border appears in the selected color.

Switching the fill color

Whether you simply don't like MapPoint's default fill color or you want to color multiple zones differently so that they show up better, you can accomplish the task in short order. The first step involves clicking the drivetime zone's border you want to recolor. Then you need to click the Fill Color arrow button on the Drawing toolbar and double-click the swatch of the color you want. The menu closes, and the selected drivetime zone is recolored as requested.

Reshaping a drivetime zone

If you examine a drivetime zone closely, you often see various sharp points (refer to Figure 5-14). They're simply a reality given the complex calculations MapPoint performs to generate these drivetime zones. You may want to clean them up a bit though, whether it's a function of aesthetics or practicality.

You have basically two options for reshaping a drivetime zone. You can either grab one of the little black square size handles and drag it into position, or right-click a size handle and choose Delete Point from the resulting shortcut menu. Either way, the quirky points of your drivetime zone will be cleaned up for ease of viewing.

Deleting a drivetime zone

Everybody makes mistakes. If the drivetime zone doesn't meet with your approval, then you may want to start over from scratch, or even scrap the whole drivetime zone idea altogether. Deleting a drivetime zone is easy — just click the drivetime zone's border to select it and then hit the Delete key. It's as simple as that!

Changing the size of the drivetime zone

In order to change the number of minutes in your drivetime zone, you first need to delete the old drivetime zone (see the preceding section). After doing that, go back and redefine the drivetime zone as described in the steps in the "Creating a drivetime zone" section.

Part III

Presenting and Analyzing Information with MapPoint

The 5th Wave   By Rich Tennant

FRANK AND LUKE PLAN THEIR FIRST
TRAIN ROBBERY WITH MAPPOINT

"Look here, Frank. You've got to aggregate
the data using multiple thematics before
knowing which stagecoach to rob."

In this part . . .

Now that you're hooked on using MapPoint (okay, maybe we're being a bit presumptuous, but if you aren't already hooked, you will be by the time we start playing with all the cool features in this part), you'll want to learn how you can customize and share these little gems.

In this part, we show you how to put together the perfect map for distribution or publication. You find out how to customize the map's appearance and extract only the parts that you want to use, and then you discover all the ins and outs of e-mailing, printing, and publishing the maps to the Web. You can even see just how easy it is to incorporate these maps into PowerPoint presentations, Publisher newsletters and brochures, and the like.

But wait, there's more! You also learn how to take your own data (be it an Excel spreadsheet, an Access or SQL Server database, or an Outlook Contact List) and craft it into a meaningful, colorful map that lets you see your data in a whole new light. You can even blend your data with Census data for additional insight.

Chapter 6

Drawing with MapPoint

• •

• •

Wouldn't it be great if you could take those beautiful MapPoint maps and draw all over them — maybe highlight alternate routes from one place to another, add arrows on the map to point to your business's driveway because it's not on the street address side of the building, or add a text box to describe landmarks or other information of interest?

Well, you can. MapPoint 2002 gives you a full set of drawing tools to take you far beyond simple Pushpins.

Putting "Pen" to Map: The When and Whys

Drawing on a map isn't for everyone. In fact, drawings that are poorly thought out and executed can detract from a map. So when should you consider using MapPoint's drawing tools? The most obvious answer is when Pushpins or data maps fail to meet your needs. But there are other situations that almost mandate pulling out your virtual pen. Consider the following:

✔ You want to draw a rough outline of a plot of land that you're selling for yourself or a client. This outline gives prospective buyers a good indication of where the land sits in relation to various points of interest.

✔ You're providing direct-mail recipients a map showing how to find your new store and you want to alert people to pesky one-way streets. Drawing arrows in the appropriate spot may be helpful.

✔ You want to place a Pushpin in a location with an address currently not recognizable by MapPoint (that is, no physical address exists for the location yet). You'll need to draw one yourself (see "Drawing a Pushpin by Hand," later in this chapter), but at least this way the location may resemble others on your company Pushpin map.

✔ You need to draw attention (no pun intended) to a specific part of town, perhaps the location of your citywide arts festival, trade convention, or other major event. MapPoint's drawing tools let you accomplish the task with ease.

✔ You've got a Pushpin map of important clients and want to send mail to those clients in a certain location about an upcoming promotion. No need to know the postal codes to extract the desired records. Simply draw the area you want to work with and export the records to Excel (see Chapter 11 for more details on exporting records to Excel).

✔ If your corporate headquarters sits in the middle of a major metropolitan area, you may want to produce a map that highlights routes to get there from various spots in the city — the airport to your building, the preferred corporate hotel to your building, and so on.

As you can see, the right tools and a bit of forethought can make a good map great. In the sections that follow, we show you how to do just that.

Presenting the Tools of the Trade

Unlike a visual artist whose tools of the trade might include charcoal, pastels, watercolors, and oils that are stored in numerous drawers or paint-splattered bins, your drawing tools of the trade are neatly organized on the MapPoint Drawing toolbar (see Figure 6-1).

From this convenient toolbar that appears at the bottom of the MapPoint window, you can literally grab your tool of choice and draw to your heart's content. If the toolbar happens to be hidden, right-click any of the toolbars on-screen and then click the Drawing option from the resulting menu.

Alternatively, you can click View⇨Toolbars from the menu bar and then click the name of the toolbar you want to display or hide.

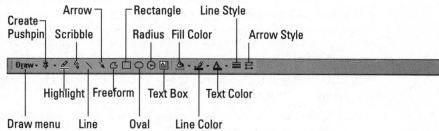

Figure 6-1:
MapPoint's
Drawing
toolbar
keeps
everything
close at
hand.

Also keep in mind that because many of MapPoint's drawing tools are flexible and easily modified to meet your needs, a few of them may start to look alike after awhile. That's just fine, because you're more than likely going to end up leaning on a couple of old favorites anyway. Our job, however, is to introduce you to all these tools and show you how to build the map you want and need with the least amount of work and the best possible results.

Does MapPoint's Drawing toolbar look familiar to you? It bears a striking resemblance to the Drawing toolbar used in the other Microsoft Office family applications, so you may have used these tools before. Even so, some of the tools have a different purpose in MapPoint, so you may still want to skim through the chapter. One of the first things you will discover is how geographically smart these drawing shapes are. After you place them on the surface of the map, they remain in the same location even if you zoom or pan the map!

Drawing a Pushpin by Hand

MapPoint is very good at drawing Pushpins on its own, provided that you give it some existing or recognizable street addresses to work with. But that isn't always possible. If the location you wish to mark with a Pushpin is under construction or even brand new, MapPoint won't have the information it needs to place the Pushpin for you. That means that you're on your own, at least for the time being.

Never fear, though. If you can find the spot on the map, adding a Pushpin is literally a mouse click away. After the area you wish to mark is in plain view on-screen, follow these steps:

1. **Click the Create Pushpin button, shown in the margin, from the Drawing toolbar; then, click the desired location on the map to set the Pushpin in place.**

The black Pushpin symbol appears by default. You can select a different Pushpin style from the get-go, however, by clicking the Create Pushpin arrow button. This gives you access to MapPoint's gallery of 256 Pushpin symbols plus any you may have created yourself (see the section titled "Designing Your Own Pushpin Symbols," in Chapter 4).

2. **Click inside the gray bar at the top of the Pushpin's text balloon to name the Pushpin.**

3. **Click inside the white part of the balloon to enter an address, phone number, or other descriptive information.**

   The section in Chapter 4 called "Working with Pushpins" gives you everything you need to know about placing and manipulating Pushpins in MapPoint.

Using Your Virtual Highlighter

College kids are famous for taking a yellow marker and drawing through lines of text in their books to highlight important bits of information. But this isn't just any yellow marker — it's a special transparent yellow marker known as a highlighter. It colors the surrounding white space in a book bright yellow while leaving the black text sharp and perfectly visible. You can get a whole rainbow of highlighter colors now: orange, pink, green, and more.

MapPoint, too, has a nice yellow Highlight tool available for you on its Drawing toolbar, and this is one highlighter that never runs out of ink! It's especially great for highlighting alternate or multiple routes on a map.

Putting the highlighter to work

To use MapPoint's highlighter, make sure that the area you wish to work with is fully visible on-screen. Then, follow these steps:

1. **Click the Highlight button on the Drawing toolbar.**

   Your mouse pointer resembles a plus (+) sign until you click the starting point, making the pointer pencil-shaped.

2. **Click and drag the highlighter to color the part of the map that you wish to highlight.**

   You'll also notice that MapPoint measures the distance as you drag the highlighter along a path. Pressing the Esc key deactivates the highlighter, restoring your mouse pointer to its default behavior.

Drawing a neat line through a road can be a real challenge because each little wiggle is accentuated on the map, giving the map a sloppy appearance (see Figure 6-2). If you need to draw a straight line, use the point-to-point procedure described in "Reading Between the Lines," later in this chapter; you'll get much nicer results. And if you must highlight a meandering path, make sure that your mouse is clean and in good working order or, better yet, use an optical mouse (one that uses light rather than the traditional mouse ball to track movement). Even then, you'll need a steady hand for best results.

Figure 6-2:
Highlights may be hard to see if they're placed behind roads and other map elements (they may be even harder to see here in black and white).

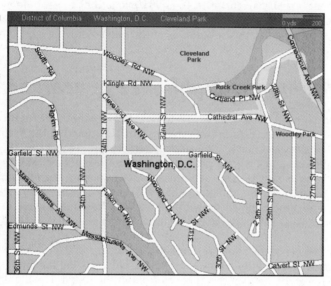

Need to highlight a single point? If it's a point of interest, a Pushpin, or another clickable element, just click it and choose Tools⇨Highlight. The place name will be highlighted with a bright yellow band of color.

You can also draw highlighted point-to-point lines by clicking the starting position and then clicking the destination point, resulting in a straight line drawn between the two points. You can repeat the process as many times as needed, pressing the Esc key to restore the mouse pointer to normal. Because drawing a straight line can be tricky at best, this is a great way to highlight routes on straight stretches of road.

Here's another useful purpose for the MapPoint highlighter. Say that you need more room at corporate headquarters and have begun looking for additional office space. You know of three or four possibilities close by but aren't sure which one is truly the closest for employees who need access to both buildings. You can highlight the routes between each new location and corporate headquarters the exact way the employees would have to travel to get there. Highlighting the routes not only lets you take advantage of various exits from the buildings but also helps you take into account shortcuts between buildings, through alleys and such. (Not that we advocate sending your employees into creepy back alleys. . . .) To find the most suitable location, look at the size of each route as expressed in yards or miles. The answer as to which property is closest should be obvious.

You may also want to use the Highlight tool to compare the relative distance to different bus stops nearby, or to any two locations that would cut down the number of steps needed, the time spent in the sweltering summer heat, the time trudging through mounds of snow, and so on.

Modifying the highlight's appearance

When you look at a highlighted stretch of road or other area on the map (refer back to Figure 6-2 for an example), you'll notice that the MapPoint highlighter behaves just like its real-world counterpart, highlighting the chosen area while remaining transparent. This feature presents a classic good news/bad news situation in that although street names, road boundaries, and such are plainly visible, the highlight itself may not be because a roadway may take up almost the entire width of the MapPoint highlighter. Seeing at first glance what is being highlighted on the map may be difficult.

If the roadways of the route you're highlighting are well known (or their specific names don't matter to the person who will be using the map), you may want to make the highlights appear in front of the roads. The highlights will then appear more as though a regular (not highlighter) felt-tip marker drew them — the road names and other elements are covered entirely by the yellow highlights. Sure, it masks the text on the map, but it's a whole lot easier to see!

To bring the highlighted line to the foreground, right-click the line and then choose Order⇨Bring in Front of Roads from the shortcut menu. You can restore the map to its previous state by pressing Ctrl+Z or clicking the Undo button or, if you've done additional editing to the map, by right-clicking the highlight and choosing Order⇨Send Behind Roads from the shortcut menu.

Draw ▾

Instead of right-clicking a drawing and using the shortcut menu to perform an action, you can click the drawing that you wish to modify and then use the Draw button at the left end of the Drawing toolbar to access the same options. In many ways, right-clicking is simplest, especially because both methods require you to click the drawing to begin working with it anyway.

Scribbling a Few Lines

"Scribbling" used to be a word reserved for art produced by young children or for the doodles generated by absent-minded adults while talking on the phone. Scribbling in MapPoint, however, is considered "freeform drawing" — a tactic that can go a long way in producing customized maps and targeted data analysis.

As its name implies, MapPoint's Scribble tool lets you draw anything you want on a MapPoint map (see Figure 6-3). Most likely, the tool is used to highlight a route, but the creative among us can use the Scribble or Freeform tool to draw a cat face over the nearest kennel, put crosses on the map to mark nearby churches for conference attendees, or draw an odd shape as a guideline for extracting address data in a certain geographic location.

 To use the Scribble or Freeform tool, you first need to center on the screen the area of the map you wish to work with. That way, you can clearly see what you're doing. Next, click the Scribble or Freeform button (both shown in the margin) on the Drawing toolbar to turn your mouse pointer into a virtual pen. Click in the starting point of your drawing and then drag the mouse pointer in the desired direction to finish your drawing. With the Freeform tool, you can also click the starting point and then click a destination point to draw a straight line between the points you clicked. Repeat as desired to keep drawing straight lines.

Scribble versus Freeform: What's the difference?

MapPoint's Scribble and Freeform tools behave quite similarly at first glance. Even the help files don't make the differences obvious. Good thing you're reading *MapPoint 2002 For Dummies*!

Both tools turn your mouse pointer into a virtual pencil — just hold the left mouse button down to draw anything you want. Now here's where the differences become obvious. When you release the mouse button in Scribble mode, the tool is deactivated. You have to click the Scribble button on the Drawing toolbar again if you want to do any more scribbling.

With the Freeform tool, you stay in Freeform mode until you press the Esc key or double-click the end point of your drawing. The Freeform also makes it easy to mix and match freeform shapes drawn by hand with precise lines. For example, if you want to draw a circle around a point and then draw a line off to the side, you click the Freeform button on the Drawing toolbar, draw the circle, and then release your mouse button at the point where you want to draw the line. You'll notice that even though the mouse button has been released, the drawing tool is still tethered to the end point of your drawing. To draw the line, simply move the mouse pointer into position. No matter where you put the pointer on-screen, MapPoint draws a straight line between the end point of your drawing and the second point you click on the map.

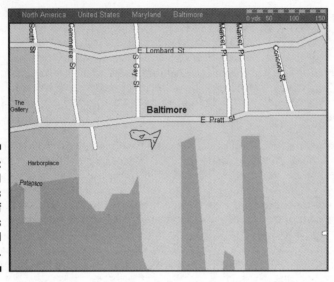

Figure 6-3:
A scribbled fish marks the spot of Baltimore's National Aquarium.

To draw a series of separate shapes (say, to put the eyes on that cat face over the nearest kennel), draw all the connected parts with the Scribble tool, click the Scribble tool again, draw the next set of connected points, and then repeat the process until all the parts of your drawing are finished. Again, achieving high-quality results is a real challenge. If the goal is to produce a map worthy of appearing on your company's Web site or of being mailed out to conference attendees, you may be better off creating a text box (discussed later in this chapter) or selecting an appropriate Pushpin from the 256 available in the Pushpin gallery, as described in Chapter 4.

Unlike the Highlight tool, which measures the distance you draw by default, the Scribble and Freeform tools require you to right-click the drawing and then choose Show Size to see the distance covered by the drawing.

Reading Between the Lines

Drawing a line (or arrow or predefined shape, for that matter) is the best way to get professional results out of MapPoint's drawing tools. Although freeform drawings offer total flexibility, unless you have an awesome mouse and the steady hand of a surgeon, the resulting squiggles can be less than satisfactory for anything other than personal use.

If you can accomplish your task with lines, arrows, or any other of the predefined shapes on MapPoint's Drawing toolbar, you'll be very pleased with the results. Consider using lines to underline important elements of your map, or use color-coded lines to underline various types of competing restaurants in your area (such as green for strong competition with your new pizzeria, yellow for minor competition, and red for no competition whatsoever).

To find out how to colorize MapPoint lines, read the section later in this chapter called, "Changing the color of lines, borders, and arrows."

To draw a line in MapPoint, center the location you wish to work with on-screen, click the Line button, and then click the starting point for your line on the map. Simply drag the mouse pointer out to the line's destination; then release the mouse button to set the line in place. A thin, 1-point black line appears between the points you clicked.

Unless you're a supermodel, being too thin may not always be best. The same holds true for MapPoint lines. The thin default lines are nice and dainty but can be very hard to see — not a good trait when you're trying to draw attention to something!

Luckily, MapPoint makes putting a little meat on those lines easy. To thicken a line from its 1 point default width:

1. **Click the line to select it and then click the Line Style button (shown in the margin) on the Drawing toolbar (see Figure 6-4).**

    You'll see a range of possibilities from which to choose along with a sample of the resulting line width.

2. **Click the line width you want.**

    The Line Style menu disappears and MapPoint redraws the line in the specified width. You can use these steps to make a fat line thin, of course.

Flat shapes on a round world

When you're working with MapPoint, the maps you see may appear flat, but MapPoint views the area as part of a sphere. Remember that you are drawing the "rectangle" onto the surface of the globe. Given that, the lines and shapes that you draw appear as straight as an, well, arrow when you look at them up close. Of course we all know that the world is not flat; it's a globe. MapPoint always takes the curvature of the Earth into account when it displays map areas, measures distances, presents your map drawings, and the like.

If you zoom out as far as you can on your map and click View⇨Globe View When Zoomed Out, you'll notice that long lines or arrows actually bow out a bit to factor in these subtle curves. That gives you a more authentic view of how the straight line would really look from afar on a round planet.

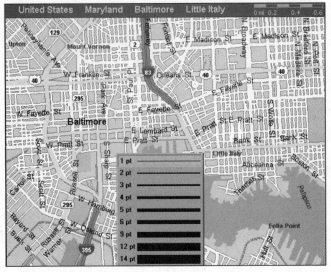

Figure 6-4:
Size can be
everything
when it
comes to
MapPoint
lines.

Pointing Viewers in the Right Direction

 Here's something you may not know: MapPoint's arrow-drawing tool is actually quite smart. Why? Because unlike other drawing tools that have predefined appearances and behaviors, the Arrow tool (shown in the margin) changes on the fly to meet your needs. Instead of the arrowhead always appearing on the right or left side of the line, the arrowhead appears in the direction you move your mouse.

For example, if you click the Arrow tool, click the bottom-left corner of your map, and then drag the mouse pointer toward the right, the arrow obviously points right. If you click the opposite corner of the screen and then drag the pointer left, you have a left-pointing arrow. So basically, the arrowhead points in the direction that you drag the mouse. Cool, huh?

 Want to change the direction of an arrow? Just click the arrow to select it, click the Arrow Style button on MapPoint's Drawing toolbar, and then click the desired arrow.

Like the Line tool, MapPoint's Arrow tool gives you professional-looking results from the onset. These arrows can be used to mark one-way streets, point to your business's delivery dock, or showcase a special location on the map, as shown in Figure 6-5. Anytime you need to show direction on your maps, this tool is the one to use.

To mark a one-way street, you need a thin arrow to fit inside the boundaries of the road. To highlight a special location on the map, however, you may need something a bit more flamboyant.

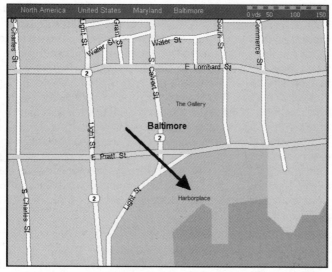

Figure 6-5:
Maps like
this make
what you
want people
to notice
more
obvious.

Or what if you want to indicate east-west or north-south movement — how in the world can you get a double-headed arrow? Piece of cake!

 First, deal with the size issue. To modify the thickness of the arrow, click it to select it; then, click the Line Style button. The Line Style menu gives you a collection ranging in size from the dainty 1-pt. thickness to a whopping 14-pt. size. Simply click the one you want MapPoint to use to redraw the arrow.

 As for the direction of the arrowhead, that, too, is an easy fix. To reverse the direction of an arrow or to make what's called a double-headed arrow (where it points to both ends), click the arrow to select it and then click the Arrow Style tool (shown in the margin) on the Drawing toolbar. Here, you can choose the direction of your arrow by merely clicking a menu option. You can even use the Arrow Style menu to change a line to an arrow or vice versa.

Whipping Your Maps into Shape

If you're known for your artistic ability, we congratulate you; you are indeed a rarity. Unfortunately, most of us have other claims to fame, leaving us in a bit of a lurch when it comes to drawing just about anything. Luckily, MapPoint gives us some handy tools to draw basic shapes such as squares, rectangles, circles, and ovals (see Figure 6-6). You can use these shapes to encase a point you want to draw attention to, or you can use it to draw an area on a Pushpin map that you want to isolate for data analysis.

MapPoint offers two shape-drawing tools: the Rectangle tool and the Oval tool (refer to Figure 6-1). Interestingly, these tools can produce squares and circles, too, depending on how you drag the mouse pointer. To make a rectangle (or square), click the Rectangle tool in the upper-left corner of the area you want to mark, then drag the pointer down and to the right. How far you drag the pointer in each direction depends on the type of shape you're trying to draw; you'll just have to eyeball that part of the process. When the shape meets with your approval, simply release the mouse button to lock it in place.

Making ovals and circles is just as easy. Click the Oval tool, click the map in the upper-left corner of the area you want to draw in, and then drag the mouse pointer down and to the right to form your shape. Again, the distance that you drag depends on the size of the shape and whether you're making an oval or a circle. Release the mouse button to set the shape in place and you're good to go!

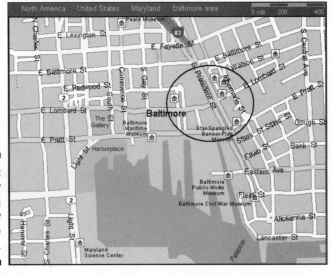

Figure 6-6:
If only
drawing
shapes by
hand were
this easy . . .

Unlocking the Wonders of Radius Circles

Radius circles? What in the world are radius circles, and why are they so "wonderful," you ask? Well, you're about to find out. Remember the drivetime zones that let you find out just how far you can travel in a certain amount of time? Radius circles let you click a center point and drag the mouse out to draw a circle that covers a certain distance.

Now that you know what they are, you can see what makes them so wonderful. Say that you have a Pushpin map based on all your store's customers. You plan to open a new location for your clothing chain and want to tell every customer within 20 miles of the new store. You can open the Pushpin map, build a 20-mile radius circle around the new sight, and then export the records to Microsoft Excel, which you can turn around and use as a data source for a targeted marketing/advertising campaign.

So how do you build a radius circle? Start with a fresh map (or open a Pushpin map if you want to go on and analyze data based on the radius circle). Then click the Radius tool on MapPoint's Drawing toolbar (refer to Figure 6-1). Next, click the center point of your radius circle and drag the mouse out until the screen tip box shows the desired distance that you want to cover. Then release the mouse button. A circle similar to the one shown in Figure 6-7 appears on-screen. See how much territory just a few miles covers?

If you right-click over the radius circle's border, you can add all the Pushpins inside the circle to an optimized route, or you can export them to Excel for later use. (In the "Data Analysis with MapPoint" part of this book and in Chapter 11, we cover how to use this specially selected data to your advantage.)

Figure 6-7:
A radius circle lets you see just how close you are to various points of interest, but most of all, it can be a powerful routing and data analysis tool.

Adding radius shapes on top of the original radius shape and varying the new shapes with respect to size and distance is a great way to build concentric rings showing the bands of area from the center point.

Adding Text Boxes to Your Maps

A map littered with unexplained doodling is not very useful. There are legends to explain markings and coloration native to the maps, but any drawings you add will be totally void of meaning unless you take the time to provide information to the contrary.

Sure, you could try to write a label or description using one of MapPoint's drawing tools, but doing so would be like putting a marker in a two-year-old's hand and asking the child to write his or her name. Endearing, yes. Professional or legible? Hardly.

When legibility and professionalism are key, consider adding a text box to your map. Not only is it easy to read but also the fonts used are the same style and color as those used in the Pushpin text balloons. This likeness gives the map a more consistent, polished feel. Text boxes also have crisp white backgrounds, making their message stand out from the map elements around it.

To add a text box to your map, follow these steps:

1. **Open the map to the location you want to add the text box.**

 2. **Click the Text Box tool (shown in the margin) on MapPoint's Drawing toolbar.**

    When you move your mouse onto the map's surface, its pointer will appear as a plus (+) sign (some people also refer to this as a crosshair shape).

3. **Move the intersection of the mouse pointer (the cross section of its plus-sign shape) to the upper-left corner of the future text box's edge.**

4. **Now click the chosen location and move the mouse pointer down and to the right to draw the text box.**

    Releasing the mouse button sets the text box in place.

    Don't worry about the height of the text box as much as the width. The width stays where you set it, but the height will auto size itself as needed.

5. **Click inside the white part of the text box and then type in the text you want to appear.**

    Remember, the width stays the same, but if MapPoint needs more room for the text you enter, it'll add lines to the text box automatically.

6. **When you finish typing, click the map outside the text box.**

    Your masterpiece awaits (see Figure 6-8)!

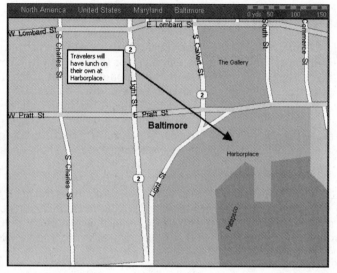

Figure 6-8:
Professional
labeling of
custom map
elements is
a snap
thanks to
the Text Box
tool.

Want the text box to pop out more noticeably? Consider changing the color of the text in your text box. From bright orange to flamingo pink, you'll find something for just about every purpose or occasion.

 To change the text color, click the text box to select it, click the Text Color (shown in the margin) arrow button on the Drawing toolbar and then click the color swatch you want to use. You'll find 40 choices available on the palette provided.

 For whatever reason, MapPoint doesn't let you modify font style or size in its text boxes, so you have to rely on colorized text and borders to make the element stand out.

Editing Your Drawings

"We're only human". . ."Things change". . . . Clichés abound in the world today, but they're as relevant today as they were before the phrases even became clichés. Because they're true, you need to know how to correct mistakes or otherwise make changes to your MapPoint drawings. Maybe you want to make a drawing a different color, move it to a new spot, make it bigger. . .who knows? You can do all this and then some to your drawings.

Enclosing your shapes

MapPoint is amazing in that you can surround a subset of Pushpins to single them out for targeted direct-mail campaigns or to build an optimized route around them. Best of all, these selected Pushpins need not fit into a perfect circle, square, or other standard shape. You can draw an area by hand that gives you the freedom to pull in stray Pushpins or exclude specific ones.

Of course, to take advantage of the data analysis and routing capabilities inside Freeform or Scribble drawings, you have to have a fully enclosed area. (Pushpins can sneak out of the tiniest cracks, you know!)

To make sure that an area has been fully closed off, draw the area you wish to work with using the Scribble or Freeform tool, then, right-click its border to open a shortcut menu. Click the Close Curve option. MapPoint pulls the two ends of the drawing together so that you may work with it more effectively.

Filling in the blanks with Fill Color

 Fully enclosed shapes drawn on a map can also be colored in. This gives you the opportunity to highlight certain parts of the map, selected clusters of Pushpins, and so on. You accomplish these actions by using MapPoint's Fill Color tool. Click the enclosed shape that you want to fill with color, click the Fill Color arrow button, click the swatch of color you want, and poof! It's all done.

After you have selected a fill color, MapPoint will continue to fill in automatically any drawings that you create with that color. Depending on your perspective, this feature can be a shortcut or a curse. To stop MapPoint from filling the drawings in automatically, click the Fill Color arrow button on MapPoint's Drawing toolbar and select the No Fill option.

By default, the fill color overlays any roads, points of interest, and the like, making them totally invisible. (Only Pushpins show through this default setting.) If, however, you want the street names, roads, and points of interest to peek through the color, you can accomplish this by right-clicking inside the colored area and choosing Order⇨Send Behind Roads.

Laying it all on the line: Changing line width

In addition to colorizing elements to call attention to them, MapPoint allows you to modify a line's width. We're not just talking about random lines that you may have drawn on the map, either. We're talking about text box borders, arrows, and drawing borders as well, making this a tremendously useful feature.

By default, lines and borders are a tiny 1-pt. hairline size, but with a few simple mouse clicks, you can thicken them significantly (up to 14 pts. in fact). Figure 6-9 shows you how tremendously different the various line widths make an arrow appear. To change line width in any of the elements described previously, simply click the element to select it and then click the Line Style tool (shown in the margin). A menu of line widths appears. Click the one you want and MapPoint will redraw the line in the desired size.

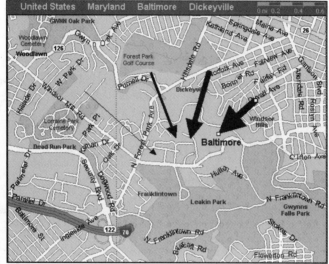

Figure 6-9:
1-, 4-, 9-, and 14-point arrows make radically different statements on a map.

You can also lengthen or shorten a line or arrow by clicking it and then dragging the little white boxes in or out as needed.

Deleting a drawing

Don't want a drawing anymore? Your wish is MapPoint's command. If the drawing was the last action you performed on the map, pressing Ctrl+Z will do the trick. Otherwise you can delete a drawing by clicking it and then pressing the Delete key.

Moving a text box or standard shape

You can't move scribbles or freeform shapes, but relocating a text box or standard shape is easy. Click the element you want to move to select it. Next, move the mouse pointer over the element's border until it looks like a four-headed arrow (see Figure 6-10).

Figure 6-10:
A four-headed arrow means that the drawing has packed its bags and is ready to go!

When the pointer takes on this four-headed arrow appearance, you can click the drawing and drag-and-drop it anywhere on the map.

Baby, the bigger the better!

If you've ever spent hours hanging pictures and trying to get them just right, you'll appreciate MapPoint's ability to resize drawings. Although you can't resize scribbles and freeform drawings (you can, however, reshape them, as we show you in the next section), you can tweak any other shape or text box. To begin making adjustments:

1. **Click the drawing you want to work with.**

2. **Hover the mouse pointer over the drawing's border until you see a double-headed arrow.**

3. **Click the drawing and drag its border in the desired direction to resize it.**

4. **Release the mouse button to lock the drawing into its new size.**

Text boxes can appear to be ornery critters, but they're really just behaving as intended. You can adjust the width of a text box at any time, however; MapPoint automatically controls the height. So try as you might to resize a text box's height, it ain't happenin', baby!

Reshaping a scribble or freeform drawing

Here's a fun one for you. Getting exactly what you want can be tricky, but you should be aware that it is humanly possibly to modify the shape of a freeform or scribble drawing.

When you click one of these types of drawings, you'll see a series of boxes along the shape's border. These boxes are known as *points*. You can delete them by right-clicking and selecting Delete Point from the menu. You can also move them by clicking and dragging them into place.

Getting the exact shape that you want without redrawing the shape can be tough, but at least now you can attempt it!

Changing the color of lines, borders, and arrows

See "Filling in the Blanks with Fill Color," earlier in this chapter, to see how to fill a drawing with color and change the color of text box text. But you're in the right place to find out how to change the color of lines, borders, and arrows in MapPoint drawings. Accomplishing this is not only possible but also downright easy:

1. **Click the line, arrow, drawing, or text box border you want to recolor.**

2. **Click MapPoint's Line Color tool and then click the color you want to appear on the selected drawing.**

   In seconds, MapPoint redraws the selected image in the color you chose.

Managing Stacked Drawings

In MapPoint, you can draw anywhere on a map, including over other drawings. Placing multiple drawings on top of each other creates a stack of drawings. Although these multiple layers can provide a wealth of information to map viewers, they can also become confusing, especially if you use fill colors. Parts of drawings can be obstructed by other drawings, making it next to impossible to figure out what's happening where.

Luckily, MapPoint has a series of Order commands designed to help you make sense of all the layers of drawings. To begin working with a stack of drawings, right-click one of the drawings, point to Order, and then use Table 6-1 to decide which command to execute.

Table 6-1	Rearranging Stacked Drawings
Menu Command	*Outcome*
Bring to Front	Puts the currently selected drawing at the top of the stack for easy viewing
Send to Back	Puts the currently selected drawing at the bottom of the stack
Bring Forward	Moves the selected drawing up one level in the stack
Send Backward	Moves the selected drawing down one level in the stack
Bring in Front of Roads	Shows fill-colored drawings only, thus blocking roads, street names, points of interest, and others from view
Send Behind Roads	Makes roads, points of interest, and such appear through any fill-colored drawings

Note that when only two drawings are in a stack, the Bring to Front and Bring Forward commands serve the same purpose. The same holds true for the Send to Back and Send Backward commands.

Chapter 7

Working with MapPoint Output

*W*hat good is a map if you can look at it only on your computer from within MapPoint? Sure, that may be fine for doing casual browsing or data analysis, but the best itinerary in the world is virtually useless unless you can print it and take it with you!

The same holds true for customized maps. When viewed from within MapPoint, they're interesting; but when included in a well-formatted Word document, a PowerPoint presentation, or a Publisher newsletter, they become truly spectacular. They go from being a uniquely helpful personal tool to being powerful messengers, telling customers where to find you, showcasing your sizable client base, even telling your company shareholders exactly where things stand with regard to annual sales.

What's nice about the tactics this chapter discusses is that they can all be used on regular maps, Pushpin maps, or even on maps you generate using data from Microsoft Excel or SQL Server.

E-Mailing Maps to Others

Whether you're e-mailing a map of your newest store's location to your most loyal customers or sending a sized pie chart map reflecting company-wide performance to your sales force, you'll love MapPoint's e-mail capabilities. Within minutes, clients, employees, or associates from around the world can see the same rich MapPoint maps you do. Best of all, these associates don't need to have MapPoint installed on their computers to view the maps, making the maps truly available to anyone.

MapPoint gives you two alternatives for e-mailing maps — one designed for recipients who have MapPoint installed on their machines and the other for those who do not. For those with MapPoint, the map file can simply be attached to the e-mail message. For others, the map will need to be sent as a picture.

If you're not sure whether the intended recipient has MapPoint, it's obviously best to assume that they don't. That way, precious time won't be wasted at either end troubleshooting the problem or resending the map.

Mailing to MapPoint users

Not surprisingly, the simplest way to send a map is to e-mail it to someone who already has MapPoint installed on his or her machine. Just follow these steps to e-mail a map to a fellow MapPoint user:

1. **Click File⇨Open to open the MapPoint map you wish to mail and make sure that the desired part of the map you open appears inside the main map window.**

   You may want to turn off the Legends and Overview pane to maximize the viewing area. You also may want to use the Select, Zoom, or Pan tool (described in Chapter 2) to get the proper area on-screen.

2. **Click File⇨Send To⇨Mail Recipient (as Attachment).**

   A new message window of your default e-mail program opens with the MapPoint map already attached (see Figure 7-1, which demonstrates how a Microsoft Outlook message may look).

   Is the Send To menu item missing when you try to follow these steps? If so, then you need to install or configure an e-mail program on your computer. For obvious reasons, MapPoint needs such a program in place to accomplish this task.

3. **Enter the e-mail address of the intended recipient along with a message explaining the significance of your map; then click the Send button.**

   If all goes well in cyberspace, within minutes, your message and the attached map are placed in the inbox of the recipient.

Should you receive a message with a MapPoint attachment, all you have to do to view the attachment is open the message, double-click the attachment icon, choose the Open option from the resulting dialog box, and click OK. Watch as MapPoint launches with the map preloaded for viewing. You can then manipulate the map just as you can any other MapPoint map.

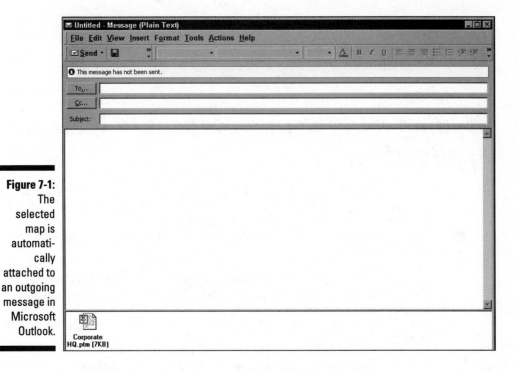

Figure 7-1:
The
selected
map is
automati-
cally
attached to
an outgoing
message in
Microsoft
Outlook.

Mailing to non-MapPoint users

As we noted previously, you can send a map for use by recipients who don't or may not have MapPoint. In this circumstance, you have two options available for sharing the map.

Assuming that you use Microsoft Outlook for your e-mail client, you can send the map as a picture. Open the desired map in MapPoint and then click File⇨Send To⇨Mail Recipients (as Picture). A new Microsoft Outlook message screen appears with a picture of the selected map in the message body. Simply address the message, give it a subject, add any notes, and send it on its way.

When the recipient opens your note, he or she sees a picture of the map just as you sent it no matter what e-mail program the recipient uses. But remember, because you sent a picture rather than a real map, recipients can't change the view or otherwise alter the map even if they do have MapPoint installed.

Not everyone uses Microsoft Outlook as his or her primary e-mail client, however. Many opt to use Outlook's little sister, Outlook Express, or even a non-Microsoft product instead. Not to worry. As long as the e-mail program supports standard Windows cut-and-paste commands and can display pictures in the message body, you're in business.

To send a picture of your map from a non-Outlook e-mail program, you'll basically need to copy the map and paste it into the message body manually. See the following section to read about the ins and outs of copying and pasting maps into various Windows applications.

Copying and Pasting Maps into Windows Applications . . .

Need to copy and paste a map into an e-mail message? Want to add a map to a PowerPoint presentation that you have to give to your board of directors? Perhaps you're needing to include a map in a grant proposal that you're drafting in Word, or hoping to provide a map to your nonprofit animal shelter in a Publisher-created brochure.

You can do all these things with MapPoint, and the process is a whole lot simpler than it may seem at first glance. If you've ever used cut-and-paste or copy-and-paste in other Windows applications, you'll find putting maps anywhere a breeze. You need to know about some MapPoint-specific issues first, however.

You can find out more about how MapPoint 2002 works with Office XP in Chapter 11.

Important copyright notice!

MapPoint maps and their related output are intended for personal use, not for resale or profit. For example, you can print maps and itineraries for your family vacation to your heart's content, but selling MapPoint-generated trip routes would be a major no-no.

This doesn't, however, mean that you're unable to use MapPoint for business-related tasks. You can use a MapPoint map in an ad showing your store's location, provided that the Microsoft copyright notice stays intact on the map. The same holds true for including a map on a flyer, brochure, or even a Web page. As long as the information on that map is not being sold and the Microsoft copyright appears, it's fair game.

(We highly recommend, however, that you consult the license agreement that came with your copy of MapPoint for full details, because some commercial uses may be unique in nature.)

Your data maps may be used for internal analysis, but they cannot be sold. Sure, the data overlayed on the map may be yours, but the map itself is not.

You should also note that copyright law does not grant you permission to include MapPoint maps in magazines or newspapers because they use advertising to generate income. You can contact Microsoft for special permission.

Copying the whole map

Sometimes you may need to send the MapPoint map along with its overview map and legend. The overview map not only shows recipients the specific location but also helps them relate it to a larger context (say, where a tiny town sits in relation to the rest of the state).

As for the legend, it becomes useful in helping the recipient interpret various map markings, points of interest, and so on. You should know, however, that you need to expand the legend elements you want available in the pasted document by clicking the plus (+) sign to the left of their respective title. If you don't expand a legend element, neither its title nor its map elements appear in the pasted location.

To copy this whole package for placement in a new location, you first need to prepare the map. This means making sure that the desired part of the map appears in MapPoint's map window. (After all, the recipient won't be able to click, pan, or zoom his or her way to a different view.) You also want to verify that any applicable legend elements are fully expanded.

When the map is ready to go, simply right-click the MapPoint map, choose Copy from the shortcut menu, move to the document into which you want to insert the map, click the mouse in the exact spot you want to paste the map, and then paste it in using your favorite Paste command (Ctrl+V or the Paste button on the Standard toolbar works for most Windows programs). The three elements — map, overview map, and legend — are copied as three separate images, so you can rearrange them in their new document if you'd like.

Whether you're mailing a map to a client or including it in a major PowerPoint presentation (see Figure 7-2), you're ready to go!

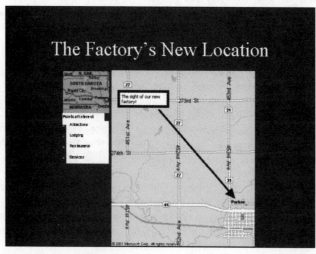

Figure 7-2:
Add
accurate,
customized
maps to
your
PowerPoint
presentation
in seconds.

Keeping the background of these pasted-in map elements white is a distinct advantage because you can't recolor the legend. (And even if you could, the background of the map element icons could easily become lost on an intense color.) Alternatively, you may want to consider leaving off the legend entirely if at all possible. That way, you can better coordinate the map slide or page with other presentation elements and still have an easy-to-read map.

Just the maps, please

Don't need a legend or overview map? No problem! Just position MapPoint's map window so that you can see everything you want to include on the map; then click Edit⇨Copy Map. The contents of your map window will be held in the Windows Clipboard until you open or create the document in which you want to place the copy of the map, place your cursor where you want to place the map, and then perform the Paste command.

Getting the map where you want it can be a real nightmare if you try to click the map's edges to position it. When you've zoomed in fully, a single click can take you a whole lot farther than you wanted to go. Try using the Pan tool instead. Just click the Pan button (shown in the margin) on MapPoint's Navigation toolbar and then click and drag the map into position. That way, you can move as much (or as little) as you want.

Pasting in parts of maps

MapPoint maps are sort of like all-you-can-eat buffets — just because mounds of ham, prime rib, stuffing, and a dozen luscious desserts tempt you doesn't mean you have to have them all! Even though you can zoom in only so far on a MapPoint map, you always have the option to copy only a portion of the map. Using this option not only gives you a smaller image file but also emphasizes the part of the map you most want viewers to see.

To begin copying a part of the map, click MapPoint's Select tool (shown in the margin) on the Navigation toolbar. When the mouse pointer takes on its plus (+) sign appearance, place the intersection of the pointer in the upper-left corner of the area you want to include; then click and drag the Select tool frame down and to the right until the desired section of the map is framed. Release the mouse button to set the frame in place. Finally, right-click inside the frame and click the Copy option on the shortcut menu. From there, you can literally paste the map into any application that will accept it.

Use caution when drawing your map parameters. If the bottom border rests on or near a road name, that road name may become obstructed by the Microsoft copyright information that appears in the lower-left corner. Such placement will make it harder for viewers to see the true scope of your map, so remember to place your borders accordingly.

Copying Driving Directions

Placing a set of driving directions into another application is even easier than pasting a map into a new location. Or at least a lot fewer decisions need to be made! Of course, to copy a set of driving directions, you first need to make those driving directions appear on-screen. Depending on your situation, you may either need to create the trip using Route Planner, or open an existing route file using the File⇨Open command. (Consult Chapter 5 for route planning information.)

In any case, a Driving Directions pane appears in the upper-right corner of the MapPoint workspace. This pane displays step-by-step instructions for taking the trip or running the route you defined. Right-click on the driving directions and choose Copy Directions from the shortcut menu. Next, move to the file or document in which you'd like to place the directions. This may be an e-mail message, a Word document, or even a PowerPoint slide. After you click the spot you want to paste the directions into, perform your favorite Paste command (press Ctrl+V or click the Paste button). The driving directions are ready for further action.

Printing MapPoint Documents

As authors, people always ask us how we feel about the future of electronic publishing (making a book available on a computer or handheld device instead of or in addition to the traditional book form). Although movement in that direction is undeniable, we argue that it can be downright impossible to get comfortable curling up next to a crackling fire with a mug of hot chocolate, instrumental music playing softly in the background, and your favorite book balanced precariously on your knees in the form of a six-pound laptop!

Sure, electronic books are wonderful for research because often you can search on words or phrases of interest, but using this type of media is just not the same as flipping through a "real" book. Although the electronic availability of books and maps is important, sometimes paper still is the best way to go.

With MapPoint's printing capabilities, you can print maps to distribute with a speech you're giving, print each account rep's route for the day (or week), include a full-page Pushpin map of clients served with your latest grant application . . . the list of possibilities keeps on going. MapPoint gives you a whole lot of flexibility for producing printed maps as well, so with a little work, you can almost always get what you're after.

Getting set up to print

If you plan to print maps or routes on a regular basis, you can configure MapPoint's print settings so that printing is ready to go at the drop of a hat. You do the majority of this work via the Page Setup dialog box, shown in Figure 7-3.

Figure 7-3:
Setting
these
options
ahead of
time can
make last-
minute
printing a
snap!

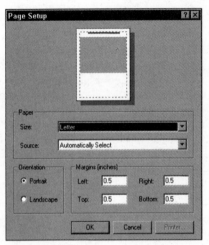

First, select the size of the paper you plan to use in your printer. The standard letter size is the default, but you can use the drop-down box provided to access a variety of options ranging from a tiny envelope to the largest piece of paper your printer can handle.

Unless you have a sophisticated printer setup, you may want to let MapPoint automatically select the paper source, as it will by default. Those using networked printers, however, may actually need to choose a paper source or even change it each time an item is printed, depending on printer traffic. Luckily, the Page Setup options are within a click of the standard Print dialog box, so making modifications shouldn't be too much of a hassle.

In this dialog box, you also have the opportunity to select paper orientation by clicking the desired option (Portrait or Landscape).

Note that when printing a route, MapPoint will try to print the route on as few pages as possible, meaning that it will automatically choose a paper orientation for you. If MapPoint's choice is unacceptable, choose the desired paper orientation in the Orientation section in the lower-left corner of the Page

Setup dialog box and then disable the automatic paper orientation option from the Print dialog box (click File⇨Print to open it). (Click the More Options button, deselect the Automatically Select Page Orientation option, and then click OK.)

Finally, you may want to set margin size. By default, MapPoint sets margins to half an inch all around, but you can easily change that number by typing a new value into the applicable margin text box.

When all the options meet with your approval, click OK to save them.

Putting your driving directions in writing

You've probably noticed this truth at meetings and conferences: Everyone has different learning styles. Some meeting attendees would be totally lost without PowerPoint slides, overhead projections, or doodles on a white-board. These visual learners want printed handouts and often can be seen scribbling notes frantically. Then there's the person who listens attentively, staring right at the speaker. He or she doesn't even take notes but just sits there soaking in every word.

When it comes to reading driving directions, the same two preferences emerge — one wants maps with the route highlighted; another wants a no-frills set of text-only directions. Luckily, MapPoint can deliver on both counts.

When it comes to printing driving directions in MapPoint, you basically have four options:

 ✔ **The Current Map View option (Figure 7-4) gives you a large, single-page map with the route highlighted (assuming that a route has been defined, of course).** Although this highlighted route is useful for providing the overall picture of your route, you need a set of driving directions as well because the roads on the map may be too small to distinguish street names, necessary turns, and such.

To print a good route overview map, the whole route should appear in the current map view. The fastest way to ensure that your current map view includes the whole route is to click Zoom⇨To Entire Route on the MapPoint menu bar.

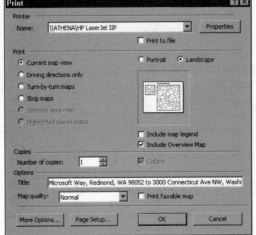

Figure 7-4:
MapPoint
enables you
to print a
large image
of your map
or route.

✔ **The Driving Directions Only option produces a text-only, step-by-step set of directions (see Figure 7-5).** This option uses minimal paper and printer toner/ink and gives the driver no image distractions whatsoever.

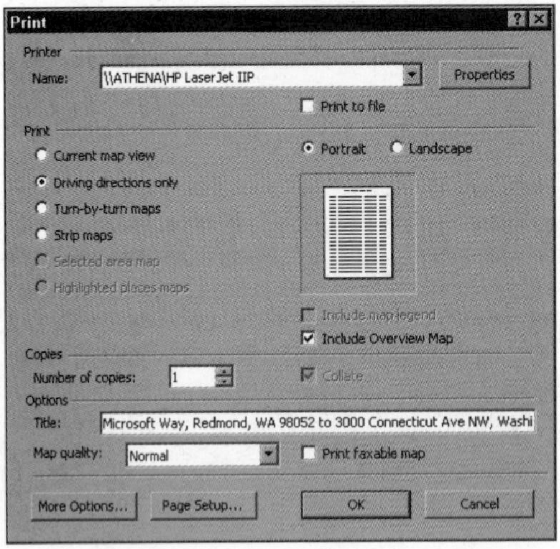

Figure 7-5:
The Driving
Directions
Only option
saves toner
and paper
as well.

✔ **The Turn-by-Turn option (see Figure 7-6) prints a tiny map along with a brief narrative for each step of your journey.** If you can't figure out whether you're a more visual learner, or you'd rather just be told where to go, this option is the perfect solution. It uses aspects of both preferences! It's also great to use if you're sharing driving or navigating duties with someone who has a different preference than you.

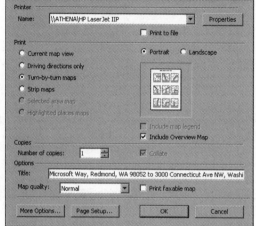

Figure 7-6: The Turn-by-Turn option is a good compromise for both learning types.

✔ The Strip Maps option (see Figure 7-7) divides the page in two with a long strip map on the left and the driving directions on the right.

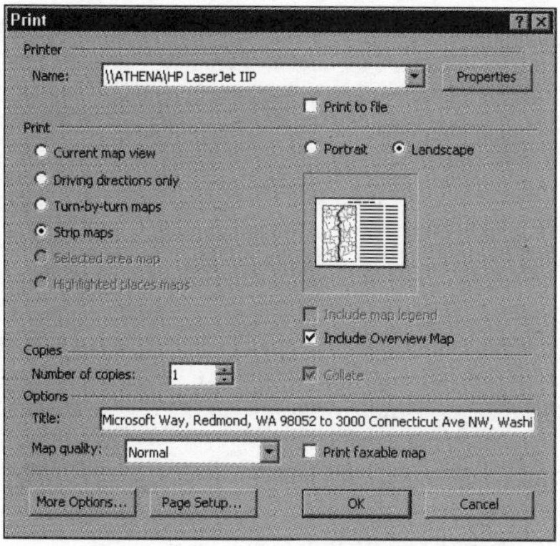

Figure 7-7: These strip maps remind some of the automobile club vacation itineraries they may have received in the past.

Remember, your preferred map type may change depending on the intended use of the printout. A field rep may like the succinct text-only output, whereas the vacationer may like the strip maps. And those trying to navigate complex routes in areas filled with odd twists and turns may find the turn-by-turn maps and directions invaluable.

Basic printing in MapPoint

Printing in MapPoint is similar to printing a document from just about any other Windows-based application. In this case, simply open or create the MapPoint map you want to print and then click File⇨Print. Refer to Figures 7-4 through 7-7 in the previous section to see the Print dialog box.

Assuming that your printer is properly configured, you should see it listed by name in the Name text box near the top of the dialog box. In the Print section, you'll need to specify how you want the driving directions printed. (See the bullets in the preceding section for details about what you get with each option.) You can also set paper orientation here, though MapPoint will automatically choose one that's optimized for the type of printout you choose. MapPoint by default prints an overview map with your selection. Just click the check box again to skip it if desired.

Choosing the number of copies needed along with the printout's title are pretty straightforward options to set. MapPoint suggests a title based on the defined route or the map location, but you can effortlessly change it by clicking inside the Title text box and typing in a new title of your choice.

Another thing you should consider adjusting, however, is the Map quality option. Using the drop-down box provided, you can print the material in Draft, Normal (default), or Presentation form. You may also opt to print a faxable copy of the material by checking the box immediately to the right of the Map quality option near the bottom of the dialog box. Click OK and your printouts will be ready and waiting at your printer!

Pages need breaks, too!

By default, MapPoint prints everything on as few pages as possible. But what if you'd like highly detailed strip maps that require more pages, or you want a separate page for each stop, or something similar?

Have we got the options for you! When viewing the Print dialog box, look for the More Options button in the bottom-left corner. Clicking it gives you access to a host of cool page-break options (see Figure 7-8).

In the More Printing Options dialog box, you can choose from the following by clicking the corresponding option:

- Print route on as few pages as possible (the default)
- Print high-detail strip maps using more pages
- Print each stop on a separate page
- Print each day on a separate page

✔ Print a new page every ___ miles (you choose the number of miles; the default for this option is 100)

✔ Print a new page every ___ hours (you choose the number of hours; the default here is 8)

✔ Include summary statistics (trip duration, cost, and so on)

✔ Automatically select page orientation (also enabled by default)

You can choose only one of the first six options for obvious reasons, but the final two can be selected or deselected as desired. Click OK to return to the standard Print dialog box, and then click OK again to send the job to the printer.

Figure 7-8:
MapPoint's
More
Printing
Options
dialog box
enables you
to customize
your
printouts
even more.

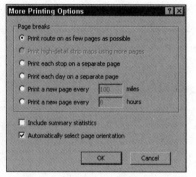

Printing parts of maps

Only want to print a portion of your map? No problem! Select it using MapPoint's Select tool, open the Print dialog box, and then choose the Selected Area Map option. After you've chosen the rest of your options, you're ready to send the map to the printer.

MapPoint on the Web

Unless you're experienced with it, designing Web pages can be quite a challenge, especially if you have an assortment of elements (maps, driving directions, Pushpins, and so on) to deal with. Luckily, MapPoint can do a lot of the work for you, so you won't find yourself copying and pasting maps, driving directions, and Pushpins into the wee hours of the night!

Before you delve into this too deeply, however, there are some things you should know about MapPoint Web pages. First, although they're nice, professional looking Web pages, they're pretty basic. The pages contain just the page's title, the elements you chose to have included on the Web page, and Microsoft's copyright notice — no fancy fonts or colorful backgrounds here (see Figure 7-9). The basics are more than adequate in most cases, but if you want the MapPoint pages to blend in with other pages on your site, you need to work with them using your favorite HTML editor (FrontPage 2002 or something similar). That way, you can incorporate a background image, special fonts, color schemes, or anything else necessary to make the pages look like the rest of your Web site.

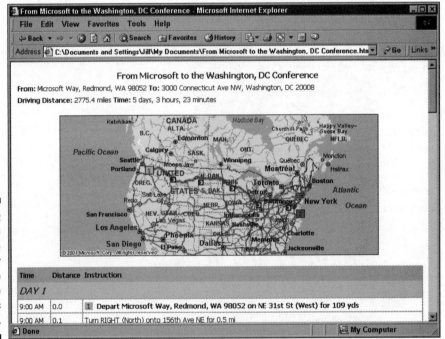

Figure 7-9: Keep the Web page as is or spruce it up a bit; the choice is yours.

That brings us to the second point. MapPoint helps you build Web pages, not Web sites. You can take the pages generated by MapPoint and add them to your current Web site or publish them on their own. Either way, however, you need an HTML editor to make the most of them. And don't expect MapPoint to help you publish those Web pages; that's not MapPoint's job. Microsoft wisely confined MapPoint to doing what it does best: create great-looking maps for use anywhere.

What can I do on the Web with MapPoint?

So, what kinds of Web pages can MapPoint build? Here's just a sampling of what you can do with MapPoint's various Web page options:

- ✔ Create a page displaying a map of your store's new location marked by a large arrow.

- ✔ Publish a map of all your clients marked with hyperlinked Pushpins. When visitors click a pushpin, they're taken to the client's Web site.

- ✔ Show visitors how to get from the airport to your bed and breakfast by having MapPoint build a page containing an overview map and step-by-step driving directions in a nicely formatted table.

- ✔ Provide visitors with a tiny map of your location that they can click to see a larger map along with a set of driving directions. You do this by creating a thumbnail page (see the following section for details) for your map.

Saving a map as a Web page

Many options are available to you when you go to create a Web page, so thinking through the purpose of your Web page before you make your selections is important. Doing so increases your chances of getting the results you want the first time around.

Because MapPoint can work only with what it has available to it, you may need to do a little setup work on the front end, so use the bulleted list that follows as a checklist for getting everything in order:

- ✔ **Want hyperlinks?** If you want MapPoint to make clickable hyperlinks available on your Web page, you first have to define those hyperlinks. See Chapter 4 to find out how to add a hyperlink to your Pushpins or check out the MapPoint Help files for additional information on using hyperlinks in MapPoint.

- ✔ **Need driving directions included?** MapPoint may be smart, but it's not psychic. If you want driving directions on your Web page, you have to calculate the route in MapPoint first.

- ✔ **Want map legends?** If the visitor could benefit from seeing a legend of points of interest icons or something similar, make sure that the Legend and Overview Map pane is shown and the desired legend is expanded. (Just click the plus (+) sign to the left of the desired legend to expand it.)

✔ **What map to use?** Use the Zoom (magnifying glass button with a plus sign inside), Pan (hand-shaped button), or Select (the button with a square and an arrow in the lower-right corner) tools on the Navigation toolbar to make sure that the area of the map you want to appear on your Web page also appears on-screen in the MapPoint map window. The map view is one element you cannot edit after you save a Web page, so make doubly sure that you're getting what you want.

Just follow these steps to begin building your MapPoint Web page:

1. **On the MapPoint menu bar, click File⇨Save as Web Page.**

   The Save as Web Page dialog box shown in Figure 7-10 appears.

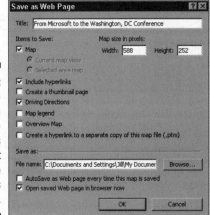

Figure 7-10:
Web page creation head-quarters (at least where MapPoint is concerned).

2. **In the Title text box, type in a title for the Web page.**

   This is the text that will appear at the top of your Web page, so choose your title wisely.

   By default, MapPoint uses the name you saved your file to as the title. If you didn't save the map, the name of the route points or the location of the map may appear instead.

3. **Set the size of your map in pixels by typing a value in the Width and Height text boxes provided.**

   MapPoint selects a size based on the size of the map as it currently appears on your screen. You can make it larger or smaller as desired; just keep in mind download times, how much you can see on the screen at a time, and so on. You can use a value between 32 and 3500 in the Width and Height boxes.

4. **Check the Include hyperlinks option if you've defined hyperlinks on your map and want them to be accessible from your Web page as well.**

5. **Click the Create a thumbnail page option to have a Web page with a smaller version of your map built.**

   The visitor clicks the thumbnail image to see a larger version of the map.

6. **Select the Driving Directions check box to include a table containing step-by-step driving directions on your Web page.**

   This option will not be available unless the map includes a calculated route.

7. **Click the Map Legend option if your Web page visitor would benefit from the presence of a legend to interpret the map.**

   Remember, the legend that you want to include needs to be open and fully expanded or you won't see anything!

8. **Click the Overview Map option to help visitors see where the location displayed is in relation to a larger area.**

   A small overview map appears at the bottom of the Web page, just above Microsoft's copyright information.

9. **Click the Create a Hyperlink to a Separate Copy of This File (.PTM) option to include a link to a copy of your map's MapPoint file.**

   Visitors with MapPoint installed can then click the link to load a copy of the map on their own machine. This way, visitors can look for nearby places of interest or otherwise manipulate the map as desired.

10. **Type a filename for your Web page in the Filename text box near the bottom of the dialog box.**

    The title is used by default; however, that may be a longer file-name than you'd like to see. Feel free to type a shorter one that serves the purpose better.

11. **Click the AutoSave As Web Page Every Time This Map Is Saved option to update the Web page every time that someone makes a change to the map.**

    Unless the Web page was saved to a shared network folder, you most likely need to go in and upload the new Web page manually.

12. **Click the Open Saved Web Page in Browser Now option to preview the Web page you just built.**

    Your default Web browser launches with the Web page you defined on-screen.

13. **Click OK to save the Web page for future use if everything meets with your approval.**

This is the time to do all of your testing before you publish the page to the Web. Do all your hyperlinks work? Is everything spelled correctly? Are the desired map elements easy to see? If so, you're ready to publish your work to the Web.

Managing saved Web pages

Because the only thing constant is change, chances are you'll find yourself needing to edit a MapPoint Web page at one point or another. Although most changes can be easily made after the fact, one can't be (easily, that is): the map view. It's not impossible, however. Read on to see how to modify your pages down the road.

Viewing a saved Web page

If you want to see a Web page created previously in MapPoint, open the map on which the page is based and then click File➪Manage Saved Web Pages. The Manage Saved Web Pages dialog box, shown in Figure 7-11, opens.

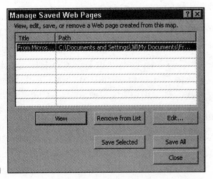

Figure 7-11:
All Web
pages
generated
as a result
of the open
map are
listed here.

All Web pages built using the current map are listed in the dialog box. To view a specific page, click its name and then click the View button. Your default browser opens with the selected Web page displayed.

Deleting a Web page from the list

Time to do a little spring cleaning? To get rid of a Web page that you no longer want, follow these steps:

1. **Open the map on which the Web page is based and click File➪Manage Saved Web Pages.**

   The Manage Saved Web Pages dialog box appears (refer to Figure 7-11).

2. **Click the name of the Web page that you want to delete and then click the Remove from list button.**

   The Web page instantly disappears from the list (though not from your computer). You can't redo this action, so proceed with caution.

Editing a previously saved Web page

Did you forget to enable hyperlinks on your Web page? Have you decided to include an overview map? You're not out of luck, thanks to MapPoint's capability to enable you to edit a Web page. Changing any of the map options presented earlier is easy (with the exception of the map view, which we cover in the next section):

1. **Open the map on which the Web page was based, make any necessary formatting changes to the map, and then click File⇨Manage Saved Web Pages (refer to the dialog box shown in Figure 7-11).**

2. **Select the name of the Web page you wish to work with in the Manage Saved Web Pages list; then click the Edit button.**

   This action launches the Save as Web Page dialog box, shown in Figure 7-10. To begin making changes, simply work your way through the dialog box, selecting or deselecting options as desired.

3. **Click OK to save the changes.**

 Just because you edit the Web page doesn't mean that you have to edit the map itself. You can make any alterations you want to the Web page, but they needn't be saved as part of your map. For example, you can open all the Pushpin balloons on your map, save them as a Web page, and then exit MapPoint without saving the map with the Pushpin balloons open.

Changing a map view on a Web page

The only way to change a map view in a MapPoint Web page is to overwrite the existing Web page. To do this, follow these steps:

1. **Open the map you want to work with and reposition the map by clicking Zoom, Pan, or Select, as shown in Chapter 2, to reflect the desired view.**

2. **Click File⇨Manage Saved Web Pages.**

   Be sure that you've selected all the options you wanted in the original Web page. And if you've selected a certain part of the map that appears on-screen, be sure to click the Selected Area Map option.

3. **Enter a filename to give the new Web page the same name as the Web page file you want it to replace.**

You must make the filename the same to make all this work. You may wish to use the Browse button to locate the file you want to replace. Verify that all the information is correct.

4. **Click the OK button.**

MapPoint alerts you that the selected file already exists and asks whether you want to overwrite it.

5. **Click Yes to have the new Web page replace the old one.**

Chapter 8

Analyzing Data with MapPoint

. . . .

In This Chapter

▶ Analyzing data with MapPoint

▶ Preparing a data source from scratch

▶ Adapting existing data sources for optimum results

▶ Defining territories manually

▶ Generating territories automatically in MapPoint

. . . .

*W*ouldn't it be great to have a crystal ball to help you make the most educated and informed business decisions possible? Well, you may have found the next best thing in MapPoint. Although MapPoint can't help you see into the future directly, it can provide some invaluable clues to what that future may hold. How? By taking your megabytes of data and turning them into more than just random bits of numbers and facts. Much like the way that Microsoft Excel can turn thousands of cells into meaningful charts and graphs, MapPoint can turn the same data into graphical maps, putting a nice geographical spin on your data. It can even overlay your data with Census-based demographic data, deepening your insight.

Analyzing Data in MapPoint

Why would you need to analyze data in MapPoint? Say that you feed your customer database into MapPoint and use the Data Mapping Wizard to color your map based on the number of customers in each area. A quick look may reveal that most of your customers are coming from an area north of your store. Should you look for a new location up north, or should you beef up your advertising campaign closer to home?

Before you decide, try an experiment. If you kept track of the amount purchased by each customer, you could recolor the map based on total sales rather than the customer's residence. That may present a very different scenario. You may have a large number of customers coming from up north, but you may find that they actually buy very little compared to those who live closest to your store. Ah . . . your store's not in such a bad place after all.

Depending on the data you kept on each customer, you could map repeat visitors, find out what types of merchandise they favored (such as clothing, accessories, or shoes), even see the average age of your customer, which could help you choose additional business locations where the demographic composition matches the profile of your average customer.

MapPoint not only tells you a lot about your customers and clients but also can help you to single out recipients of targeted offers, thus maximizing your direct-mail advertising budget. For example, you can mail customers within five miles of your new store about the store's grand-opening celebration by using the Radius Circle drawing tool on your Pushpin map. Or you can find everyone in the state who bought shoes from you and e-mail them about your latest shipment of hot new styles.

If you'll let your imagination wander a bit, we bet you'll find dozens of questions you'd love to ask of your data but until now haven't had the ability to do.

Considering the (Data) Source

Whether you have existing data you'd like to analyze or need to start collecting the data from scratch, you'll want to know from which applications MapPoint accepts files. Your choice of data source can include any of the following:

- Microsoft Access database files
- Microsoft Excel files
- Microsoft Outlook contact files
- Relational database files (SQL Server, or any other OLE/ODBC-compliant database)
- Plain-text files (TXT, CSV, ASC, or TAB format)
- Microsoft Streets and Trips Pushpin files (STP)

Even if your data doesn't exist in one of these forms, chances are that it can be easily converted. Check your application's documentation or Help topics to see how best to accomplish this.

If you need to begin gathering the data from square one, the application you choose to collect it in will most likely be one you already have available to you and are comfortable using. Beyond that, your choice is almost irrelevant. As long as you keep the data source design tips that appear in the next couple of sections in mind, you should be in great shape.

Of course, you may need to consult documentation or online Help topics during the quest to create your data source in the chosen application. That's to be expected, because you may not have undertaken such a project in the past. And even if you have created a data source before, the design tips we share in the following sections may require you to do things in a slightly different manner. Don't let the process frustrate you; rather, focus on all that great information you'll have at your fingertips in the near future!

Discussing Data Types

MapPoint recognizes several types of data the moment it sees them. Before it begins working with your data, MapPoint scours your worksheet or database table for certain column headings. If it finds some that it understands, it translates the respective information to data that it can easily map. If MapPoint finds any questionable column headings, it asks you to assign them a data type manually (select a data type from the drop-down boxes provided) while working your way through the Data Mapping Wizard.

In Figure 8-1, you'll see an Excel worksheet full of data ready to be used by MapPoint. We've included the worksheet, SampleAddresses.xls, on the CDs that comes with this book, so you have a nice chunk of data to play with from the start if you don't already have your own data.

Microsoft Excel - SampleAddresses.xls

File Edit View Insert Format Tools Data Window Help Acrobat

Arial — 10 — **B** *I* <u>U</u>

C470

	A	B	C	D	E	F	G
1	ID	Name	Address	City	State	ZipCode	Value
2	1	Anas Abbar	1745 Bonanza	Gering	Nebraska	69341	1
3	4	Michael Meng	3304 Glen Royal Rd.	Raleigh	North Carolina	27612	2
4	9	Steve Clayton	1111 Andersen Drive	Pittsburgh	Pennsylvania	15220	3
5	10	Stuart Theodore	15205 E. 114th St. N.	Owasso	Oklahoma	74055	4
6	12	Tanya Van Dam	1856 Corporate Drive Suite 17	Norcross	Georgia	30093	5
7	14	David Goodhand	15w236 fillmore	elmhurst	Illinois	60126	6
8	16	Bill Sornsin	180 N stetson Avenue	chicago	Illinois	60601	7
9	18	Bethany O'Hara	24313 Hunt Ct	Hollywood	Maryland	20636	8
10	19	Darlene Mangione	615 s 9th	st joseph	Missouri	64501	9
11	21	Michael Emanuel	2231 Palestra #2	Maryland Heights	Missouri	63146	10
12	23	Jay Connelly	2121 w Main st #1050	Mesa	Arizona	85201	11
13	25	James Wilson	15 st charles	little chute	Wisconsin	54140	12
14	26	Steven Levy	112 w 11th ave	Emporia	Kansas	66801	13
15	27	Amy Bott	690 country squire ct	columbia	Missouri	65202	14
16	29	David Perera	326 Alexander Avenue	Greensburg	Pennsylvania	15601	15
17	31	Andrew Miller	1151 Gills Drive	Orlando	Florida	32824	16
18	32	Steve Masters	630 smith # 10	pasadena	Texas	77504	17
19	33	Kari Sherman	3562 w. Shakespeare	Chicago	Illinois	60647	18
20	36	Amy Meyer	2409 Cattleman Dr.	Brandon	Florida	33511	19
21	38	Scott Jones	2 New Dawn	Irvine	California	92620	20
22	40	Karen Berge	18900 Detroit Extension #503	Lakewood	Ohio	44107	21
23	42	Anne Hooper	287 Kootenai Dr	Libby	Montana	59923	22
24	45	Rob Daum	395 Dolores Way	South San Francisco	California	94080	23
25	46	Garrett Vargas	1546 Metropolitan Blvd	Tallahassee	Florida	32308	24

User Updates \ **Customers**

Ready — NUM

Figure 8-1: This clearly labeled worksheet will work well with MapPoint.

Notice the succinct column headings across the top of the worksheet? MapPoint will be able to recognize the vast majority of them instantly, meaning that you won't have to define them manually when you go to work with the data later on.

Table 8-1 gives you a brief rundown of these recognized data types and their respective column headings.

The data type indicates the type of data contained in a column of data. MapPoint uses this information to match the records to the map. For columns containing location information, choose the appropriate data type (such as State or City) from the drop-down box provided. For columns containing identifiers, select Name or Name 2 as the data type. For columns containing information other than location information, choose <Other Data>. To skip a column and not import it into the current map, choose <Skip Column>. As you work your way through the various data mapping wizards, you will eventually choose which of these columns will be displayed on the map.

Table 8-1	Data Types Supported by MapPoint 2002
Data Type	*Column Headings*
Name data	Name, Name 2
Location data	Address1, Address2, Address3, City, County, State, Country/Region, ZIP Code, 3 Digit ZIP Code, Census Tract, Metropolitan Area, Latitude, Longitude
Other data	Anything other than name or location data that doesn't fit into any other category, including hyperlinks
Territory	List the name of the record's territory (or its account rep, etc.) in this column; MapPoint can call on it to build territories

If you were to use a database containing the data types listed in Table 8-1 to build a Pushpin set of your clients or customers in MapPoint, the name data would be the information that appears on the gray title bar of the record's Pushpin balloon. The location data would be used to place the Pushpin in the proper position, as would the Territory data type.

To map a data source to territories, you must first define valid territories in MapPoint. See the section called "Establishing Territories," later in this chapter, for more details.

The more your data source conforms to these data types, the easier you'll find performing quick and accurate data analysis to be.

Preparing Your Data for Mapping

As you prepare (or create) your data for use by MapPoint, you can do several things to make it a bit more MapPoint-friendly. By MapPoint-friendly, we mean structuring it in such a way that MapPoint can quickly and easily identify your data fields and draw the desired map. A well-structured data source not only speeds up the map drawing process but also can potentially give you even more insight than a haphazardly organized data source.

Consistency counts

Analyzing data can be challenging enough without having to overcome organizational problems. When examining your data or planning for its collection, make sure that you have a consistent format for data fields. For example, consider using an Address 1 field for street or physical addresses, and an Address 2 field for Post Office box numbers. In other words, separate the location information MapPoint uses to match the data to the map from other information.

You also want to make sure that vital elements such as the city, state, and ZIP code have a uniform location and are treated as individual fields or columns in your files because that's what MapPoint will look for to perform its data mapping.

Head in the right direction

MapPoint is smart. It can recognize such column headings as City, State, and the like, so use that capability to your advantage. If you give your data columns clear, meaningful headings such as Name 1, Name 2, and so on, MapPoint will be able to detect the type of data held within that column without your having to go in and manually tell MapPoint what's what in the Data Mapping Wizard. It may seem trivial now, but when you need to analyze data quickly, this feature can save you precious moments.

Insufficient data to complete this request . . .

Perhaps you have a hodge-podge of records available to you. Some have a complete mailing address whereas others simply contain a city and state. Although MapPoint will try its best to map those incomplete records with the others, it may be best to extract them and then import or link them to your map separately. That way, MapPoint can do its job swiftly and accurately.

Address problems ahead of time

At first glance, placing a record's full address in a single field may seem to be a great idea. After all, the fewer data fields, the better, right? Wrong! By splitting up a record's location data, MapPoint can report statistics based on city, state, ZIP code, or something similar.

If all this address information were lumped together in a single data field, it would be next to impossible for MapPoint to make much sense out of it beyond possibly creating a Pushpin to mark the record's location on the map.

The more location data fields, the merrier!

The more location data fields you can define for your records, the more flexible your MapPoint data analysis options will be. You'll easily be able to analyze your data from the country, region, state, or city level if all these elements are subdivided in your data source.

The existence of numerous location data fields also serves as a data filter of sorts. For example, if you want to find out where your biggest customers are in California, the presence of a State data field lets MapPoint search through only the California records rather than have to hit every single record in the database. Doing so not only speeds up data mapping but also puts less of a demand on computing resources.

Go international

If your records deal with more than one country, you can make life a whole lot easier on yourself (and MapPoint) by adding a Country field or column of data. Doing so can serve as a powerful data filter when you're trying to examine a specific country, and it can save MapPoint a lot of processing time trying to guess where the address provided is located.

Make it unique

Every good database of information contains a primary key for each record. A primary key is just a fancy way of saying that each record should have a unique identifier, such as a customer ID number, which is stored in its own field or column. This unique identifier ensures that a record's complete file stays intact whether the account holder gets married and changes her name, moves to another state, or otherwise changes circumstances.

This unique identifier is especially important if you link your data to a MapPoint map down the road. If a record is changed without the benefit of a unique identifier, it may become difficult (if not impossible) for MapPoint to merge the changed record with the existing MapPoint record. With a unique ID number, MapPoint can reconcile the records in no time.

Even if you simply go to refresh an imported MapPoint data map later on, the absence of a unique identifier can cause unexpected glitches. Creating a primary key early on is definitely worth your time. And while you're at it, consider putting this primary key in the first column or field of your data table; that way, it's the first thing MapPoint sees in the record.

Text file considerations

If for whatever reason you find yourself working with a text file of data, make sure there are separators (also known as delimiters) in place to mark where one field ends and another begins. Valid separators include a tab, semicolon, or comma. Just make sure you're consistent in your use of delimiters, or MapPoint may have some trouble mapping your data.

Speedy primary key generation in Microsoft Excel

If you don't already have a primary key for your data and are using Microsoft Excel for your data source, we have a quick solution for you. First, launch Excel and open the worksheet containing the records you want to work with.

From there, you'll need to add a new column to the front of your worksheet. To do this, click the A column heading to select the first column; then click Insert⊅Columns from the Excel menu bar. A new blank column A appears and your other columns are renamed. In the top cell, enter a column name for your primary key — something like Customer ID, ID, or whatever is appropriate given the type of data you're working with.

Now it's time to enter the primary keys. Don't worry: You won't have to go in and type each number manually; Excel's AutoFill feature does the trick nicely. To begin working with AutoFill, you first need to type the starting number for the series of primary keys in the cell below the primary key column heading. In the cell beneath that, enter the next number up in the series. (For example, you may enter 1 in the first cell and 2 in the next, or 5000 in the first cell and 5001 in the next if you want to create the illusion of a large customer base. Because these numbers aren't typically public information, however, you may want to stick with 1 and 2 for simplicity's sake.)

With those numbers in place, click the first cell and drag the mouse downward until both cells are highlighted. Release the mouse button and move your mouse to the lower-right corner of the bottom cell. The pointer takes on the appearance of a plus (+) sign. When you see the plus sign pointer, click and drag the mouse down the column of data until the cell next to every record is highlighted. When you release the mouse button, every selected cell will have its own unique number.

Dollars and sense

Given the nature of data analysis, at least some of your columns or fields more than likely will contain money-related information. If you're working with Microsoft Excel, you'll want to make sure that entire columns are formatted as currency rather than single cells because inconsistent formatting can really throw calculations and mapping off. In an era when "time is money," who needs the extra delays, especially when they can so easily be avoided?

To show currency symbols in data tips in MapPoint, the columns or fields containing currency information in your source data must be formatted as Currency. Because each program does it a bit differently, you may need to consult the documentation for your spreadsheet or database application to learn how to do this.

Establishing Territories

With MapPoint, a territory is considered to be a set of user-defined geographic boundaries. These geographic boundaries (based on census tract, ZIP code, state, or metropolitan area) are typically used to denote service areas, delivery zones, marketing regions, coverage areas, sales districts, and the like for businesses large and small.

Dividing a list of customers or geographic locations into meaningful territories can be a nightmare without a tool such as MapPoint. For starters, ZIP codes that are sequential may not be physically located next to one another. (As an example, College Park, Maryland has a 20740 ZIP code, whereas Beltsville — the town immediately to the north — uses 20705.) Logical territories therefore can't be assigned based on a ZIP code alone. This is where feeding your data into MapPoint comes in.

You can create territories in one of two ways in MapPoint: by using your data source or by manually selecting territory coverage areas on the map.

The following sections deal with using more common data sources such as Microsoft Access, Microsoft Excel, and so on. MapPoint can also work with large relational databases such as SQL Server, and other OLE/ODBC-compliant databases. We devote a whole chapter, Chapter 10, to getting MapPoint to talk to SQL Server databases. After you have everything in place, you can use MapPoint with SQL Server just as easily as you can use it with Excel or Access.

Automatically generating territories

If your data source has a territory name field or column (a sales rep's name, for example) for each record along with a complete physical address (including a state and ZIP code at bare minimum), MapPoint can build the territories for you.

After your data source is adequately prepared to map in territories, follow these simple steps to have MapPoint's Create Territories Wizard build a map of territories based on your data:

1. **Launch MapPoint and click the Territories button on the Standard toolbar.**

   The Method dialog box of the Create Territories Wizard opens (see Figure 8-2).

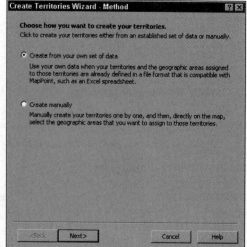

Figure 8-2: Two choices await you in the first dialog box of the Create Territories Wizard.

2. **Because you'll be working with your own data source, click the Create From Your Own Set of Data option and then click Next>.**

   The Import or Link window, shown in Figure 8-3, appears. You need to decide whether to import or link to your data source.

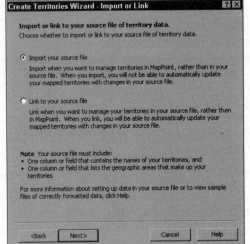

Figure 8-3:
To import or
link . . . that
is the
question.

Importing versus linking territories

Deciding when to import versus link your data to the Create Territories Wizard can pose some interesting challenges. First, consider the differences between the two techniques. Importing the data basically takes the records from your source data and pulls them in to MapPoint, enabling MapPoint to take a geographical snapshot of your territories as they exist at the time the map was generated. Linking, on the other hand, points MapPoint to your data, which it can then use to build a territory map. Following are some of the pros and cons of each approach.

Importing data gives you a bulkier MapPoint file because MapPoint needs to package the data along with the territory map. Importing is a more flexible option than linking, however, in that it enables you to manage the territories from within MapPoint. That means you can draw and redefine territories as needed rather than have to go back to the data source and make the edits there. Importing is a good option for creating territories that seldom change, and for building "portable" territory maps that you can take on

the road with you whether you have access to your data source or not.

Linking gives you a nice tidy MapPoint file because linking requires MapPoint to merely point to the data it needs. In addition, linking gives you access to the most up-to-date information out there. So what's the downside? If you want to modify your territories, you have to go back to the data source, make the necessary changes, and then rebuild your territory map. That's an awful lot of work when time is of the essence. But for companies and organizations who are constantly adding customers to their sales rep territories, linking may be the best way to keep everything up-to-date. Just remember, though, that linked territory maps take significantly longer to load than their imported data counterparts because the data needs to be found each time. And even though you create a linked territory map, that map is still a snapshot of your company's status at the exact point in time the map was generated. To get the most current information, you need to click Data⟳Update Linked Records from the menu bar.

3. Select the desired option and click the Next> button.

You'll be taken to a standard Microsoft Office Open dialog box like the one shown in Figure 8-4.

Figure 8-4:
If you needed further proof that MapPoint is part of the Microsoft Office family, here it is!

4. Navigate to the data source file you want to use. When you see the file listed, double-click it to open it.

A window similar to the one in Figure 8-5 opens. In the case of an Excel workbook, the worksheets or named ranges of the workbook are listed so that you can easily choose the data in your source file that you want to work with.

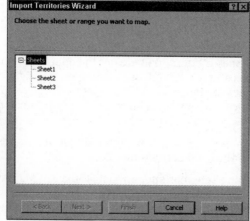

Figure 8-5:
Pick and click the data that you'd like to work with.

5. Double-click the data you wish to work with (for example, sheet 3 of your Excel data source).

The window in Figure 8-6 appears. This is where you'll define the data types of your column headings/fields.

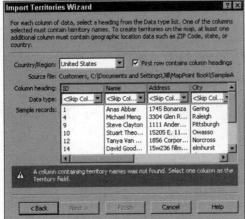

Figure 8-6:
MapPoint warns you if your data source is not properly formatted for importing territories definitions.

6. **First, click the arrow to open the Country/Region drop-down box and select the name of the country or region you'll be working with.**

   If your data spans multiple countries, choose <Multi/Other>, the first item on the list.

7. **If the first row of your data source does *not* contain column headings, you need to deselect the First Row Contains Column Headings option.**

   If your column headings aren't labeled at all and you fail to deselect this option, the first record in your database will be omitted from the territory map.

   MapPoint is a smart tool. Even if you haven't labeled your data source columns, MapPoint may attempt to figure out the data type on its own. For example, if it "sees" a column full of state names, it assigns State as the data type so that you don't have to. Don't let that fool you, however. If your data source does not contain column headings, you need to execute Step 7 no matter how many data types MapPoint can assign on its own.

8. **Click the down arrow buttons below each column of data to choose a data type for any unlabeled column headings.**

   If you used the naming schemes suggested in Table 8-1, MapPoint should have been able to select all the data types for you. And if a column has no relevance to territory construction, keep the <Skip Column> data type in place.

9. **Click the Finish button after you have labeled all the fields.**

   The window in Figure 8-7 keeps you apprised of MapPoint's status in building your territory map.

Figure 8-7:
MapPoint
keeps you
informed of
its progress
in building
the territory
map.

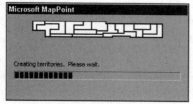

If MapPoint has trouble mapping any of your data records, a dialog box appears to guide you through problem resolution. For example, Figure 8-8 shows you how MapPoint deals with an unidentifiable ZIP code. In this case, MapPoint assumes that you may have made a typo, so it gives you several possible ZIP codes from which to choose. If you find the correct one, select it in the window and click OK. Alternatively, you can skip the record in question or cancel the process all together and rectify the problem in your data source.

Figure 8-8:
A typo or an
oversight?
MapPoint
helps you
decide.

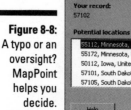

Building territories manually

If you don't have an existing data source with territory-compatible fields in it, you may find creating the territories manually to be easiest. Although you have much flexibility with the territory boundaries, you still need to choose a geographical unit of measurement (such as a state, ZIP code, or metropolitan area) for your territories. You should always choose the smallest geographic unit that you may want to use. Such a decision will give you far more flexibility as you fine-tune your territories.

To create territories manually, you again call on the Create Territories Wizard. You should note, however, that only one territory set can exist on each map. Launch MapPoint and follow these steps to begin working with the Create Territories Wizard:

1. **Click the Territories button on the Standard toolbar to open the Create Territories Wizard.**

   The Method dialog box, shown back in Figure 8-2, appears.

2. **Choose the Create Manually option in the Method box and then click the Next> button.**

   The Geography dialog box, shown in Figure 8-9, opens, asking you to select the geography on which you'd like to base your territories.

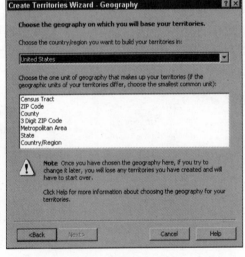

Figure 8-9:
Unless your territories cover an entire state, ZIP codes may be the best way to go.

3. **Click the drop-down box provided to select the country or region you want to build your territories on; then click the name of the smallest unit of geography on which your territories are based (typically ZIP codes or states).**

4. **Click Next> to continue.**

   In a special Manual Creation Tips window, the Create Territories Wizard gives you a few tips for creating territories.

   Metropolitan areas may seem to be a good geographical unit on which to base territories, but using this unit has one major drawback: areas outside a metropolitan area cannot be included on the map, leaving vast geographic areas untouchable by your territories unless you go in and redraw the boundaries by hand.

5. **Click the Finish button to exit the wizard and begin defining territories.**

   The Territory Manager pane, shown in Figure 8-10, opens, ready for you to begin defining your territories. The type of map you see here will depend on the geographical unit of measurement you chose as the basis of your territories. This figure illustrates a map based on metropolitan areas.

6. **Give your territory set a meaningful name by clicking inside the text box provided and typing in the desired name.**

   Do not attempt to save the territory map until at least one territory has been defined. Without one or more territories in place, literally nothing exists for MapPoint to save, so all that work in the Create Territories Wizard will have been for naught.

Figure 8-10:
You'll work with the Territory Manager any time you need to modify a territory map.

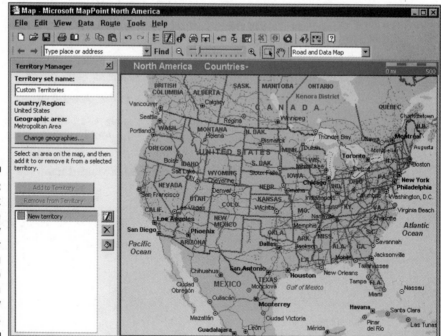

7. **Click the New Territory button in the legend window to enter the name of your first territory in the text box provided.**

   In many cases, a territory will bear the name of its account rep, marketing manager, or something similar. By default, MapPoint labels a territory "New Territory." To change the name to something more meaningful, click New Territory on the Territory list and enter the desired name in the resulting highlighted area (the spot where the old territory name appeared).

8. **Click the Zoom button to zoom in on the area you wish to work with so that you can clearly see the ZIP codes, state names, or whatever geographical unit you chose.**

   You may also need to use the techniques described in Chapter 2 to get to the appropriate location on the map.

9. **Click the applicable ZIP code, state name, or other relevant label to select the first geographical area to include in the first territory.**

   The otherwise black letters of the area you've chosen will become highlighted and framed in white, leaving no doubt what area you've selected.

10. **Click the Add to Territory button in the Territory Manager.**

    MapPoint colors in the selected area in the color displayed on the Territory Manager next to the territory's name. Repeat Steps 9 and 10 as many times as needed until the first territory is completely defined.

11. **Click the New Territory button (the top button to the right of the territory legend) to begin defining a second territory.**

    Click the New Territory label to give the territory a meaningful name; then enter the name desired into the resulting highlighted area.

12. **Repeat Steps 9 and 10 to assign areas to the new territory.**

    Continue following these steps as necessary until all your territories have been laid out as desired. Eventually, you'll end up with a nicely labeled, color-coded territory map like the one shown in Figure 8-11.

13. **Click File⇨Save As to give the map a meaningful name and save your work.**

    MapPoint takes a few moments to build your new map. You'll also find that the territories in your legend have been rearranged in alphabetical order for easy reference.

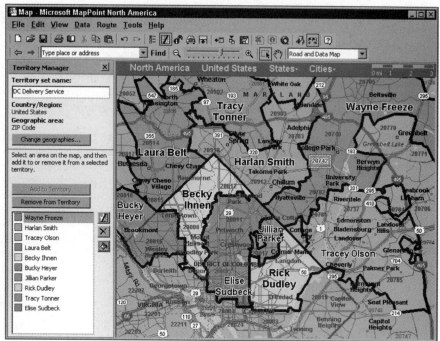

Figure 8-11:
Each of your
territories is
labeled and
shaded with
a different
color.

Manipulating Territories

Something not quite right about that territory map you created? Perhaps
colors in adjacent territories are too similar to be easily spotted, or maybe
you've lost a couple of account reps and want to dissolve their territories.

Whatever the case, you'll be happy to know that editing territories in
MapPoint is a breeze. Before you get started, however, we need to offer a few
caveats. Although you can modify imported and manually created territories
with little thought, about the only change you can make to linked territories
is the territory's color on the map. Again, that's because any changes made
to a linked data source need to be made in the data source, not in MapPoint.

 To modify a territory map, you need to open the map and call on the
Territory Manager, as shown in Figure 8-10. The Territory Manager pane
should open with the territory map. If you've closed it to perform other tasks
on the map, you can access it again by clicking the Territories button (shown
in the margin) on the Standard toolbar. Now you're all set to begin editing
your territory map!

Adding geographical areas to a territory

Basically, you have two ways to add coverage area to a territory. The first involves selecting the name of the territory that you want to add to on the territory legend, clicking the appropriate data label (ZIP code, state name, or other) on the map and then clicking the Add to Territory button in the Territory Manager pane. The map is instantly re-colored to reflect the addition.

 The second alternative is great for filling in holes in coverage or for selecting areas whose labels may be hard to click because of the presence of other map elements (intersections, points of interest, and the like). Click the territory's name that you want to edit in the territory legend; then click the Select tool on MapPoint's Navigation toolbar. Use that tool to select an area on the map that's to be added to the selected territory (click the upper-left corner of the area you want to include; then drag the mouse down and to the right to draw your square or rectangle.) After the appropriate area has been marked, click the Add to Territory button. Any ZIP code (or whatever geographical unit of measurement you're using) that falls within the selected area will be pulled into the chosen territory.

Deleting areas from a territory

Just as you need to add areas to a territory in the exact geographical units that you specified in creating the map, you need to remove them that way as well. That is, you can delete only whole states from a territory that uses states as its fundamental unit of measurement. The same holds true for cities, ZIP codes, metropolitan areas, and other available geographical units.

The easiest way to remove a geographical area is as follows:

1. **With your territory map on-screen, open the Territory Manager by clicking Data⇨Territories from the menu bar.**

2. **Select the name of the territory that contains the area you want to remove.**

3. **On the map, click the label of geographic unit that corresponds to the area you want to remove from the territory.**

   At this point, the Remove from Territory button should now be available in the Territory Manager pane.

4. **Click the Remove from Territory button to remove the area from the selected territory.**

Remember that if you select the wrong area and notice it the instant after you click the Remove from Territory button, you can bring the area back with ease by pressing Ctrl+Z — the Undo command that you may have grown to know and love in other Office applications. You can also click the Undo button (shown in the margin) on MapPoint's Standard toolbar.

Renaming a territory

Staff turnover is a fact of life in the workplace, and if you identify territories by employees' names, you may find yourself occasionally needing to rename a territory.

To rename a territory, simply double-click its name in the Territory Manager pane. Doing so highlights the name and surrounds it with a frame of thin black lines. Click inside that frame and type in the new name for the territory. Press Enter or click elsewhere on the screen to lock the name in place and have it appear on the map.

Of course, you'll also want to save your territories map after making a change like this one.

 If you've linked to your data source, you won't be able to change this information in MapPoint. You'll have to go back to your data source to do it.

Changing the color in which a territory appears

It may seem like a simple matter of aesthetics at first glance, but the color of your territories really can impair the legibility of your map. Even though each territory is outlined with a thick black line, similar colors next to one another make things harder to see than they need to be.

MapPoint does its best to select colors that don't look similar to one another, but a map with many territories that span convoluted areas may result in similar colors being adjacent to one another.

 You can change the color of a territory no matter how you created them (linked-data people, this one's for you) by clicking the Change Color button — the bottom button on the right side of the territory legend (shown here in the margin). The Change Colors dialog box like the one shown in Figure 8-12 appears.

Does your new choice look better? Don't forget that if the dialog box hides the territories you're working with, you can click the dialog box's title bar — the strip at the top labeled "Change Colors" — and drag it out of the way so that you can see everything you need.

Figure 8-12:
Fifty color
choices
await you,
though
many of
them are
only subtle
variations of
the five
basic colors
MapPoint
provides.

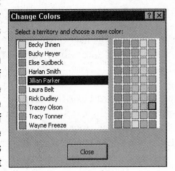

Click the name of the territory whose color you want to change, and then click the desired color swatch in the right side of the Change Colors dialog box. When you're happy with your selection, click the Close button to close the dialog and save your changes.

Deleting a territory from your map

 Want to get rid of a territory on your MapPoint map? Just click its name on the Territory Manager pane and then click the Delete Territory button (shown in the margin).

Remember, this action deletes the territory only on your territory map; it doesn't reassign the records in your source data that are subsequently without a territory. To see which (if any) of your records are now "homeless," run the Create Territories Wizard on the newly defined map.

Chapter 9

Using the Data Mapping Wizard

*H*aving heaps of data tucked away on databases or spreadsheets is fine and dandy, but without a way to interpret or communicate that data effectively, you may as well not even have it at all!

MapPoint offers countless ways not only to show what your data means, but also to produce highly detailed maps that are destined to become permanent fixtures in your reports, grant applications, publications, Web pages, and presentations.

Choosing a Map Type for the Job

Keeping the types of data you've collected in mind, one of the first decisions you need to make is what type of data map is best suited for making your point or helping you gain better insight into your business or organization.

Three basic types of data maps are available in MapPoint 2002: maps that display locations without any associated numerical data (Pushpin Maps and Multiple Symbol Maps), maps that tie a single piece of numerical data to each location (Shaded Area Maps, Sized Circle Maps, Shaded Circle Maps, and Multiple Symbol Maps which is new in MapPoint 2002), and maps that have multiple numerical values for each location (Pie Chart Maps, Sized Pie Chart Maps, Column Chart Maps, and Series Column Chart Maps, all of which are new in MapPoint 2002).

These new map types add even greater depth to MapPoint's data mapping capabilities in that it is now possible to map multiple fields of numeric data for each location.

After you've narrowed down the range of possibilities, use information in the following sections to help you make your final decision. You can always change your mind or try something different later (and there's no need to rerun the entire wizard to do so, as you can see in the section titled "Editing Your Data Maps," later in this chapter), but at least it'll give you some solid options to start with.

It can be difficult to come up with a legend label that's short enough to fit on-screen yet describes the map to its fullest. Given that, we have a couple of tips for you. First, when sharing a MapPoint map electronically, you can hover your mouse over a legend label ending in "..." to produce a screen tip (a little gray box) with the entire label name displayed. It may also be worth adding a narrative to the map (paste it into Word and add a paragraph description) as you distribute it to make your intentions perfectly clear.

For your convenience, the following sections present the map types in the order they appear on MapPoint's Data Mapping Wizard.

Shaded Area Maps

The Shaded Area Map breaks up a map into different geographical areas, such as states, counties, or ZIP or postal codes, and then shades each area based on a value you specify from your data source. This type of map is very useful when analyzing statistical data that spans larger areas such as counties or states. It's also good for analyzing demographic data because you can easily spot areas with a high population, high income, and the like.

Shaded Area Maps also give you a great foundation on which you can overlay additional data for a valuable comparison and contrast. For example, you may want to build a Shaded Area Map that reflects the density of high-income households in your target area, and then overlay Shaded Circle Maps displaying annual sales for your small chain of high-end boutiques. Does a correlation exist between sales and income? Is there a higher-income location you may want to consider expanding to? These are only a few of the insights you can gain about your business using Shaded Area Maps. Figure 9-1 illustrates a sample Shaded Area Map.

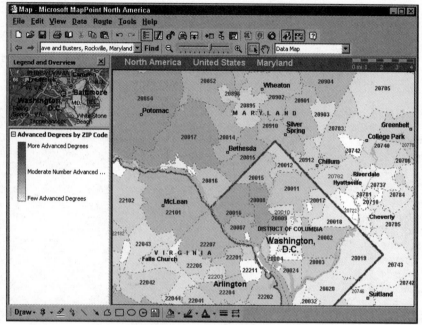

Figure 9-1:
This map
shows
where the
suburban
Washington,
D.C.
neighbor-
hoods with
the greatest
density of
advanced
degrees are.

Shaded Circle Maps

These maps are great for illustrating a relative value in a single location. For example, you may create Shaded Circle Maps to reflect the concentration of high-income families within a given ZIP code. Each ZIP code's circle would be an identical size; however, by default, the darker the circle's color, the higher that location's concentration of high-income households. If you wanted a good map type to use with a Shaded Area Map foundation, this would be a terrific choice because it's clear and easy to read.

In Figure 9-2, we've created a sample of a Shaded Circle Map for you. This particular map helps target the most educated metropolitan areas for a proposed pre-teen computer camp, technology museum, or other education-dependent initiative.

Sized Circle Maps

The Sized Circle Map is a variation of the Shaded Circle Map discussed previously, only instead of marking a site's value with a shaded circle, it makes the circle larger or smaller depending on the value being mapped.

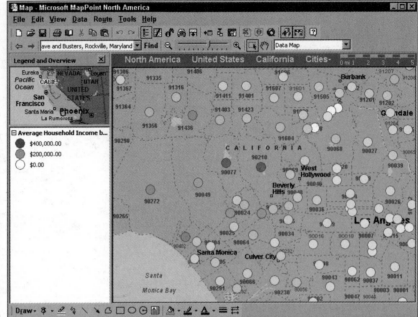

Figure 9-2:
Use a
Shaded
Circle Map
to get a
quick feel
for how one
location
ranks in
relation to
another.

These maps are great overlays for a Shaded Area Map, and an additional strength lies in their ability to show a single site's value. Whereas Shaded Circle Maps are a good choice for mapping a significant number of sites that are close together, Sized Circle Maps can draw attention to high-value sites that may be scattered across the country. Take a look at Figure 9-3 to see a sample of a Sized Circle Map.

Multiple Symbol Maps

You know how many nonprofit organizations have various membership levels? For example, you contribute $20 and you're an Associate, $50 and you're a Contributor, $100 and you're a Donor, and so on. Well, a Multiple Symbol Map is the perfect way to demonstrate an organization's range of support graphically and geographically.

For each data point (typically a member's mailing address), MapPoint posts a color-coded dot (or Pushpin depending on your selection), which corresponds to the member's contributed dollar amount. You can also use Multiple Symbol Maps to differentiate between your standard and full franchise locations, your standard and "super" stores, or any other distinction you may have.

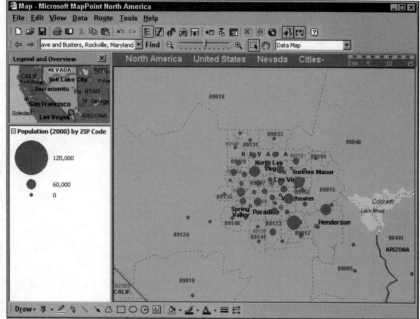

Figure 9-3:
Sized
Circle Maps
can be
effective at
comparing
ZIP codes
demo-
graphically.

Pie Chart Maps

If you've ever made charts from your data in Excel, then you may be familiar with pie charts in which each pie represents a location, customer, and so on. Each slice may correspond to a store's various product line sales, or maybe even the annual sales for each of the last four years to see whether all years were equal or got progressively better. Basically, this type of chart map plots statistics for each point or location's values simultaneously. No comparison is made between points on the map. If you want to see how one performed in relation to another, take a look at the Sized Pie Chart Map option described in the next section.

You can bring these pie charts to multiple locations in MapPoint, as shown in Figure 9-4. In that figure, you can see a comparison of a small mail-order firm's clothing versus shoes sold in various states.

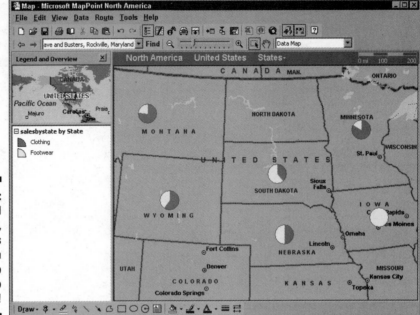

Figure 9-4:
As an added
bonus,
these pies
come with
zero
calories, so
enjoy!

Sized Pie Chart Maps

Using the example of the stores mentioned in the previous section, in addition to seeing how the sales of two or more product lines compare to one another, Sized Pie Chart Maps make it possible to compare the bottom line of each store with one another (see Figure 9-5). The locations with the highest values display the largest pies, and those with the smallest values display the smallest pies. And, of course, each pie in the Sized Pie Chart Map is still subdivided just as the standard Pie Chart Map is.

Sized Pie Chart Maps are a terrific way to illustrate vast amounts of data. You not only can view specifics about a particular point, but also how all those points compare to one another.

Column Chart Maps

All the other map types are great, but what happens if you need to map a negative value? Column Chart Maps are the only type of map that will let you adequately display a negative number value. Beyond that, they can chart performance at each data point where no comparison between them is needed.

Figure 9-6 shows you what a map of this type may look like. This one shows how various product lines perform within each state. In this type of map, each column is a different color, which serves as a reminder that each block of data should be considered individually.

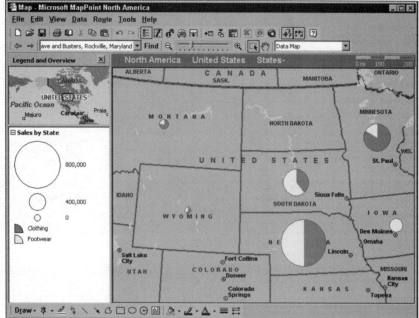

Series Column Chart Maps

Let's just get it out in the open — Series Column Chart Maps are a whole lot like Column Chart Maps. In fact, they're pretty much identical except for one tiny difference: All the columns in a Series Column Chart Map are the same color. What makes that difference so powerful, though, is the fact that it encourages viewers to see the data as one statistic viewed over time.

Try looking at Figure 9-6, and then take a look at Figure 9-7. Although they display trends over time, they have a different feel, don't they? The Column Chart Map's different-colored columns appear to divide the data into chunks, whereas the Series Column Chart Map's columns move your eye from left to right, encouraging you to see the data as a series of snapshots taken over time.

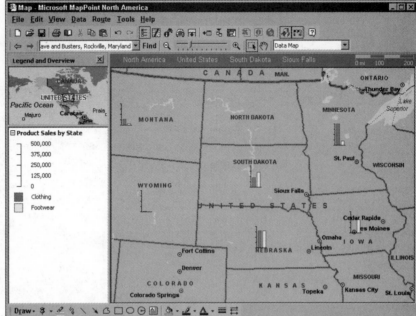

Figure 9-6:
Although no negative values are presented here, that's really this type of map's strength.

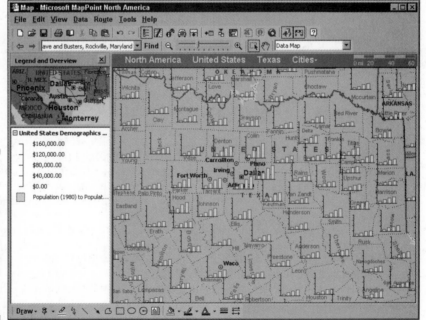

Figure 9-7:
See how the average household income in these counties has changed over time?

Pushpin Maps

Whether you want to mark the states you own stores in, need to mark all of your members' locations, or want to create a Pushpin map of your customers from which you can create routes for your sales reps, you'll find that Pushpin Maps are your best bet. They don't work for demographic mapping, but they're almost unbeatable for marking a single location on the map.

And we should note that after you create a Pushpin Map of your customers, members, clients, or whatever, that Pushpin Map becomes invaluable. Using MapPoint's Drawing tools, you can select certain groups of Pushpins and turn them into routes, export the selected addresses to Excel for targeted direct mail or e-mail advertising campaigns . . . there are some terrific possibilities here. Figure 9-8 shows you what a Pushpin Map might look like.

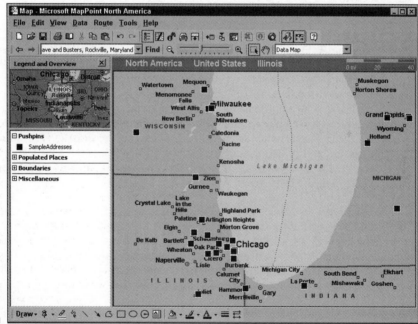

Figure 9-8: Black squares can replace standard Pushpins to enhance visibility of data points.

Choosing Whether to Import or Link Map Data

After you've determined what type of map you want to use, the next major decision to make when you go to build a data map is whether you want to import the data or link to it. We touch on this a bit in discussing territories in Chapter 8. Here, the considerations for building a data map are different.

When you import data to MapPoint, that information is actually extracted from your data source and pulled into MapPoint. You can even modify imported data as needed to map it properly. Importing is great for mapping stats that are static or change relatively infrequently, such as a Pushpin map of your store locations or a Sized Pie Chart Map of each store's performance during the previous year.

Importing is also a great way to take successive snapshots of your data over time. Just import an updated data source into the same map parameters, give the map a new filename, and you've marked your place in time. Additionally, importing is the best way to compare apples to apples. After you've imported the data into MapPoint, you can use it to make an assortment of maps, knowing for certain that each map reflects identical data or statistics. And that brings us to the downside of importing data, which is the fact that you have to import the data source all over again if you want to see an update. Of course, depending on your perspective, that can be perceived as extra work or as a built-in safety feature!

Linking is a bit of a mixed bag, too. Because it references your data rather than pulls it into MapPoint, the data the map uses will change every time an edit is made to the data source and the map file is updated by clicking Data⇨Update Linked Records. For records that remain more static such as store location lists, this changing may not pose a problem, but if you attempt to link to your customer database that's updated in real time with each order placed, creating a map that says something meaningful and specific is like shooting at a moving target. Sure, it gives you the most current information possible, but it also makes comparing apples to apples a bit tricky because the data is always changing, and you can't be certain who's looking at what version of the data, when.

You could be doing a collection of maps for your company's annual report and in the time it takes you to finish the first map and move on to creating the second, several more orders could be placed meaning there's no way the first map could — with a hundred percent degree of certainty — agree completely with the data presented in the second map. Linked data cannot be edited in MapPoint either, meaning that you'll always have to return to the data source to fix any problems you may find. If, however, you want a data map that your sales force can access to see how they're doing in relation to one another, then linking may be the perfect option. That way, all they have to do to get the freshest data is click Data⇨Update Linked Records; they won't have to import the entire database all over again.

Remember, no matter which method you choose, the maps you create are like snapshots taken at a specific point in time. Even linked maps won't change before your eyes when the map is on-screen unless you click Data⇨Update Linked Records from the menu bar.

Which Wizard to Use When?

MapPoint offers three data-mapping wizards: the Data Mapping Wizard, the Import Data Wizard, and the Link Data Wizard. The primary difference among them pertains to the order with which you execute the required steps. The Data Mapping Wizard requires you to select the type of map you want to create first, whereas the Import Data Wizard and Link Data Wizard ask you to define your data source first.

Because the Import Data Wizard and the Link Data Wizard eventually drop you into the Data Mapping Wizard, the three wizards can almost be considered identical (with the exception of where you start in the process, that is). You should also know that if you want to tap in to MapPoint's extensive demographic data, you want to use the Data Mapping Wizard. Beyond that, there really isn't a "best" wizard for certain tasks; the choice comes down to a matter of personal preference.

To eliminate unnecessary redundancy and to conserve space for other MapPoint goodies, we walk you through the Data Mapping Wizard only. Because the Import Data Wizard and the Link Data Wizard merely rearrange the steps of the Data Mapping Wizard, you should be in great shape with a single walk-through.

Running the Data Mapping Wizard

The Data Mapping Wizard opens the door to nine different data map types, as described earlier in the chapter in the section "Choosing a Map Type for the Job." The wizard guides you every step of the way, but the subtleties of some of the decisions you have to make may get a bit complex. When complexity is potentially an issue, we include more details to help you make the best decision possible given your needs and circumstances. In some cases, we include sidebars that explain how certain options work.

To begin creating your data map, just launch MapPoint 2002 and follow these steps:

1. **Open the Data Mapping Wizard by clicking Data⇨Data Mapping Wizard from the menu bar, or click the Data Mapping Wizard button on MapPoint's Standard toolbar (shown in the margin).**

   The Map Type window of the Data Mapping Wizard opens, as shown in Figure 9-9.

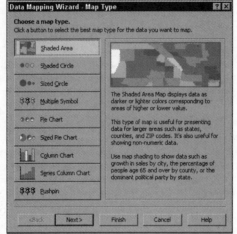

2. **Click the name of the map type you want to create and then click the Next> button.**

   When you click a map type, a description of the map along with a sample image of mapped data appears on the right side of the wizard. After you've clicked the Next> button, the Data Set window, shown in Figure 9-10, appears.

3. **Click the appropriate option to choose whether to import or link to your own data by and then click the Next> button to continue.**

   You're taken to an Import Data Wizard or Link Data Wizard window that resembles a standard Microsoft Office Open or Save As dialog box.

We discuss the demographic-specific option in a section titled, "Dealing with Demographics," later in this chapter.

These steps are applicable to standard data sources such as Excel spreadsheets, Access databases, Outlook contact lists, and the like. Tapping into a larger relational database such as SQL Server, Oracle, or Informix require a bit more work. All of Chapter 10 is devoted to working with such data sources using MapPoint.

4. Navigate your way to the desired data source, and when its filename appears on-screen, double-click the name.

A dialog box like the one shown in Figure 9-11 opens, asking you to choose the range of data you want to work with. (If you have a single data source, this screen may not appear.)

Figure 9-11:
This window corresponds to an Excel data source and will look different if you're working with an Access database, Outlook contact files, or other supported source file.

5. Double-click the name of the data range you want to use for the data map.

After a few moments of processing (the bigger the data source, the longer the process), a dialog box like the one shown in Figure 9-12 appears. This dialog box is where you define the most appropriate headings for each column or field of data. You also want to make sure that the Country/Region box specifies the correct area. If multiple countries or regions are covered in your data, be sure to select <Multi/Other> from the drop-down box.

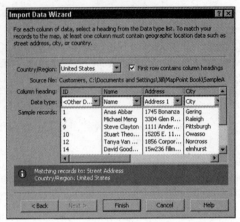

Figure 9-12:
MapPoint
is pretty
good at
identifying
most
types of
information
provided by
the data
source.

6. **Click the arrow button next to each of the drop-down box to select the appropriate data type for each column or field of information; click Finish when you're done.**

   If you imported the data, you can choose a <Skip Column> option that tells MapPoint to ignore the data in the respective column or field. And if you linked to the data, MapPoint prompts you to choose a primary key column to uniquely identify each record. After a bit of processing time, the Data Fields window shown in Figure 9-13 opens.

7. **Click the field you want when the Data Fields window asks you to select the data field or column you want to map (but note that this information will not be requested for Pushpin maps).**

   The selected field is the field you want to look at in greater detail. It might hold the number of customers from various ZIP codes, the total annual sales for a store, or some other piece of information. MapPoint can add, count, or average this information for you.

8. **Click the arrow button next to the drop-down box provided to divide the data by a second field of data (please see the sidebar "Avoiding Data Field disasters" for more details).**

   This option, which will not appear for Pushpin Maps, is useful primarily if you want to analyze your market penetration in various areas. For example, you can opt to map Customer IDs and then divide them by population. Depending on how you tell MapPoint to show the data, you get a map that illustrates your company's market penetration by ZIP code, county, state, or other geographical unit. This is extremely useful information when you're evaluating your marketing efforts and plans.

   Examining real numbers only can be deceiving. Having 20 customers from Baltimore County, Maryland, is no big deal because of its large population, but having 10 customers in more sparsely populated Berkshire County in western Massachusetts is a commendable accomplishment for a national scale business.

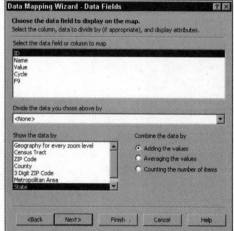

Figure 9-13:
You can do
a lot from
within the
Data Fields
window.

9. **Click the name of a geographical unit from the box at the lower-left side of the window to tell MapPoint how you want the data shown.**

   MapPoint displays the information in the geographic unit specified, giving you the opportunity to view data by state, ZIP code, metropolitan area, or other available geographic unit. You may also be interested to know that you can vary the appearance of data by zoom level as well, meaning that if you're looking at the map close up, you may see ZIP code or county stats; at medium range you'd see state-wide stats; and at the highest level you'd see country-wide data where available.

10. **Specify whether you want the data added (the default), averaged, or counted by selecting the desired option; click Next> when you're done.**

   When it comes to this option, MapPoint is one smart cookie. If you choose a non-numeric field in the Select the Data Field or Column to Map window at the top of the dialog box (something like a Name or Address field), MapPoint automatically recognizes that it cannot add or average the data, so it grays out those options and counts them automatically. After you click Next>, the Legends window shown in Figure 9-14 appears.

   Use extreme caution when working with customer IDs or primary keys. If they are numbers, MapPoint may attempt to add them rather than count them, which could give you inaccurate results. Before clicking the Next> button, be sure to double-check the Combine Data By options to make sure that Counting the Number of Items is selected.

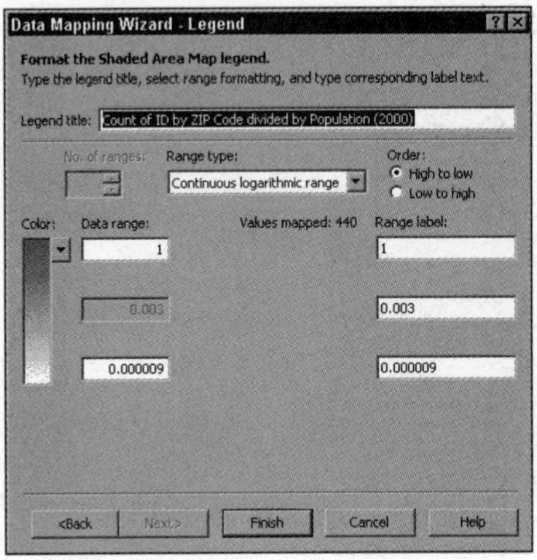

Data Mapping Wizard - Legend

Format the Shaded Area Map legend.
Type the legend title, select range formatting, and type corresponding label text.

Legend title: Count of ID by ZIP Code divided by Population (2000)

No. of ranges: Range type: Order:
                  Continuous logarithmic range ▼   ○ High to low
                                                       ○ Low to high

Color: Data range: Values mapped: 440   Range label:

          1   1

          0.003   0.003

          0.000009   0.000009

    <Back   Next>   Finish   Cancel   Help

Figure 9-14:
The labels
you choose
here can
go a long
way toward
making
your maps
easy to
understand.

11. **Click all the desired options, and then click Finish to have MapPoint build your map.**

A variety of collection techniques are used, including drop-down boxes, text boxes, and radio buttons. The options you'll work with will depend on the type of data map you choose. The data attributes form varies depending on the options you select; however, all forms contain these elements:

- **Map Title:** Holds the title of the map.

- **Range Type:** Describes how the information is drawn on the map. You can choose from any of six different ranges or you can create your own custom range.

- **Order:** Enables you to choose whether the highest values or the lowest values are displayed with the darkest color.

- **Colors:** Enables you to choose from one of 16 different color schemes. Eight start with a single solid color (say, dark blue or purple) that fades to white depending on the data value. Five fade to yellow from a single color. Of the remaining three, one is red to white to blue, one is gold to green, and the last is rainbow.

You can also type in more descriptive Range labels in the text boxes provided. Meaningful labeling will do wonders for the viewer's ability to interpret the true meaning of your map's data.

And don't forget, you can create a Shaded Area Map as a foundation and overlay a second batch of data over the top by simply re-running the Data Mapping Wizard. Use the same data source with a different spin, or choose a different data source altogether; the choice is yours.

Dealing with Demographics

MapPoint is phenomenal at mapping data you've collected, and it gives you access to some pretty awesome demographic data as well. When you use it in combination with your own data, you can gain some pretty powerful insights into your business's strengths and weaknesses. For example, if your business caters to high-income families, you may want to make a Shaded Area Map reflecting the average household income, and then overlay a Sized Circle Map based on your customer database. Does the bulk of your customers come from the highest income areas? Are high-income areas nearby that you may want to consider running more ads in? These are just a few of the questions you potentially can answer with such a map.

MapPoint comes with more than eight million pieces of information in more than 136 categories covering the United States and Canada, and as many as 43 categories for other countries worldwide. Of course, the availability of data from all countries may not be equally plentiful, but the U.S. and Canada are extremely well covered, as you can see in the sections "U.S. demographic data available in MapPoint" and "Canada demographic data available in MapPoint," which appear later in this chapter.

MapPoint comes with a fair amount of data, but you can always purchase or download more. In fact, we've given you some more to play with on the book's CDs.

Demographics and the data mapping wizard

Running the Data Mapping Wizard against the demographic data included with MapPoint takes you through a series of steps that may be slightly different than the steps you'll see using your own data.

For example, when you select the Add Demographic Data to the Map option, you need to use the drop-down box provided to select U.S. (the default for MapPoint's North American Edition), Canada, or Worldwide demographic data. After you click the Next> button (as you do in Step 3 of the "Running the Data Mapping Wizard" section presented earlier in the chapter), you actually skip ahead to that section's Step 7, which involves working with the Data Fields screen. Refer to that section to make sure that you understand each of your choices and how they interact with one another. Note that the Combine the Data By options are all grayed out. MapPoint assumes that you want to count any demographic groupings you may form in your maps.

Beyond that, the Data Mapping Wizard behaves identically no matter what type of data you work with or what method you use to access it from within MapPoint.

You cannot map demographic data with the Pushpin map type.

U.S. Demographic data available in MapPoint

U.S. demographic data, which is provided by Claritas, can be divided into two general categories: Population and Households/Housing Units. Each bit of data also typically has four values:

- ✔ Estimated 2000 values based on the 1990 Census
- ✔ Data collected from the 1990 Census
- ✔ Data collected from the 1980 Census
- ✔ Projections for 2005 based on the Census and other sources

Because tables listing all the bits of data and their corresponding breakdowns are readily available in MapPoint's Help files, we just touch on the highlights here:

- ✔ **Population:** These bits of data let you examine an area's population by age, median age, race, level of education completed, and so on.
- ✔ **Households/Housing Units:** View information about the typical household's annual income, how many people rent versus own their homes, when the homes in that area were built, and the average household's size.

With careful planning, analyzing demographic maps of your business's area can help you maximize your advertising dollars and marketing efforts. For example, a remodeling company may look for areas where the majority of homes are older and thus more likely to need repairs, and the company can launch a telemarketing campaign based on that ZIP code. (Sorry, you'll have to get the phone numbers somewhere else.) Or a high-end fashion boutique chain may scout out wealthier neighborhoods for its next major newspaper advertising campaign. A wealth of possibilities exist no matter what your business's target market is.

Canada demographics available in MapPoint

A company called Compusearch provides MapPoint's Canada demographic data. In addition to the typical age of population breakdowns and the like, you find unique statistics such as the average number of rooms in a dwelling, population by home language, immigration period, and population by occupation.

Canada data is typically pulled from the 1991 and 1996 Census with the exception of total population and average income, for which there are also figures for 2000 and projections for 2005. A few statistics (such as home language and population in the workforce) are derived from a 20 percent sampling only, so you may want to make decisions based on that data with caution.

Also note that the Canadian postal service significantly changed the Forward Sortation Area (FSA) boundaries between 1997 and 1998. If this change affects you, you may want to browse the MapPoint Help files for details on how MapPoint deals with this change.

Worldwide country data available in MapPoint

Worldwide country data examines countries as a whole, and not every country has data available for every single category. Worldwide country data comes from a variety of sources and can be divided into five general categories, as follows:

- ✔ **Population:** Includes such data as population density, number of males or females in various age groups, population growth rate, and projected population for 2025 and 2050.
- ✔ **Health:** Presents figures for each area's infant mortality rate.
- ✔ **Economy:** Covers such data as the Gross Domestic Product (GDP) along with various breakdowns of GDP by type, imports, exports, tourist expenditures, labor force participation, and the like.
- ✔ **Communications and Transport:** Displays the number of computers connected to the Internet per 10,000 people, cell phone subscribers per 1,000 people, daily newspaper circulation in the thousands, along with TVs, personal computers, and motor vehicles per 1,000 people.
- ✔ **Education:** Includes each country's literacy rate (where available) as well as the number of years that individuals in various countries typically stay in school as well as male and female breakdowns.

You can find some pretty nifty statistics, to be sure! Be aware, however, that worldwide country data offers country-level statistics only, so unfortunately we won't be able to hone in on high Internet use within specific ZIP codes with the data that comes with MapPoint. That doesn't mean you can't get hold of it somewhere else and pull it into MapPoint, though.

Avoiding Data Field disasters

The Data Fields window gives you four different elements to work with (refer to Steps 7 through 10 of the "Running the Data Mapping Wizard" section). Although the enormous number of options gives you a great deal of flexibility, it can also be overwhelming and downright confusing, especially when you try to decipher how one option affects another. We try to reduce some of the potential confusion for you here.

Take a spreadsheet as an example. The first item — the field you want MapPoint to map — corresponds to the column of your spreadsheet that you want to look at in greater depth, such as amount of sales, number of items purchased, or something like that. The Divide the Data You Chose Above By option lets you express the data in the form of a percentage, which is great for evaluating your company's market penetration in a certain geographic area. For example, you might divide the Customer ID field by Population (2000) — an area's population according to the year 2000 Census — to begin extracting a percentage. Note that this divide function is useful only for a select few purposes.

In the vast majority of cases (with the exception of a market penetration analysis), the option can be left at its default of <None>.

The Show Data By option comes next. To keep with the spreadsheet analogy, this option performs the grouping of the spreadsheet records (that is, it groups all the records by ZIP code, county, state, and so on). These are the groupings from which MapPoint will perform its calculations. If the data is mapped by Customer ID and grouped by state, MapPoint sorts all the records so that calculations can be performed on each group (that is, the customers in every state can be counted, and so on).

Finally, you must decide which operation MapPoint should perform on the data selected. If the data represents a recognizably non-numeric field, MapPoint grays out your choices and assumes that you want to count the records in each group. If the field is in fact numeric, you can opt to add, average, or count the items in each group.

Obtaining more demographic data

Don't see what you're looking for in the data provided with MapPoint? Well, you can find a lot more data where that came from, especially if you're looking for U.S. data! By visiting the Claritas Web site (www.claritas.com), you can browse a number of data solutions compiled for a specific industry (restaurants, real estate, and the like). You can also gain free access to 2000 Census data online.

Don't forget that any table of data you find online can potentially be converted for use with MapPoint. Either copy and paste the data into Excel, or use Excel's Web Query tool to do the gathering for you. The information can then be imported to MapPoint using the Data Mapping Wizard.

Just because the data appears on the Web, however, doesn't mean that it's free for the taking. Copyright laws still apply. Government Web sites can potentially offer valuable information that's a matter of public record.

Hey, mister, what's your range type?

MapPoint includes two continuous ranges, four discrete ranges, and a custom range that you define for yourself. For those of you who aren't hard-core mathematicians or statisticians, the range names and their implications may have little meaning. Here is a brief rundown of the options available, including what they do and how they work:

✔ **Continuous range:** Selects the largest and smallest data values you want to map and distributes the values evenly throughout the range. This range is great if your data is distributed evenly.

✔ **Continuous logarithmic range:** Selects the largest and smallest data values you want to map and distributes the values using a logarithmic scale. This approach is ideal if your data is distributed in groups close to the beginning or end of the range.

✔ **Discrete equal ranges:** Examines your data to determine the size difference between the largest and smallest data values. Then it breaks this size value evenly into up to eight individual ranges.

✔ **Equal data points (quantiles):** Examines your data and creates up to eight ranges so that an equal number of data points is in each range.

✔ **Discrete logarithmic ranges:** Similar to the continuous logarithmic range, but it groups the data in up to eight discrete ranges. Your data must contain only positive numbers.

✔ **Unique values:** Enables you to assign a color for each unique data value. You should use this range if you have non-numeric values you want to chart. Note that you cannot chart more than eight values.

✔ **Custom:** A variation of the discrete range option. It enables you to specify a starting and stopping value for each range rather than use equal or logarithmic ranges. If none of the standard distributions meets your needs, simply select the one that comes closest and then change the range value to whatever you need. MapPoint will convert the range to Custom.

You should also note that in a number of circumstances, MapPoint chooses an appropriate range type for the task at hand.

Finally, continuous ranges use all possible colors to represent your data, whereas discrete and custom ranges map your data values into different categories depending on the data value.

Editing Your Data Maps

When it comes to editing your data, MapPoint is pretty easy to get along with. You can change the data you're looking at, readjust the data grouping from state level to ZIP code level, change the wording of your legend, alter the colors used on the map, and perform other editing. You name it, it's easy to change — even after the fact.

Tweaking the data

To change the data that's being mapped, right-click the data map legend and choose Data Fields from the shortcut menu. Choosing this option takes you to the Data Fields screen (refer to Figure 9-13, shown previously). Make the desired changes and then click the Finish button. Or if you'd first like to make some adjustments to the new map's legend, click the Next> button, modify the desired entries, and then click Finish.

If you want to try a new map type on for size, right-click the data map's legend and choose the Map Type option. Take your pick from the Map Type screen and then click Finish. If you desire any other changes, click Next> instead and then make your way through the rest of the Data Mapping Wizard as usual.

Modifying the appearance of the legend

Whether you want to reverse the order of your legend from high-to-low to low-to-high or you need to change the type of data range you're using, you can do so at any point via MapPoint's Legend dialog box. (Refer to Figure 9-14 to see the settings you can work with in this dialog box. The options available to you will vary depending on the map and data range types you've chosen.) To begin working with the settings in this dialog box, right-click the data map's legend and then choose Format Legend from the shortcut menu.

If you merely want to change the labels on your Sized Pie Chart Map legend (either the legend's title or the map elements), you can do so by right-clicking the data map legend and clicking Labels from the shortcut menu. The dialog box shown in Figure 9-15 appears.

Figure 9-15: You can give your data fields more explicit names if you'd like.

To change a legend label, click the text box to the right of the data field you wish to work with; then, delete or add text as desired. You also can change the legend's title from this dialog box. After you have made all the necessary changes, click the Finish button to save your edits and exit the dialog box.

Showing fields in balloons

As we describe in Chapter 4, you can show information about a Pushpin in a Pushpin balloon. You can do the same for each MapPoint data point (see Figure 9-16).

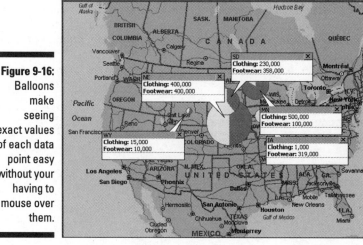

Figure 9-16: Balloons make seeing exact values of each data point easy without your having to mouse over them.

Follow these steps to tell MapPoint what information you want to see in these balloons:

1. **With your data map on-screen, right-click the name of the mapped data in the legend and choose Properties from the shortcut menu.**

   The General tab of the Properties dialog box opens.

2. **Click the Balloon tab to open it.**

3. **Place a check mark next to the fields you want to appear in the balloon, verify that the Display Selected Field Names in Balloons option is checked, and then click OK.**

   The dialog box closes and you're ready to open each data point's information balloon.

To open a data point's balloon, right-click the data point on the map, and then choose Show Information from the shortcut menu. The balloon you defined appears on-screen. Repeat as necessary until all the data points you want to see have balloons on-screen. To close a balloon, click the Close (X) button in the upper-right corner of the balloon.

Are your balloons cluttering up the screen or covering one another up? You can change the orientation of problem balloons by right-clicking their title bars, pointing to Orientation on the shortcut menu, and then clicking the desired orientation of the balloon.

Displaying data tips

When you mouse over a data point on your data map, a gray box called a *data tip* appears (see Figure 9-17). In it, you can see a summary of the selected data point's information. These data tips appear by default, but should you find them bothersome, you can easily turn them off. To do so, click Tools⇨Options from the MapPoint menu bar and deselect the Show Data Tips option. Repeated the process to enable the data tips again.

Figure 9-17: Mouse over a selected data point on-screen for a quick summary of the information it conveys.

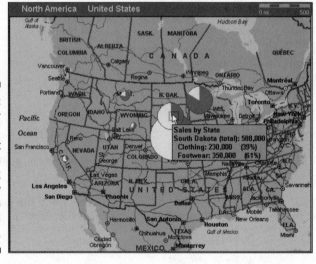

Chapter 10

Importing Data from SQL Server

· ·

· ·

*W*hen it comes to using MapPoint with your favorite relational database (SQL Server, Oracle, Informix, DB2, and so on), things can get a bit tricky. In this chapter, we attempt to demystify the process by explaining how MapPoint accesses and uses your data. We then arm you with everything you need to extract only the data you want from your database.

Although this chapter's steps and examples focus on SQL Server databases, you can use similar techniques to tap into Oracle, Informix, DB2, or other relational databases. (You will need to consult your database vendor's documentation for specifics, however.)

We work our way from a simple example that can be used as is up to more complex examples that deal with creating a new database table or view. In the end, however, you'll see that data in a whole new light, er, map!

More Linking versus Importing

When you run MapPoint's Data Mapping Wizard (covered in Chapter 9), you have a choice of importing data or linking to your data. Importing your data creates a local copy of that data in the MapPoint .PTM file. Because the imported data is local to MapPoint, you cannot automatically update the data should the data in the database change. If you want the map to reflect recent changes to the database, you have to import the data again.

On the other hand, when you link to your database, MapPoint stores information about how to locate the source of the data rather than the data itself. Keeping this memory of the source allows MapPoint to refresh the data without having to load all that data a second time. Note, however, that, if you update the data in your database, the data displayed in MapPoint will not be updated unless you explicitly refresh the data (click Data⇨Update Linked Records). When you refresh the data, MapPoint is smart enough to detect when records were added or deleted from the database as well as to update any values that may have changed in the existing records.

In general, you may prefer to use imported data rather than linked data. Although doing this means that you have a static view of the data as of the time you imported it, it also means that the map won't change unless you explicitly import the data again. Why is that a good thing? Because if you're sending a map of company performance to a board member for discussion on the phone, a map based on imported data is the only way to ensure that you and the recipient are seeing the exact same set of numbers.

Importing data also makes the MapPoint files easier to exchange with others because the files are self-contained. Linking to your corporate database is useless if you're trying to access it from your laptop on the road (unless, of course, you have wireless Internet and/or the ability to access the database over the Internet remotely).

If you have a map that needs to be frequently updated with information from the database, consider using linked data, because the amount of work (not to mention wait time) needed to update the data is less than what is needed to import it all over again.

You can update linked data in MapPoint by using the following command from the Command Prompt window (from the Windows Start menu, click Programs⇨Accessories⇨Command Prompt): `c:\Program Files\Microsoft MapPoint\MapPoint.exe /U "<filename>"`, where `<filename>` contains the full path name of the file you want to update. If you use this command as part of a scheduled job in Windows, your data will automatically be updated for you.

Accessing Your Database

No matter whether you made the decision to link or import your data, MapPoint's Data Mapping Wizard (or the Import Data Wizard or Link Data Wizard, for that matter) asks you to specify the name of the file containing your data. Chapter 9 discusses how to specify a sheet within an Excel workbook, but here you need to specify the name of a Data Link file (`.UDL`). The Data Link file contains the information necessary to connect MapPoint to your database server. Assuming that you already have a connection to your database, just specify the name of the .UDL file and continue on with the Data Mapping Wizard.

If this is the first time that you have tried to access the database, you need to create a Data Link file. The easiest way to create it is to use Windows Explorer to find the folder where you want to keep the new file; then, right-click in Windows Explorer and choose New➪Text Document from the pop-up menu. Next, change the default name from `New Text Document.TXT` to a more meaningful filename followed by `.UDL`, such as `Athena.UDL`, where `Athena` is the name of your database server. Windows may warn you that changing a file-name extension may make the file unusable. When asked to confirm whether you really want to make the change, respond by clicking the Yes button.

After you create the file, right-click the UDL file's icon in the Windows Explorer and select Properties from the pop-up menu. Doing so displays the Properties dialog box for the file. Then select the Provider tab to see the list of OLE DB providers available on your system (see Figure 10-1). Choose the appropriate provider for your database server. In the case of SQL Server, choose Microsoft OLE DB Provider for SQL Server.

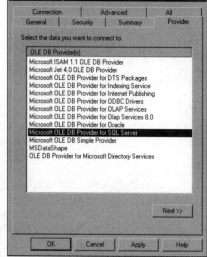

Figure 10-1:
Choosing an
OLE DB
provider on
the Provider
tab of the
Data Link
Properties
dialog box.

If your database doesn't support OLE DB, choose Microsoft OLE DB Provider for ODBC Devices as the OLE DB provider. Then use the appropriate connection information for your database server. See your database administrator for more information about how to connect to ODBC databases.

After selecting the OLE DB provider, click the Connection tab of the Data Link Properties window (see Figure 10-2). Although the details of this window will vary depending on the database server you're using, you generally have to enter these four pieces of information:

 ✔ **Server:** Specifies the name of the computer that runs the database server

 ✔ **User name:** Specifies the user name that you will use to log onto the server

 ✔ **Password:** Specifies the password associated with the user name

 ✔ **Database:** Specifies the name of the database on the server that you want to access

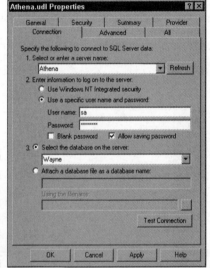

Figure 10-2:
Enter the connection information into your data link file.

All this information is unique to you or your organization. Typically, your database administrator provides you with the necessary values to enter in this window. In the case of SQL Server, you have to choose between Windows NT Integrated security or supplying a specific user name and password.

If you choose to enter the specific user name and password, you must check the Allow Saving Password check box to store the information in the data link file. Because MapPoint won't prompt you for your user name and password, they must be stored in the .UDL file for you to connect to your database.

It is possible that if you are using Windows XP, 2001, or NT your logon user name may automatically give you access to SQL Server. If this is the case, you can select the Use Windows NT Integrated Security option. Check with your system administrator or database administrator to determine whether you have NT Integrated security access to the server and database to which you want to connect. You can verify that the information you supplied is correct by clicking the Test button. If everything is correct, you will receive a message saying that the test connection succeeded. Otherwise, you receive a message indicating an error without necessarily explaining what is wrong. If you receive an error message, verify that you entered all the information correctly and try again.

Finally, click the OK button to save this information into the .UDL file. If you check the Allow saving password check box, you'll see a message that recommends against saving your password into the file. Click Yes to save the information, even though it will not be secure.

The information that you provided is kept in a .UDL file, which is open to anyone with access to the computer on which it is stored. Because this information is stored as plain text, anyone with access to your PC will be able to get the user name and password information that you supplied. This access in turn makes it possible for someone to access the database server using your user name and password without your permission.

A better approach would be to have MapPoint store all this information (except your user name and password) in the .PTM file. Then, before MapPoint connected to the database, it could prompt you for the user name and password. As long as MapPoint didn't keep a copy of the security-related information (and you close MapPoint when you have finished accessing the database), no one could use your computer to access the database server without your permission. We hope that this potential security leak will be changed in the next version of MapPoint.

This problem exists even if you select the Use Windows NT Integrated Security radio button in the Data Link Properties window, because anyone having physical access to your computer may be able to access the database using your security information, even though no password information is stored in the UDL file.

Using Database Tables in the Data Mapping Wizard

After you've told MapPoint how to reach your SQL Server database, you can run the Data Mapping Wizard against it. Just launch MapPoint and follow these steps to begin working with an existing SQL Server database table:

1. **Click the Data Mapping Wizard button on MapPoint's Standard toolbar.**

   The Data Mapping Wizard opens, presenting you with a list of data map types from which you can choose.

2. **Now click the button corresponding to the type of map you wish to create from the data; then click Next>.**

3. **Click the appropriate option to choose whether you want to import or link to your database; click the Next> button to continue.**

   You are presented with a dialog box that resembles a traditional Microsoft Office Open dialog box.

4. **Navigate to the directory in which you stored the .UDL file you created; double-click its name to select it.**

   Note that you may need to use the File of Type drop-down box to select Microsoft Data Link (.UDL) as the file type to make the file appear on-screen.

5. **Choose the table or view of your database you'd like to work with, and then continue with the Data Mapping Wizard as presented in Chapter 9.**

Although the data link file allows you to access a particular database, your data is actually stored in a collection of tables and views. Use the dialog box shown in Figure 10-3 to choose which table or view you wish to use.

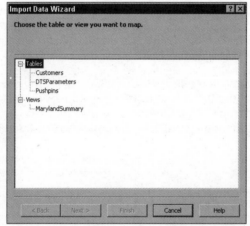

Figure 10-3:
Choose the table or view that contains the information you want to map.

A table is similar to a worksheet in Excel. It contains a number of columns and rows. Each column stores a particular field of data such as a ZIP code or the name of a state. Each row contains a particular instance of the data. For example, a row can contain your name, address, city, state, and ZIP code among other items of data.

Typically, one of the fields stored in a table can be used to uniquely identify a particular row in the table. This field is known as the primary key. Some common primary keys include customer ID and social security number.

Primary keys are important when you let MapPoint link to your data instead of importing it. MapPoint uses the primary key to determine when a row in the table has been updated, added, or deleted when you refresh the data in MapPoint. If a particular primary key value exists locally in MapPoint and it also exists in the database, then any changes made to the information in the database are copied to MapPoint. Likewise, if a particular primary key value exists locally in MapPoint but doesn't exist in the database, MapPoint deletes the copy of the local record. Finally, if a primary key value exists in the database, but not MapPoint, the refresh process adds the new row locally. Of course, this process may result in unmatched address records in MapPoint that will need to be resolved through MapPoint's Unmatched Records dialog box.

As far as MapPoint is concerned, a view is the same thing as a table. As does a table, a view contains a series of columns and rows. In contrast to a table, a view doesn't have a physical existence. Instead, the data in a view is derived from one or more tables and views. Because MapPoint processes all the data in a table or view, you can use views to reduce the amount of work that MapPoint has to perform (meaning that you'll get your end result a whole lot faster with minimal wear and tear on your equipment and network).

Not surprisingly, MapPoint works best when you design your database with MapPoint in mind. MapPoint works best when you store your address information in separate fields such as Name, Address, City, State, and ZIP. Luckily, those are fairly common database design techniques, so even existing databases should be in decent shape. This is because MapPoint analyzes the names of your data fields and attempts to translate them into column names that it understands. These fields include: Name; Name 2; Address 1; Address 2; Address 3; City; County; State; Country/Region; ZIP Code; 3 Digit ZIP Code; Census Tract; Metropolitan Area; Latitude; Longitude; and Territory.

If you have a field that is not in this list, MapPoint still makes the data available for statistical processing using the same techniques outlined in the previous chapter.

Summarizing Data for MapPoint

MapPoint can import complete address information from your database and summarize it while generating a map, but this may not be the most efficient use of MapPoint. For example, if you want to summarize sales of a particular product by state, you may be dealing with hundreds of thousands of records of information. Rather than force MapPoint to resolve each address to a location on a map, you can summarize the data on the database server and then import only the summarized data into MapPoint.

A database server is optimized to deal with large volumes of data, so summarizing hundreds of thousands of rows of data in the database server is a whole lot quicker than forcing MapPoint to deal with every record whether you need/want it or not. The time to compute the summary data on the database server is a very small fraction of the time it would take MapPoint to resolve each particular address and then summarize the data.

How you summarize the data depends on how you want to show the data on your map. You can choose to let MapPoint pick the appropriate value to display depending on the level of zoom, or you can choose to display data by increasing geographic area: ZIP code, county, metropolitan area, state, or country. This implies that you need to summarize data by ZIP code and let MapPoint aggregate the data to create the larger geographical areas. However, if you want to see data only at one particular data level, you should summarize the data at that level if practical to reduce the total number of records MapPoint must process.

The easiest way to summarize data on the database server is to create an SQL query using the Select statement. The Select statement allows you to choose rows containing only certain values in particular columns, or summarize the data and present it as if the data represented the contents of a single table (or it can do both). In addition, the Select statement can access multiple tables, combining or summarizing (or both) data as directed.

Because MapPoint doesn't support data retrieved from an SQL query, the next best way to summarize your data is to create a view in your database. A view is simply an SQL Select statement that has a particular name associated with it. MapPoint can in turn access a view and return all the rows associated with it. Refer to the step of the Data Mapping Wizard depicted in Figure 10-3 in the previous section. That's where you'll select the desired view.

MapPoint doesn't allow you to create a new database view, so you need to use a different tool, such as Query Analyzer. Query Analyzer is a tool associated with SQL Server that allows you to enter and execute various SQL statements on the fly, such as the Select statement. You can use Query Analyzer to develop a Select statement that returns the rows you want to import into MapPoint and then add the Select statement to your SQL Server database as a view.

Most database servers include a tool similar to Query Analyzer that allows you to execute SQL statements interactively. Refer to your database administrator for more information about the particular tools available for your database server.

Introducing Query Analyzer

You can start Query Analyzer in Windows by choosing Start⇨Microsoft SQL Server⇨Query Analyzer. Then you will be prompted to enter the name of the database server plus your connection information (see Figure 10-4).

Figure 10-4:
Enter your connection information for Query Analyzer.

To use Query Analyzer, you need to install the SQL Server client tools on your computer. These tools are distributed as part of the SQL Server database package. See your database administrator for more information.

After choosing your database server and filling in the connection information form, click OK to connect to your database and start Query Analyzer. Doing so displays a window similar to Figure 10-5. Here is a list of some of the key parts of this window:

- **Query pane:** Contains the SQL statement you wish to run.

- **Results pane:** Contains the results of the last SQL statement you ran. If you haven't run an SQL statement yet, this pane won't be visible.

- **Object Browser:** Contains a list of databases available to you on the database server and the objects contained within each database. It also contains a list of common functions that you can drag into the query pane as part of the SQL statement you want to build.

- **New Query:** Opens a new query pane, where you can enter an SQL statement such as the Select statement.

- **Load SQL Script:** Enables you to choose a text file (usually with a file type of .SQL) and load it into the query window.

- **Save Query:** Enables you to save your current SQL statement into a text file with a file type of .SQL. If your cursor is in the Results Pane, pressing this button saves the results to a report file (.RPT) containing a text-formatted version of your data.

✔ **Clear Window:** Clears the current window and leaves it ready for you to enter another query.

✔ **Execute Mode:** Determines how the results are displayed in the results pane. By default, the results are displayed as a data grid; however, you can choose to display the results as a series of text lines. Other options are available to display information about how your query ran or to save the results directly to a file.

✔ **Parse Query:** Enables you to verify that the structure of your SQL statement is correct before you execute it. Parsing your query doesn't find some types of errors, such as misspelled table names and column names, but it can find out whether you managed to put all the symbols and keywords in the right place.

✔ **Execute Query:** Actually runs your query. It begins by parsing your query and then resolving all the column and table names. If everything is correct, it runs the query and returns the results in the Results pane.

✔ **Cancel Query Execution:** Stops a query while it is executing. Because a query can take minutes or hours to run, this button can be a very useful thing.

✔ **Current database:** Contains a drop-down list of databases that you can access on your database server. The one displayed is your current database. You can change the current database by picking another one from the list.

It is very important that you check the current database drop-down box when you start Query Analyzer. By default, it will pick the database called Master, if you have access to it. Unfortunately, this is the worst possible default database because SQL Server uses it to store information about all the other databases in the database server. We don't recommend accessing this database unless you are the database administrator. Even then, changing the wrong data in it could corrupt the entire database server.

Selecting Rows with Query Analyzer

The Select statement is the most complex statement in SQL; you rarely need all the capabilities, however. To retrieve all the rows from the Customer table, you can use this Select statement and you will see the results shown previously in Figure 10-5.

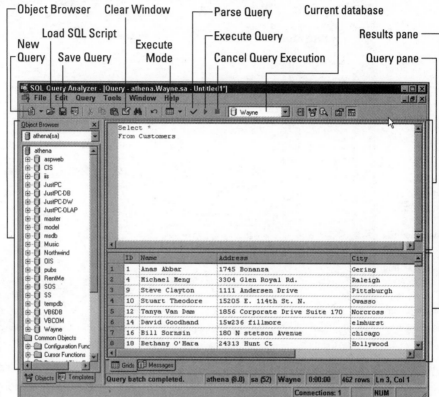

Figure 10-5: Viewing the Query Analyzer window.

```
Select *
From Customers
```

The asterisk (*) means that all the columns in the table should be retrieved. The From clause specifies the name of the table containing the rows, which in this case is the Customers table.

You can retrieve only the rows from the database for Maryland by using this Select statement with the Where clause (see Figure 10-6).

```
Select *
From Customers
Where State = 'Maryland'
```

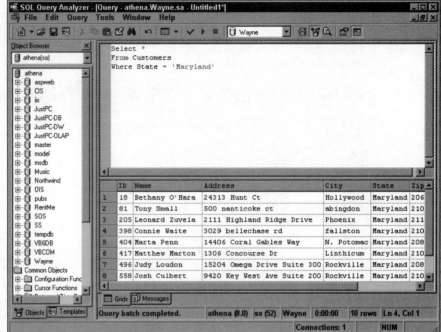

Figure 10-6:
Selecting
customers
in the state
of Maryland.

Note that we use single quotation marks (') around the value we're searching for. Double quotation marks aren't allowed and will cause an error.

You can retrieve rows from multiple states using the In operator in the Where clause, like this (see Figure 10-7):

```
Select *
From Customers
Where State in ('Maryland', 'Washington', 'South Dakota')
```

You can also select ranges of values using the Select statement. For example, the following Select statement chooses all customers added during the first six months of 2001.

```
Select *
From Customers
Where DateAdded >= '1-January-2001' And Date < '1-July-2001'
```

You need not retrieve each column from the table. Instead, you can supply a list of columns you wish to retrieve immediately after the Select keyword, like this (see Figure 10-8):

```
Select ID, Address, City, State, ZipCode
From Customers
```

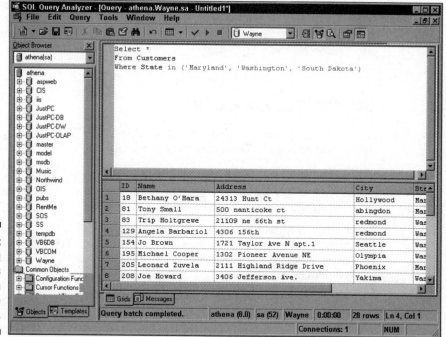

Figure 10-7:
Selecting customers from multiple states.

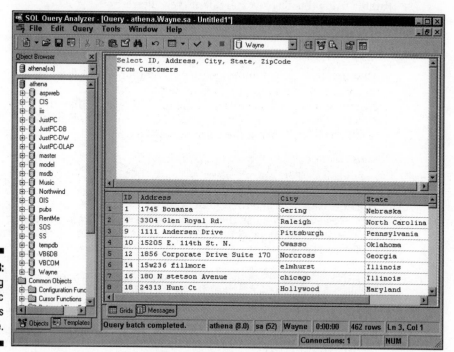

Figure 10-8:
Selecting specific columns from a table.

For more information about the Select statement and SQL in general, see *SQL For Dummies,* 4th Edition, by Allen G. Taylor. You may also want to consult *Microsoft SQL Server 2000 For Dummies,* by Anthony T. Mann, for more information about Query Analyzer.

Summarizing Data

Four key aggregation functions can be used in the Select statement that summarize your data. These functions include:

- ✔ **Sum:** Totals the values contained in specified column over all the rows retrieved. Obviously, you must supply a numeric column name with Sum or you will get an error message.

- ✔ **Count:** Returns the number of rows selected. Because Count returns the number of rows selected, it doesn't matter which column you specify, so most people use the shortcut Count(*) rather than use a specific column name.

- ✔ **Min:** Returns the minimum value of the specified column.

- ✔ **Max:** Returns the maximum value found in the specified column.

You can use the Count function to find out how many rows are in a particular table using this Select statement (see Figure 10-9):

```
Select Count(*)
From Customers
```

Although the Count function returns the number of rows in the table, it creates a new column without a name, as you can see in Figure 10-9. You can give the column a name by using the function name, then the keyword As, then the new name, as follows. Note that, as shown in Figure 10-10, the results pane shows that the column now has a name.

```
Select Count(*) As CustomerCount
From Customers
```

The downside to using these functions is that they return a single row of data. However, if you use the Group By clause, you can summarize your data by the value you specify in the Group By clause using this statement (see Figure 10-11):

```
Select Count(*) As CustomerCount, State
From Customers
Group By State
```

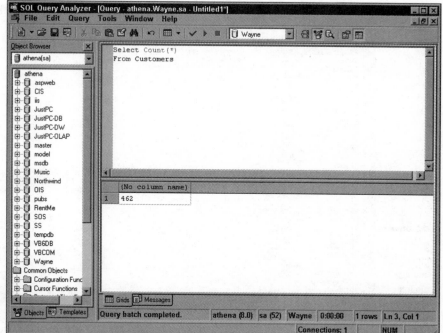

Figure 10-9:
Counting
rows in the
Customers
table.

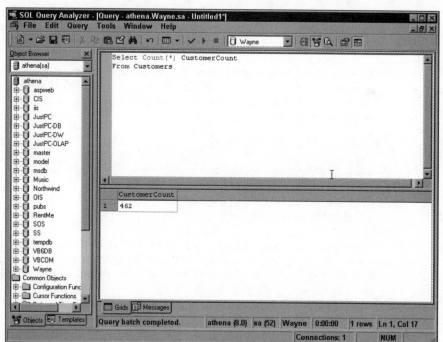

Figure 10-10:
Assigning
the new
column a
name.

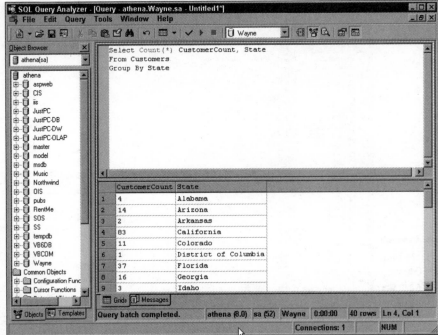

Figure 10-11:
Counting the number of customers in each state.

This `Group By` clause sorts your data by `State` and then applies the count function over each group of rows with the same state value. Using this technique, you can quickly summarize your data to a specific geographic level.

The columns listed in the `Group By` clause determine when a row will be summarized. In this case, each time the value of `State` changes, a new row will be output. You can specify multiple columns in the `Group By` clause like this (see Figure 10-12):

```
Select Count(*) As CustomerCount, State, ZipCode
From Customers
Group By State, ZipCode
```

Then a row will be returned for each unique set of values for the columns listed in the `Group By` clause.

The `Group By` clause imposes some limitations on the columns you return. Each column returned must be used with an aggregation function or must be listed in the `Group By` clause. Otherwise, you will get an error message.

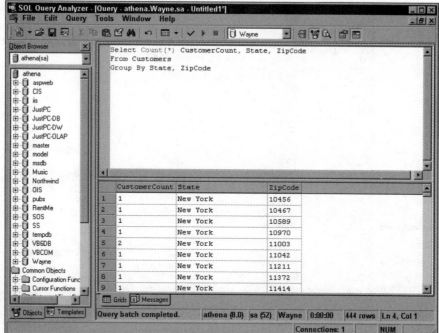

Figure 10-12:
Using
multiple
columns in
the Group
By clause.

Finally, you can combine the Group By clause with the Where clause so that you retrieve only some of the data (see Figure 10-13). For instance, the following Select statement retrieves information only for the state of Maryland:

```
Select Count(*) As CustomerCount, State, ZipCode
From Customers
Where State = 'Maryland'
Group By State, ZipCode
```

Creating Views

After you are satisfied that your Select statement is returning the data you want, you can turn it into a view by using the Create View statement. For example, you may create a view that selects summary information for Maryland using this statement (see Figure 10-14):

```
Create View MarylandSummary As
    Select Count(*) As CustomerCount, State, ZipCode
    From Customers
    Where State = 'Maryland'
    Group By State, ZipCode
```

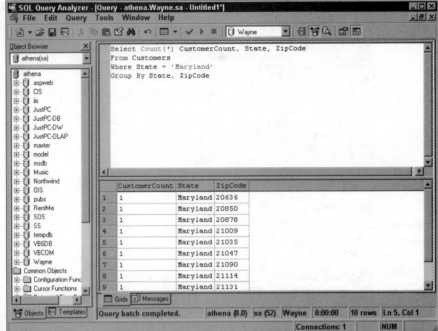

Figure 10-13:
Selecting
summary
information
for
Maryland.

Figure 10-14:
Creating a
view that
summarizes
the infor-
mation for
MapPoint.

After you have created the view, it will appear in the Select table or view dialog box, as shown earlier in the chapter in Figure 10-3.

You can delete a view from your database using the Drop View statement (see Figure 10-15).

```
Drop View MarylandSummary
```

After a view has been deleted, you must use the Create View statement to add it to the database again. To make this easier, you should always save the Create View statement to a disk file using the Save Query button discussed earlier in this chapter. Then you can load it back into Query Analyzer using the Load SQL Script button and execute it again to recreate your query.

You can check whether your view is working by running a Select statement on your view. The statement

```
Select * from MarylandSummary
```

should give you the exact same results as the Select statement contained in the view. Views, once created, can be used exactly like tables, and that includes the ability to select from them.

When dealing with complex views that process very large amounts of data, you need to be concerned with performance. If the view takes more than 60 seconds to open, MapPoint will be unable to read the data.

Now that you have determined what rows and columns in your database you want MapPoint to display, and have created a view that efficiently subsets your data on the server, you can import or link to that view. In the Choose the Table or View You Want to Map dialog box of the Data Mapping Wizard (refer to Figure 10-3), views are listed in a separate section than the tables, but you can still select them. Any views that you create in Query Analyzer will appear in the views section of this dialog box and are ready for importing or linking using MapPoint.

Part IV

Using MapPoint with Other Products

The 5th Wave   By Rich Tennant

"Hold on. I've got PocketStreets... the nearest clinic is only 300 miles away."

In this part . . .

*U*sing MapPoint will quickly become habit forming when it comes to calculating routes and mapping your sales and demographics data. Using the application is as easy as using any other Microsoft Office family member.

Being a family member also requires one to play nicely with your siblings and also with your offspring and other relatives. In the following chapters, you find out how to tightly integrate MapPoint with the in-the-box applications in Office 2000 and Office XP applications. You also can see how to integrate with satellites and attach a GPS device to your laptop so that you can wander out into the world tracking your every move.

The world can also fit into a very small place. This part shows how to move the portions of the map from MapPoint on to your Pocket PC using the Pocket Streets application that comes with MapPoint. Now you can take the streets and roads along with you when you hit the streets and roads.

Chapter 11

MapPoint and Office 2000/XP

● ●

In This Chapter

▶ Using the MapPoint Office COM Add-in

▶ Embedding into or linking maps with an Office program

▶ Using MapPoint with Office Smart Tags

▶ Importing and exporting with Excel

▶ Mail merge using Microsoft MapPoint, Word, and Excel

● ●

*B*y now you have experienced how the MapPoint 2002 user interface is loaded with Microsoft Office styles and the convenience wizards. This likeness is very much by design; MapPoint 2002 is an "out-of-box" member of the Microsoft Office family. Although MapPoint is not bundled with any version of Office, you will experience just how natural it is to use with other Office programs.

Fitting in with the Office Family

To be a member of the Office family, a program must share more than the Office look and feel. The program must be tightly integrated with other Office members, providing smooth interaction and flow of data and information.

Family ties are very important to MapPoint. In fact, as you learned in chapter 6, without other Office applications MapPoint would be a lonely and powerless orphan lost without a source of support.

Without Access, Excel, and Outlook, MapPoint would be hard up for data to map, but the great news is that's where most data with addresses are stored today! Although the application could have been designed to support its own native data storage system that would just require you to copy your data to yet another place.

Each Office family member must also have an object model to provide programmability. We discuss programming MapPoint in Chapters 14 through 18.

MapPoint Office COM Add-in

When you install MapPoint, the integration of MapPoint with many Office programs is provided automatically by the MapPoint Office COM Add-in. This add-in automatically installs toolbar buttons or menu items to many Office programs. Figures 11-1 and 11-2 show the MapPoint icon added to the standard Microsoft Word toolbar and the Insert menu.

Figure 11-1:
The MapPoint toolbar button displayed in the Word standard toolbar.

Figure 11-2:
A MapPoint menu item displayed in the Word Insert⇨ Picture menu.

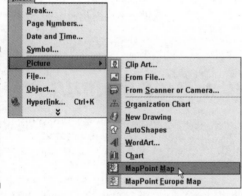

The MapPoint Office COM Add-in does its magic only if you install MapPoint after you have installed other Office family members. If you upgrade Office from 2000 to Office XP, you must reinstall MapPoint 2002.

Other features of MapPoint will work with Office 97 applications, but the MapPoint Office COM Add-in works only with Office 2000 and Office XP.

With the simple click of a button, you can embed a MapPoint map into the following Office 2000 and Office XP family members:

✔ Microsoft Word

✔ Microsoft Excel

✔ Microsoft PowerPoint

✔ Microsoft Publisher

✔ Microsoft Visio

✔ Microsoft Outlook

From inside Microsoft Outlook, you can create a map displaying the address of your contacts.

Embedding or Linking a Map into an Office Program

Use the following steps to embed a new map into a Word document. You can perform the same tasks from within Excel, PowerPoint, Publisher and Visio.

1. **Place your cursor at the location within the Word document where you want to place a map.**

2. **On the menu bar, click Insert⇨Picture⇨MapPoint Map.**

3. **A MapPoint frame will appear and the Word toolbar and menu will be replaced with the MapPoint toolbars and menus.**

You may also want to embed a new map or link to a previously created map that is saved in a MapPoint file (.PTM) or template (.PTT) file, as follows:

1. **Place your cursor at the location within the Word document where you want to place a map.**

2. **On the menu bar, click Insert⇨Object.**

3. **Click the Create from File tab.**

4. **Check the Link to file check box to link to the file.**

   This feature enables you to make changes to the MapPoint file that will automatically be updated in the Word document. The downside is that you lose the ability to update the map if you delete the MapPoint file.

5. **Type the name of your MapPoint file in the text box under File name, or click the Browse button to locate your file in the Windows Explorer.**

6. **Click OK.**

Linking Program Features: The Smart Way To Play Tag!

Smart Tags are a cool new invention included with Office XP. These intelligent hyperlinks on steroids not only link together features of different programs but also provide valuable insight into what type of action or feature you can access from a simple text or numeric string.

MapPoint installs Smart Tags in the English versions of Microsoft Word XP and Microsoft Excel XP. A Smart Tag icon appears when a text string is recognized as a possible address.

Using Smart Tags in Microsoft Word

Here is a sample that shows you how to activate a MapPoint Smart Tag in Word:

1. **Type the address** 21635 Devonshire St. Chatsworth, CA 91311 **into a new Word document.**

   The Smart Tag Icon will appear.

2. **Hover the mouse cursor over the Smart Tag icon until an arrow appears next to the icon; then, click the arrow to display the list of actions that can be performed on the related content.**

   Using MapPoint is just one of many things you can do with Smart Tags.

3. **Select Insert MapPoint Map or Plan Route in MapPoint as highlighted in Figure 11-3.**

If you also have the English version of the MapPoint Europe edition installed on your machine, the Insert MapPoint Europe Map and a Plan Route in MapPoint Europe options will also appear.

Smart Tags work on continuous text contained within a single paragraph. If you want to create a map or a route for an address contained on multiple lines, such as the way an address appears in a letter, use soft carriage returns rather than paragraph markers to separate the lines. You create a soft carriage return by pressing Shift+Enter.

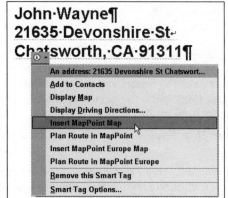

Using Smart Tags in Microsoft Excel

Whereas MapPoint Smart Tags in Microsoft Word act on individual addresses, MapPoint Smart Tags in Excel add the power of numbers and can map out a complete table of addresses. Figure 11-4 shows a Smart Tag as it appears in Microsoft Excel 2000 and XP.

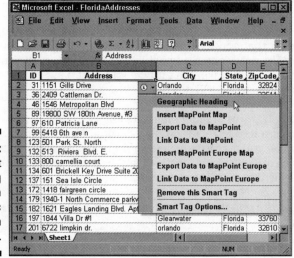

When you use Excel as a database and use column headings that appear to be geographic, Smart Tags will appear. Key words that MapPoint recognizes include Address, City, State, ZIP Code, Postal Code, Country, and Region.

To activate the Smart Tag in Microsoft Excel, follow these simple steps.

1. **Hover the mouse cursor over the Smart Tag icon until an arrow appears next to the icon; then, click the arrow to display the list of actions that can be performed on the related content.**

2. **Choose Insert MapPoint Map, Export Data to MapPoint, or Link Data to MapPoint.**

   A MapPoint map will then be inserted into Excel on the currently active worksheet and the Excel menus will switch to those of MapPoint. You can make any adjustment you desire. When you are finished, just click the worksheet outside the map and the menus will return to those used by Excel; the map will become a stationary image.

   You can reactivate the map and make additional edits by clicking it. You also can move the image around on the active worksheet by mousing down and dragging. You can even go so far as to move it to a different worksheet within the same Excel file.

Exporting Data to Excel

Excel is the preferred provider of data from MapPoint for some people, but you might discover that Access or even SQL Server better suits your needs. No matter where the data comes from, after it is in MapPoint, it can provide you with crucial insight, but wouldn't it be cool to get back to a tabular view of the data that you want to drill down on?

One of the neatest features of MapPoint is its ability to take data out of MapPoint and return it to Excel for tabular viewing. This feature is much more powerful than you may first believe; it's a brilliant spatial analysis tool that allows you to drill into your locations and find specific locations that you have defined within a geographical area.

Figure 11-5 shows the pop-up menu for a drivetime zone with the Export to Excel menu item.

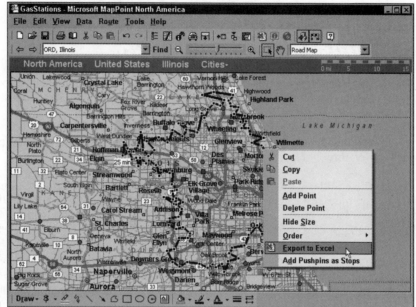

Figure 11-5:
The Export
to Excel
menu using
a drivetime
zone shape.

The most basic approach to getting back to the details is as follows:

1. **In MapPoint, use the Select tool from the Navigation toolbar to outline the area that contains the data you want to export.**

   After you have drawn a rectangle on the map, release the mouse button.

2. **Click Data⇨Export to Excel.**

   You can also right-click inside the rectangle and click Export to Excel from the context menu.

   MapPoint then launches Excel and creates a new Excel file that contains a summary worksheet and an individual worksheet for each dataset within the rectangle displayed on your map.

Rectangles are nice but the real power of this feature is that the same Export to Excel feature is accessible from many of the drawing shapes. You can export data contained in a rectangle, oval, free form or even a drivetime zone! Imagine being able to identify the subset of your customers that are within 25 minutes of your store.

Mail Merge Using Microsoft MapPoint, Word, and Excel

The MailMerge sample included on the CD does all the normal customization of normal mailmerge but also calls on MapPoint for a much more personal touch.

In this example, each target address is matched to the nearest of five stores and then a custom letter is generated that includes a custom map and the driving directions.

You could use this approach for a direct mail promotional event but you also can modify it a little and use it to help direct job applicants to the best location for an interview. You could even go so far as to recommend the time that the applicant should leave for the appointment.

You should feel free to play with the code for this example and modify it to your unique needs. You can also use it "as is" by modifying the basic text of the Word document and by replacing the store locations and customer address with your own.

1. **Start Word and open the MapPointMapMerge.doc document.**

   A dialog box will appear if this is the first time you are using the sample.

2. **Click the Find Data Source button.**

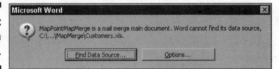

Figure 11-6:
Find Data
Source.

Microsoft Word	×
? MapPointMapMerge is a mail merge main document. Word cannot find its data source, C:\...\MapMerge\Customers.xls.	
[Find Data Source...] [Options...]	

3. **Select the data source by navigating to the Customers.xls file.**

4. **Select the CustomerList$ table for the file.**

Figure 11-7:
Select the
Customer-
List$ table.

Select Table				? ×
Name	Description	Modified	Created	Type
Address		6/2/2001 6:36:15 PM	6/2/2001 6:36:15 PM	TABLE
City		6/2/2001 6:36:15 PM	6/2/2001 6:36:15 PM	TABLE
CustomerList$		6/2/2001 6:36:15 PM	6/2/2001 6:36:15 PM	TABLE
Name		6/2/2001 6:36:15 PM	6/2/2001 6:36:15 PM	TABLE
NewStores		6/2/2001 6:36:15 PM	6/2/2001 6:36:15 PM	TABLE
NewStores$		6/2/2001 6:36:15 PM	6/2/2001 6:36:15 PM	TABLE
State		6/2/2001 6:36:15 PM	6/2/2001 6:36:15 PM	TABLE

☑ First row of data contains column headers   [OK]   [Cancel]

5. **Right-click any toolbar and select Mail Merge from the menu.**

   A new toolbar will appear.

6. **Select the Map Merge item to run the mail merge routine.**

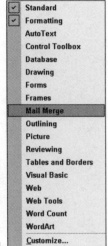

	Standard
	Formatting
	AutoText
	Control Toolbox
	Database
	Drawing
	Forms
	Frames
	Mail Merge
	Outlining
	Picture
	Reviewing
	Tables and Borders
	Visual Basic
	Web
	Web Tools
	Word Count
	WordArt
	Customize...

Figure 11-8:
Add the
MailMerge
toolbar.

Chapter 12

Tracking Your Position with GPS

● ●

In This Chapter

▶ Introducing GPS

▶ Considering the uses of GPS with MapPoint

▶ Understanding GPS receivers

▶ Installing GPS support in MapPoint

▶ Seeing your current position using GPS

▶ Routing and GPS — what's good and what's not yet available

▶ Troubleshooting GPS

● ●

*W*ay back in the mid-nineties, thanks to the United States Department of Defense, mere normals were given access to a satellite-based radio navigation system that was originally designed to help in the delivery of smart bombs. This system creates a convenient way of calculating your physical location anywhere on the earth with a degree of accuracy to within a few meters.

With any relatively inexpensive GPS receiver, you can tap into this $12 billion investment. By receiving signals from at least 3 of the 24 satellites orbiting above Earth at 11,000 miles, you also can plot your location on a map. With a little research, you can fill your head with many details about the sophistication of this system, but for the purposes of this book, we will deal only with the basics and cover how easy GPS is to use with MapPoint.

Figure 12-1 shows the basic concept of how GPS works. All you need is MapPoint on a laptop, a GPS device, and a clean "line of sight" view of at least three of the 24 satellites that make up the system.

Think of the GPS system as being nothing more than a space-age, Dr. Gizmo, line-of-sight, triangulation measuring thingee. Simple geometry shows that you can figure out the location of an unknown point by drawing a line to the point from three known locations. In this instance, the three or more known points just happen to be expensive GPS satellites, and a third dimension is included in the formula.

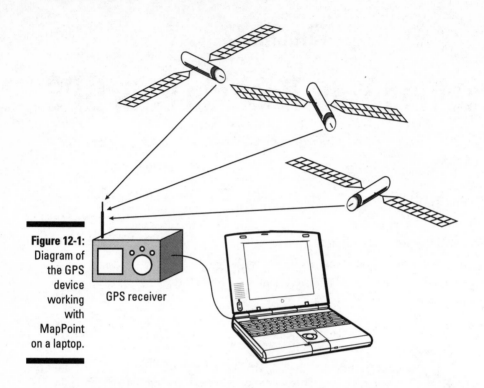

Figure 12-1:
Diagram of
the GPS
device
working
with
MapPoint
on a laptop.

GPS receiver

Out and About and Needing Guidance

We have a friend, we'll call him Joe, who believes that the use of a GPS device is a mandatory aspect of every little journey or trek he takes. He spent many hours studying the manual that came with his GPS device, hikes around in the back country recording waypoints every few hundred yards, and then labors over the results by exporting them to his PC after he gets back home. He even uses it when he goes to the local convenience store that he has visited 1,000 times. Using the MapPoint object model, Joe has even created a COM Add-in allowing him to import these waypoints into MapPoint.

We want to be clear from the start: This type of GPS activity is not what MapPoint is designed to support right out of the box and, for the majority of users, it is true overkill. We argue that Joe's use of GPS is equivalent to my use of my SUV. Nice to have and great for impressing the neighbors but of little real value in a business sense.

So why would you want or need GPS support with MapPoint? Here is where the reasoning and nicely enough the implementation are both simple and clean. GPS in MapPoint helps you to identify your location and is most valuable when it comes to figuring out where you are in reference to the 6.4 million miles of routable streets and roads in North America or the 4.8 million kilometers of routable streets and roads across Europe. It's particularly useful when you are driving in unfamiliar areas. It has saved us time and frustration more than once.

What GPS Device Is Right?

Today, many GPS devices are available online, at computer stores, and at sporting-goods stores. Because GPS device discussions tend to be loaded with the "Mine's better than yours!" arguments, we cut to the quick and follow two simple rules in making our decision on which one to buy:

✔ MapPoint requires the use of a GPS device that supports NMEA 0183 version 2.0 or later format. This is a very common standard but many popular devices also support proprietary formats, and you may need to change a setting on the device. Read the manual that came with the device or contact the manufacturer for more information.

✔ Before you purchase a GPS device to work with MapPoint, make sure that the device supports a link between it and the communications port of your laptop. If you already own a device and do not have a cable but the device has a port for one, you should be able to get the necessary cable.

Installing GPS in MapPoint

Microsoft has completely revamped the installation for GPS in MapPoint 2002 to make it easier to use:

1. **Connect your GPS device to your computer on which MapPoint is installed.**

   The connection between the PC and the GPS device is made through one of your communications ports. The dialog box shown in Figure 12-2 will appear.

2. **Click Tools⇨GPS⇨Configure GPS Receiver . . . ; choose the COM port where the GPS device is located.**

3. **Verify that the GPS device is set to support the NMEA 0183 version 2.0 or later format and set the baud rate to 4800.**

   The important thing here is that the baud rate on your GPS receiver matches the baud rate of the COM port to which it's connected.

   It's that simple. If for some reason you selected the incorrect COM port, you can always go back and change it by following the same simple steps.

Stationary GPS Receivers

Using GPS with MapPoint on a desktop PC may be a great onetime thrill but the excitement lasts fewer than 10 seconds at most. In the early days of working with GPS, Microsoft actually installed a GPS antenna on one of its buildings as the only logical means of keeping on schedule as employees coded modules. It is not all that unheard of for MS programmers to be wandering out on the roads to do coding but it was deemed much more cost effective and safer to bring the satellite signals inside especially when it rains, which is a good part of the year.

Interestingly enough, in my travels I have run into many other companies that have a similar set-up.

But does stationary GPS have other uses? Even with this great technology it did not even come into play when Seattle went through its recent earthquake. The building where it was installed just did not move enough! The team has since moved offices and the cost of moving the antenna was compared to the cost of umbrellas and the umbrellas won!

Figure 12-2:
COM port
listing.

Tracking Your Current Position

You are now ready to reap the benefits of the $12 billion investment. The following steps take you through tracking your position. Make sure that your GPS device is on and receiving signals (most of the handheld devices have their own display that will show you how many satellites are being received); then:

1. **Go to Tools⇨GPS⇨Track Position. If all is working correctly, the map centers on your current location and a small red car symbol indicating your location appears.**

   MapPoint samples the GPS location once every 15 seconds and moves the symbol to the new location. As the symbol approaches the edge of the map, MapPoint automatically recenters the view and continues tracking your movement.

2. **Click Tools⇨GPS menu and check the Always Show Position and GPS Sensor options, if desired.**

   When checked, the Always Show Position setting keeps the maps centered so that the car icon showing your location is always displaying on the screen.

   The GPS Sensor (shown in Figure 12-3) provides statistics concerning your current location relating to latitude, longitude, altitude, time of the fix, and status of the GPS device.

Using MapPoint GPS support while driving down the road can be very dangerous if you are doing so without the aid of a passenger. If you think your cell phone is distracting, think about the loss of driving focus that can take place when you look across to your laptop sitting on the passenger seat and work to focus on the brightly colored maps while trying to get perspective. Doing this while the car is parked or listening to a play-by-play coming from a passenger may damage the ego of the males in the audience but it's the only way to go. Practice safe GPSing!

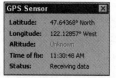

Figure 12-3: GPS Sensor.

GPS Sensor	
Latitude:	47.64368° North
Longitude:	122.12957° West
Altitude:	Unknown
Time of fix:	11:30:46 AM
Status:	Receiving data

Bringing Routing and GPS Together

So, it's road-trip time. Grab your laptop with MapPoint and a GPS device with NMEA 0183 version 2.0 or later format. You also need a communication port connection and cable and a trusted companion for assistance when using it while the wheels are turning and off you go. In this case, the "trusted companion" should be human in that it is rare to find a dog that can read maps! If you know of one, please tell us about him or her.

Follow these steps to put together a dynamic route using the MapPoint routing functionality and the live GPS sensing.

1. **Verify that the cable is attached and the GPS is on and receiving signals from three or more satellites.**

   If you are having problems getting clean reception, make sure that you are not close to buildings, trees, or other obstacles that may be blocking your line of sight to the stars.

2. **Open MapPoint and click Tools⇨GPS⇨Track Position.**

   Within a few seconds you should see a map with the car icon showing you where you currently are located.

3. **Click the Route Planner icon on the Standard toolbar.**

4. **Click the car icon on the map.**

   Right-click to get the shortcut menu and choose Route⇨Add this location as Start, or click Route on the main menu bar and choose Add as Start.

   Either of these actions adds this as the start of your route.

5. **Temporarily uncheck the Always Show Position item in the pop-up menu so that the map does not jump back to your current location as you complete the following steps.**

   You should do this before you identify the route's end and any intermediate stops.

6. **Add any number of stops and an end to your route as outlined in Chapter 5.**

7. **Click Get Directions on the Route Planner.**

   This action adds the green highlights to the map and displays the turn-by-turn directions.

8. **Check the Always Show Position menu item from the Tools/GPS menu to turn this option back on.**

   Figure 12-4 shows the car icon tracking along the path that you are traveling.

9. **Read over the directions before you depart, or have your riding companion start reading the instructions; then, away you go.**

   The map will track along as you go, showing your current location.

Troubleshooting Your Connection to GPS

Every now and then, you may experience trouble getting the GPS functionality to work. Here are a few quick things to check that should get you back on the road. Additonal trouble shooting tips can be found in the MapPoint online help.

  ✔ Although this sounds so basic, check to make sure that your GPS device is turned on and working. Some of these little devices can be real battery hogs and just the little act of forgetting to turn it on is not very reassuring to a companion you may have with you. Trust me: I've been there before!

✔ Make sure that the input/output format (interface) on your GPS receiver is set to support the NMEA 0183 version 2.0 or later format. Check your GPS device manual for details.

✔ Check the GPS cable and make sure that it is securely plugged in, both to the GPS device and your laptop's (COM) communications port.

✔ Make sure that the correct COM port is selected. On the Tools menu, click GPS⇨Configure GPS Receiver and then choose a COM port from the list. Try each of the available COM ports if your first selection doesn't work.

✔ Make sure that the baud on your GPS receiver is set to 4800 (or that it matches the baud rate of the COM port to which it's connected).

✔ Close other applications that use the same COM port you have configured for the GPS receiver.

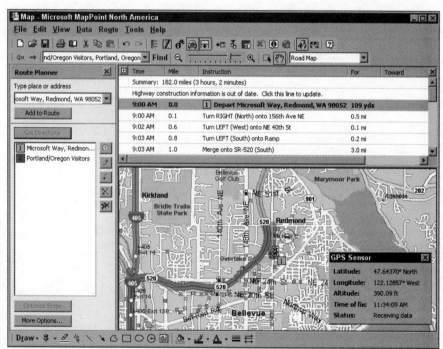

Figure 12-4:
GPS position displayed over MapPoint Route.

Is MapPoint GPS a good replacement for an in-car navigation system?

The answer to this question depends much on the features you really believe you must have and the investment you are willing to make. In-car navigation systems that come with many higher-end cars today provide added features that MapPoint cannot support, yet the price tag of these systems is many times higher and the added features may not be necessary. Then again, on some new models the feature is built-in and you have no choice but to leave it there. You may as well use it.

Having a nice voice politely providing upcoming turn information costs more money but may be better than having your mom telling you where to go (not a suggestion, Gracie!). Being able to recalculate a route should you get off track is good, but the same feature is available just by having a friend help you or by pulling over, adding a new stop point, and then getting directions again.

Another benefit that falls on MapPoint's side is the ability to detect and use the GPS device away from the vehicle. What you can't do with today's in-car navigation systems is download and integrate captured locations with MapPoint. Both sides of the debate have their pros and cons.

Chapter 13

Taking MapPoint on the Road with Pocket Streets

*T*he world of computing is getting smaller and more powerful each year with the popularity of the Pocket PCs overtaking all other forms of hand-held computer gadgets. What's cool is that the MapPoint CDs include a Pocket PC application named Pocket Streets. This little gem will allow you to take the streets and roads along with you when you hit the streets and roads! If fact, with very little effort you can take along segments of any of the 6.4 million miles of streets and roads in North America or the 4.8 million kilometers of streets and roads across Europe. Average mileage per trip will vary depending on the size of memory on your Pocket PC!

To make sure that you are not misled, be warned right up front that Pocket Streets is *not* a miniaturized version of MapPoint. It is designed to allow you to work with rich street-level maps (the lowest level in altitude and highest detail coverage within MapPoint maps) without having to lug around your desktop or laptop computer. It also supports address and place searches and simple Pushpin addition and display. With this version, it does not support the business mapping functionality of MapPoint.

Putting the World in Your Pocket

Many American males can attest to the belief that the next best thing to knowing naturally where they are going is the ability to resist stopping and asking for directions as they reach down into you're their trusty stack of maps garnered from gas stations. They unfold them (with difficulty) still hoping to recover lost dignity by impressing their passengers with their map-reading and navigation skills.

Two of the biggest dilemmas the (male) author of this book always encounters are the problems he has in refolding the maps and in locating the correct map. The challenges of these left-handed origami exercises are compounded by the number of wrong guesses he inevitably makes trying to use this big, unruly sheet of paper. All the hand-waving and other efforts to distract his passengers as he tries to get his bearings with the map usually turns into a complicated dance.

Using Pocket Streets eliminates those awkward folding episodes. The new cool service pack release for Pocket Streets 2002 (available for download to licensed owners of MapPoint 2002 at `http://www.microsoft.com/pocketstreets/`) even helps to minimize the "where am I exactly?" problem with the new GPS device support, but be forewarned you will still need to make sure that you have the correct maps along with you when you need them.

The Pocket Streets program that comes with MapPoint is identical to the version available as a companion product to the consumer edition of Microsoft mapping products. This program includes Streets & Trips 2002 for North America and Auto Route 2002 for Europe. Figure 13-1 shows a map appearing on a PocketPC.

Figure 13-1:
Pocket Streets Map of San Francisco, California, viewed on a Pocket PC.

Installing Pocket Streets

If Microsoft ActiveSync was detected on your desktop or laptop PC when you first installed MapPoint and you elected to install Pocket Streets, you are good to go. If you have yet to install MapPoint you can learn more about the installation details in Appendix A and install Pocket Streets at the same time.

It is also possible Pocket Streets could be missing from your PocketPC if you interrupted an earlier installation or decided not to install it with MapPoint. Either way, if you have already installed MapPoint and you have not installed Pocket Streets, rest assured that you can easily get up and running. To install Pocket Streets:

1. **Verify that your PocketPC is connected to your desktop or laptop PC and that Microsoft ActiveSync is installed on that PC.**

   You can do this by launching the ActiveSync applet by double-clicking either the Microsoft ActiveSync shortcut icon located on your desktop or by double-clicking the WCESMgr.exe file, typically located in the C:\Program Files\Microsoft ActiveSync\ folder. The ActiveSync dialog box will appear as shown in Figure 13-2. You should see text in the main status window that indicates whether you are connected.

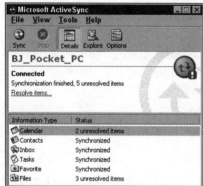

Figure 13-2: Microsoft ActiveSync applet.

2. **Place the MapPoint Setup CD in the CD drive of your desktop or laptop PC.**

   If a dialog box appears telling you that you need the MapPoint Runtime CD to run MapPoint, just click Cancel to close it. MapPoint does not need to be running when you install Pocket Streets.

3. **In Windows Explorer, navigate to the Pstreets folder on the CD.**

4. **Double-click Setup.exe and follow the online instructions.**

Now that you have Pocket Streets loaded, you need to export a map from MapPoint and copy it to your PocketPC.

We strongly recommend that you uninstall older versions of Pocket Streets before installing Pocket Streets 2002. The readme file in the Pstreets folder on MapPoint CD1 explains how you can run two versions on the same PocketPC, but be warned the file format has changed and you cannot read 2001 files with Pocket Streets 2002, or vice versa. You will be required to recreate any special maps you have, but the benefits of having newer maps should ease the pain somewhat.

Exporting a Map for Pocket Streets

We like to think of MapPoint as the mother ship and Pocket Streets as a remote scouting ship. MapPoint comes with a complete map of the world and, with a little preparation and a magical transport, you can move detailed segments of that world to the PocketPC.

Creating Pocket Streets maps on your own provides a degree of flexibility, but you will save time by copying any of the 42 North American maps or the 19 European maps already saved on the install CD1 of the respective editions. If you have the space to do so on your hard drive, you can copy all these files over to it and save yourself the hassle of having to drag the CDs around to get to the maps later.

To export a map from MapPoint, follow these steps:

1. **Open MapPoint.**

2. **Use the Select tool (or any other navigation tool) to navigate to the area you want to export; make sure that the view includes the entire area you want.**

   The lower in altitude you are, the less spatial coverage you will export. There is a maximum file size that depends somewhat on the density of the road network that will limit the select size. If the area you select is too big, MapPoint will warn you and advise you to select a smaller region.

3. **Click File⇨Export Map for Pocket Streets.**

   You will see a dialog box that estimates the size of the file. Make sure that you have sufficient space on your Pocket PC to handle the size of map you're exporting.

4. **Click OK to continue.**

   You will then be prompted to provide a filename for the file.

The maximum size of a Pocket Streets file is regulated by the way spatial data is stored inside the MapPoint maps. This maximum varies depending on the density of the road network within the desired region. For example, you will cover more road miles in Los Angeles than the central part of Kansas but you will get the same maximum amount of square miles.

Providing that you have the storage space on your PocketPC, the nice thing is that you can export multiple maps that are side-by-side and open them as needed in Pocket Streets.

If you have created Pushpin sets on the map that you're exporting from, and one or more of those Pushpins are within the selected region, they also will be exported and stored as Pushpin (.PSP) files in the same folder as the map (.MPS) file. The .PSP file will automatically share the same name as the .MPS file.

Be aware that the maximum length of both the title and body of the text that appears in the Pushpin balloon (explained in Chapter 4) will be truncated to a maximum length of 128 characters. Also, none of the additional fields selected in the Pushpin Properties dialog box will be exported.

After you click OK, a window appears, telling you the approximate file size for the map area you've selected. Be sure that you have enough space available on your PocketPC for the map you're exporting. Consult the documentation that came with your PocketPC if necessary.

Copying the Exported Map to Your PocketPC

Now that you have the export file, you need to get it onto the PocketPC before you can use it with Pocket Streets. This process is easy, but you need to make sure that you copy it to the right destination for it to work.

1. **Connect your PocketPC to your desktop or laptop PC using ActiveSync.**

   You can do this through a standard cradle connection or you can use an IR-Infrared connection. Check your PocketPC manual for details.

2. **Click the Explore tool on the Standard toolbar or choose Explore from the File menu.**

   If either of these choices is inactive (grayed out), you do not have a good connection.

You will be presented with a Mobile Device folder for your PocketPC (see Figure 13-3).

3. **Navigate within the Windows Explorer until you locate the map (.MPS) and any Pushpin (.PSP) files that you want to move to the Pocket PC.**

   Note that any Pushpin (.PSP) file that goes with a map (.MPS) file will share the same name.

4. **Move the files to the My Documents folder on the PocketPC.**

   If you are copying files to a compact flash card, you must first create a My Documents folder on the compact flash card and then copy the files to that folder.

Figure 13-3:
The Mobile Device window.

You use the same process when moving both the Pocket Streets maps that are already created on the MapPoint CD1 and any exported maps that you create.

Using Pocket Streets

Now that you have installed Pocket Streets on your PocketPC and exported and moved maps over to the My Documents folder, it's time to throw away your gas-station maps and prepare to wow your passengers.

Opening Pocket Streets and Opening a Map

Opening Pocket Streets is easy after you know where it is located on the PocketPC. Begin by clicking Start in the upper-left corner of the PocketPC Programs window and then choosing Programs. Click the Pocket Streets icon (see Figure 13-4).

Figure 13-4: PocketPC Programs window.

You are then be presented with a list of Pocket Streets .MPS files from which you can choose (see Figure 13-5).

If you already have Pockets Streets open and are viewing a map, you can open another one by clicking Tools and then selecting the Map option in the lower-left corner of the window. You will find the list of available maps at the bottom of the menu.

Figure 13-5: Open a map file from within Pocket Streets.

Zooming, Panning, and Copying Maps

Click Tools⇨Map (see Figure 13-6) to find the commands that control map zooming and panning, as follows:

- ✔ **Pan Arrows:** This option toggles on and off with a check mark. When it's checked, you see the arrows located in the lower-right corner. When you can pan in any of the four directions, the arrows are black. When you cannot pan in a given direction, the relevant arrow turns grey.

- ✔ **Zoom Full:** This option zooms the map out to the highest altitude that displays the entire map.

The Map menu also includes a Copy Map command that copies the map to the Clipboard for use with other programs on your Pocket PC.

Figure 13-6: The Pocket Streets Map menu.

Finding an address or place with ease

For starters, check out how easy it is to find something on this map. No more looking at the back of the map for the alpha listing of streets. To find an address or a place, just click Tools and choose the Find Address or Find Place menu option. The Find Address dialog box will appear (see Figure 13-7).

You can then type in as much of the address as you can and click the OK button in the upper-left hand of the window. Just like its big brother in MapPoint, the Find function provides a list of possible addresses or places matching the text you provide. You can then select the desired one and click OK to view the selection on the map.

The message There are no matches is displayed if an address search fails completely. If the search is successful, a map will be displayed (see Figure 13-8).

The place search includes locating points of interest (POIs) and any Pushpins either exported with the source MapPoint file or created later right on the PocketPC.

Figure 13-7:
The Find
Address
dialog box.

Figure 13-8:
Searched
address
displayed on
the map.

Hiding and Seeking POIs

Maps exported from MapPoint to Pocket Streets contain the complete listing of all the points of interest (POIs). Open the Tools menu to choose the Points of Interest option. You can then check which Points of Interest to display or to hide (see Figure 13-9).

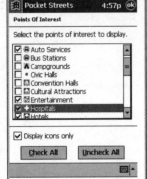

Figure 13-9:
The Points
of Interest
dialog box.

Pocket Streets substitutes and displays three overlapping squares icons at any location where two or more POIs overlap; these overlapping squares display instead of the individual icons for each POI. Be aware that all icons appear only when you are at a low zoom level. To identify and select just a single POI that is included within the overlapping group, click the three overlapping squares icon. You will be presented with a list from which you can click the one you want (see Figure 13-10).

Figure 13-10:
The Pocket
Streets POI
list.

Adding Pushpins to Pocket Streets

Along with the POIs that come with the exported map and any Pushpin that you created in MapPoint, you can also add Pushpins right on the PocketPC, as follows:

1. **Click the Pushpin button in the toolbar at the bottom of the Pocket Streets window.**

2. **Click the location where you want to place the Pushpin.**

   The Pushpin Properties dialog box appears (see Figure 13-11).

3. **Enter the name you want to use for the Pushpin in the Name box.**

4. **Enter any notes you want to make about the Pushpin in the Notes box.**

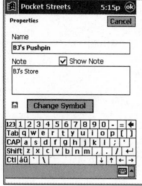

Figure 13-11:
The Pushpin Properties dialog box enables you to name your Pushpin and make notes about it.

5. **Click the Change Symbol button.**

   The symbol palette shown in Figure 13-12 appears. Notice that the Pushpin selection is limited compared to MapPoint. You also cannot use custom Pushpin symbols.

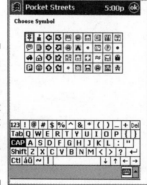

Figure 13-12:
Use this palette to select different Pushpin symbols for your map.

6. Press the OK button when you are finished making your selections.

The map appears with the new Pushpins (see Figure 13-13).

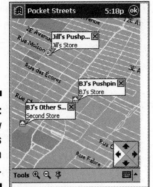

Figure 13-13:
New
Pushpins
displayed on
your map.

So now you have the power of the world stuck into your pocket. Time to burn the paper maps and finally clean out the glove compartment.

Part V

Programming MapPoint

The 5th Wave   By Rich Tennant

"Okay, Darryl, I think it's time to admit we didn't load the onboard mapping software correctly."

In this part . . .

After you master the rich set of MapPoint features, you may wish that you could automate the repetitive steps that you take each time you create a route or a business map or be able to explore extending the functionality of the MapPoint technology. As you'll see in the next few chapters, MapPoint provides the hidden power of object model programming. These chapters show how to build simple COM Add-ins to extend and automate the MapPoint application and to embed the MapPoint ActiveX Control into your mission-critical applications.

You will also get a chance to answer that age-old question about whether MapPoint is a GIS system with enough horsepower to do real things. We include this chapter to help the cartographer types in the desire to have good explanations as to why they would really wander away from GIS in some instances.

Warning! Although nonprogrammers can gain insight into how MapPoint can be extended, the following chapters are directed to the reader who has a basic understanding of Visual Basic programming.

Chapter 14

Unleashing the Hidden Power of MapPoint

The many out-of-the-box features of MapPoint provide the power needed by an above-average user. Each time you sit in front of your screen, you can discover new and valuable insight into your geographic-based data and you can tap into the functionality using the menus, dialog boxes, wizards, and direct interaction with the map in any order or to any extent you desire. Sometimes it's nice to switch on the cruise control and let MapPoint do the driving automatically. But as you may feel sometimes with a hard-working car or delivery truck, the time may come when you want to go into overdrive and accelerate into the hidden power of MapPoint. The new, enhanced object model of MapPoint 2002 provides a means to step on the gas and seek out the benefits provided by the rich automation and extendibility.

Introducing MapPoint's Hidden Powers

The under-the-hood-power mentioned in the previous section comes in the form of the greatly enhanced object model. If you are familiar with the art of Visual Basic programming or have used Visual Basic for Applications (VBA) with another Office family member, you will have an understanding of the power that an object model provides. The MapPoint object model is no different than the object model in other Office family applications; it just gives you access to the entire world. If you happen to be a novice programmer and would like to learn more about Visual Basic 6.0 programming, we highly recommend *Visual Basic 6 For Dummies*, by Wallace Wang (published by Hungry Minds, Inc.).

This chapter offers an overview of the important aspects of the MapPoint object model, but space precludes providing a detail-by-detail roster of all that is available. Reading this and playing with the code samples in the Chapters 15, 16, and 17 will give you a running start. Exploring the power at your own pace is what will keep you going.

We like to think of the MapPoint object model as the "MapPoint My Way!" feature. This hidden-power link to the world of business mapping allows for the automation of numerous steps in a recurring task and lets you go beyond basic MapPoint into a whole new world of functionality. Objects are the building blocks of an object model; think of them as named items. Each object can have a collection of associated properties, methods, and events. The MapPoint 2002 object model is greatly expanded and for the first time contains events, making programming MapPoint all the more powerful.

The MapPoint user assistance (known as online Help files to mere normals!) provides a detailed explanation and completed code samples that highlight the object model in action. For your enjoyment, we have included working Visual Basic projects for many of these samples on the enclosed CD1 so that you can save yourself from typos. We highly recommend keeping them near by for quick cut-and-paste sessions into your own projects. Figuring out how they work is important, but watching them work for real is the easiest way to understand what they are doing. You can also get great online technical support and samples from `msdn.microsoft.com/mappoint` and numerous online user groups. You will find a current listing of online places to go at BJ's Web site: `www.dataweave.com/mappoint`.

Now you can dig a little deeper and explore how objects in the object model work together to send us into overdrive.

Understanding the Object Model

Think of the MapPoint object model as a toolbox of gizmos that fit together as building blocks to achieve specific, repetitive tasks. Put them together correctly and you can master the world. At first glance, any object model can look like a Rubik's cube but joining together these gizmos (known as *objects* in computer terms) is easy. The pieces work together to produce results outside the application user interface. This toolbox of gizmos includes such goodies as maps, datasets, routes, directions, shapes, Pushpins, symbols, and Find results (see Figure 14-1). When acted upon, the individual objects result in the creation of routes, shaded area maps, result sets from queries, and the many other fruits of your labor. Contrary to the ad hoc way that you may use MapPoint, the object model allows you to do things in a specific order and with a specific degree of detail as defined in the code you create. When you have created the code that acts upon the object model, you can go back and repeat the required steps without having to remember or repeat each step in the process every time you want to do the task again.

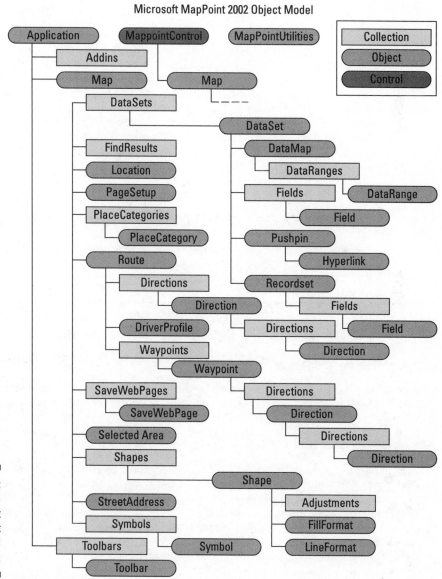

Figure 14-1:
The
MapPoint
object
model
overview.

Children need their parents

All the objects in MapPoint are part of a hierarchical parent-child structure and require an awareness of their parents before you can get them to act properly. The MapPointUtilities object is the only parent with no children. You use it to create picture objects or return programmatic identifiers when using Visual Basic. We think of it as the footloose and fancy single in the crowd. It gets to do cool things but has no responsibility when it comes to others.

So, how do you use this hierarchical structure? Think of it as a family tree. For example, you can't get to the Location object without identifying its parent, the Map object. Furthermore, you cannot get to a Map object without first identifying its parent, either the MapPoint Application object or the MappointControl object. MapPoint matches life in this respect: Children behave best when they know you know their parents! Children get their identity from their parents. Taking the analogy one step further, responsible people make sure that a child's parents are aware of tasks they ask the child to perform or information they need about the child.

Collection of treasured objects to behold

The MapPoint 2002 object model contains 24 objects, classified into collections. Table 14-1 provides a brief description of each of them.

Three-in-one: The MapPoint Application, MappointControl, and MapPointUtilities objects

You will notice that the object model diagram for MapPoint has three objects located at the very top of the diagram. Each is a unique front-end to the rich power contained within the MapPoint engine and should be used for different purposes.

The MapPoint Application and MappointControl objects provide access to almost all the same functionality but from different development approaches. From the Application object, you can use the object model to build COM Add-ins that extend MapPoint or to integrate MapPoint with

other Office applications. The MappointControl allows you to access the object model from within a Visual Basic project when you want to embed the power of MapPoint into a mission-critical application.

Finally, MapPointUtilities is an additional object used to create picture objects or return programmatic identifiers from within Visual Basic applications. After you gain an understanding of how the object model fits together, see Chapters 15, 16, and 17 to find out when each approach comes into play.

Table 14-1	MapPoint Objects
Name	**Description**
Application	The root of the MapPoint object model hierarchy
MappointControl	The root of the Microsoft MapPoint Control 9.0 ActiveX Control object hierarchy
MapPointUtilities	Used to create picture objects or return programmatic identifiers that can be used in Visual Basic
Map	The document object of MapPoint; the map that you see when you open the application or use the ActiveX control
Location	A place, an address, or latitude/longitude coordinates
PageSetup	The various options for printing; similar to those found in the More Options dialog box
Route	A calculated route of connected waypoints (start point, stops, and end point) and a set of driving directions
DriverProfile	The preferences for generating routes, such as travel time, methods for determining route costs, and preferred roads
SelectedArea	A rectangular selected area on the map; equivalent to using the Select tool on the map.
StreetAddress	An address separated into its atomic parts: street, city, other city, region, country, and postal code
Symbol	The custom or standard symbol used for a Pushpin, Pushpin set, or Multiple Symbol map
Shape	A single drawing object on the map: line, freeform, text box, radius, oval, or rectangle
FillFormat	The color and visibility properties of the fill formatting for a shape
LineFormat	The line and arrowhead formatting for a shape
WayPoint	A start point, stop, or end point of a Route object
Direction	A single line in the route itinerary
AddIns	A collection of any Add-ins currently connected to MapPoint.
DataSet	Imported or linked data from an application (such as Excel) or a file (such as a text file), manually created Pushpins, or mapped demographic data

(continued)

Table 14-1 *(continued)*

Name	Description
DataMap	A set of read-only properties that describe how a data set is mapped
Pushpin	Marks a place on the map or represents data
Hyperlink	The hyperlink properties associated with a Pushpin
Recordset	A list of all records that match a query used to create the record set
Field	A specific field or column in a data set
SavedWebPage	A single Web page saved from the map file

Each object also has a set of associated properties. All properties can be set during the design mode of development. A subset of them can be changed during runtime of your final COM Add-in or Visual basic application, whereas others are read-only during the runtime mode. The read-only ones are identified in the MapPoint Help section.

The objects you will find used the most include the Application, Mappoint Control, Map, and Location objects, described in the following sections.

Application object

The Application object represents the MapPoint application and allows access to the application window. It also enables you to open map files, add or remove COM add-ins commands, and quit the application.

This object remains valid after the map is closed and then reopened.

MappointControl object

Think of the MappointControl object as providing access to the object model in a similar manner as the application except that it is used to embed MapPoint functionality into your Visual Basic applications. It is one of the parents of the universe (or at least the Earth). You place it on a Visual Basic form and use Visual Basic code to control it and its children to add MapPoint functionality to your own application.

Map object

When you have an Application or MappointControl object, you need to create a map to work on. This is appropriately named the Map object. You can have only one map object open at a time.

Location object

So, you've got a map. Now you need to identify one or more locations if you what to do some real work. The Location object is one of the most powerful objects in MapPoint. Gain control of locations and you gain control of the world.

Using the Methods (of Your Madness)

Collecting objects is a nice hobby, but getting these objects to do something is much more valuable and fun. You get objects to take action by using methods. Methods get objects to perform such exciting activities as querying shapes, moving to a specified location on the map, adding Pushpins and demographics data to a map, finding addresses and places, or selecting various objects to take additional action on.

The MapPoint 2002 object model contains 86 individual methods. See Chapters 15, 16, and 17, to find out how to put many of these to work. Here, we cover five of them just to touch on the meaning behind the madness of methods. The methods we present here are not necessarily the most used or important methods, but after you gain an understanding of these, you will find it easier to understand the remaining 81.

For your convenience, we have included simple MapPoint ActiveX Control code samples that demonstrate some of the Distance and AddDrivetimeZone methods. Not much to write home about, but remember the number one rule of programming: Steal code whenever you can! You can find these samples on the CD with this book labeled CD1 in the \Code Samples\Simple Methods\ folder.

Before you can do anything with a map, you need to open an existing one or create a new one.

- ✔ **NewMap method:** The `NewMap` method by default uses the MapPoint default template. If desired, you can also create a new map and use a template that you have created. Following is the syntax for the `NewMap` method:

```
object.NewMap([Template])
```

- ✔ **OpenMap method:** The `OpenMap` method opens an existing map. It also displays the Save dialog box if another map is currently active and has not been saved. This method, whose syntax follows, is not available when MapPoint is embedded into a Word or Excel document.

```
object.OpenMap(Filename, [AddToRecentFiles])
```

✔ **Distance method:** Calculate the distance "as the crow flies" between two locations in GeoUnits (miles or Kilometers) with the `Distance` method, as follows:

```
object.Distance(StartLocation, EndLocation)
```

✔ **AddDrivetimeZone method:** Adds a freeform, closed shape representing the driving distance from a point on the map within a specified amount of time using this syntax:

```
object.AddDrivetimeZone(Center, Time)
```

✔ **SaveMap method:** Saves the specified map or template. If the map was opened from a template, then the map is saved as Map.ptm in the My Documents directory (This method can be used only with the MapPoint ActiveX control and not the MapPoint application). Here's the syntax:

```
object.SaveMap
```

Getting a Grip on Hot Events

Prior to this version of MapPoint, a user was really at a loss when it came to programming using events. The new enhanced object model finally contains 18 events that will make life much easier. An event occurs at some predictable point in time, usually triggered by some action initiated by the end user such as a mouse click or caused to occur from within the MapPoint application. MapPoint fires an event just before the mouse is clicked and even fires events when the mouse button is going up or going down or the mouse pointer is being moved across the map. Not so obvious yet still very important are the events that take place when the user makes a selection change on the map or when MapPoint has just completed calculating or optimizing a route.

These events are meaningless if you do not know how and when to use them and if you do not put code behind them. For now, we summarize the events in Table 14-2. In Chapters 15, 16, and 17, we put them into play.

Retiring Functions

With the extensive enhancements made to the MapPoint object model compared to the 2001 version, it is of little surprise that some of the old ways of doing things had a tendency to get in the way or become outdated. Microsoft was kind enough to keep them around to provide a level of backward compatibility, but using them going forward is a not a wise idea. We would even go so far as to say that you should do a search for each method or property listed in Table 14-3 and retrofit any existing old code with the new approaches. Doing a little housecleaning is always a worthwhile undertaking.

Table 14-2	MapPoint/MappointControl Events	
Name	*Occurs ...*	*Object*
BeforeClose	Before the map closes	Application
BeforeSave	Immediately before the map is saved	Application
New	When a new map is created	Application
Open	When a map is opened	Application
AfterRedraw	When MapPoint is finished repainting the map on the screen	Map
AfterViewChange	When the view of the map has changed and the map is done repainting to that viewpoint	Map
BeforeClick	After the user clicks the map but before MapPoint has processed the action	Map
BeforeDblClick	After the user double-clicks the map but before MapPoint has processed the action	Map
DataMapChange	After data mapping properties are changed for a data set	Map
MouseDown	When a mouse button is pressed while the pointer is over the map	Map
MouseMove	When the mouse is moved while the pointer is over the map; a button does not need to be pressed for this event	Map
MouseUp	When a mouse button is released while the pointer is over the map	Map
NewDataSet	After a new data set is created	Map
RouteAfterCalculate	After the route has been calculated	Map
RouteAfterOptimize	After the stops on the route have been optimized	Map
SelectionChange	When a selection on the map changes	Map
ReadyStateChange	When the state of the MappointControl has changed	Mappoint Control

Table 14-3		MapPoint Object Model Events
Retired Function	*On object . . .*	*Use this instead*
DataField property	DataMap	Use the DataFields property on the DataMap object to return an array of Field objects representing the fields the user wants to data map.
Find method	Map	Use the FindResults method on the Map object to return a collection of Location and Pushpin objects (a FindResults collection) that are possible place and address find matches. Use the FindPlaceResults method on the Map object to return a FindResults collection of possible place find match results.
FindAddress method	Map	Use the FindAddressResults method on the Map object to return a collection of Location objects (a FindResults collection) that are possible address find matches.
FullName property	Application	The FullName property is now valid only for Map objects. Use the Path property on the Application object to return the path, excluding the final separator and name of the object. Use the Name property on the Application object to return the name.
GoTo method	Pushpin	The GoTo method is now valid only for Location objects. To go to a Pushpin, first obtain a Location object by using the Location property on the Pushpin object. Then use the GoTo method on that Location object.
GoToLatLong method	Map	The GoToLatLong method is no longer available. Use the GetLocation method on the Map object.
RecordCount property	DataRange	The RecordCount property is now valid only for DataMap and DataSet objects. To return the number of values in a data range that were mapped, use the ValueCount property on the DataRange object.

Chapter 15

(COM) into My World!

*T*he ability to build extensions using the MapPoint object model opens the door to extending the functionality and the automation of repetitive tasks. The natural features of MapPoint enable you to perform many day-to-day tasks, but there will come a time when you find yourself or your users repeating many steps in an identical manner to do day-to-day work. You can save yourself and your users time by automating many tasks with a Component Object Model (COM) Add-in. This chapter shows you how to do that, as well as how to use a COM Add-in to incorporate a feature or function into those provided by MapPoint applications.

Creating a COM Add-in in Visual Basic 6.0

You can create Component Object Model (COM) add-ins using many different programming languages, but by doing so in Visual Basic 6.0, you can use the same Add-In Designer you would use to build a Visual Basic 6.0 add-in, saving you both time and headaches. This designer automatically incorporates the IDTExtensibility2 interface so that you do not have to implement it yourself. The Visual Basic Add-in Designer also automatically registers your add-in for you so that MapPoint can find it when you go to use it.

If all this sounds foreign and you are in a hurry to build your first MapPoint COM Add-in, don't fret. We include the complete source code for this Visual Basic on the enclosed CD1 in the code samples folder and you can just copy it over, use it, and figure out how it works later.

Our very first rule of coding is a time-trusted treasure that we all do or should do but few of us talk about: "Cut and paste all existing code if you really want to save time!"

Here are the 18 easy steps to building your first MapPoint COM Add-in:

1. **Start Visual Basic 6.0.**

2. **The New Project dialog box will appear (see Figure 15-1).**

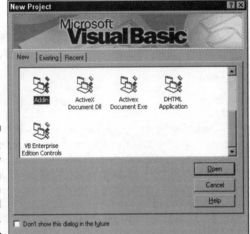

Figure 15-1:
Open a new
Add-in
project in
Visual
Basic.

3. **On the New tab in the New Project dialog box, scroll down if needed and click Addin; then click Open.**

   Doing so adds a designer class (Connect) and a new form (`frmAddIn`) to your project.

4. **Open the Connect Property dialog box located under MyAddIn in the Project window by clicking the + symbol under the Designers folder and double-clicking Connect (see Figure 15-2).**

Figure 15-2:
Double-click
Connect.

5. **Go to the Application drop-down box, click Microsoft MapPoint, and then in the Application Version drop-down box, click Microsoft MapPoint 9.0, which is version 2002.**

6. **Go to the Initial Load Behavior box and click Startup.**

7. **Close the Add-In Designer by clicking the Close button in the upper-right corner.**

8. **Go to the Project menu and click References.**

   The References dialog box will appear (see Figure 15-3).

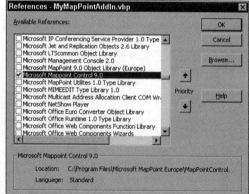

Figure 15-3:
References -
MyMap
PointAddIn
window.

9. **Scroll down as necessary and select the check box next to Microsoft MapPoint 9.0 Object Library and then click OK.**

   If you have installed the North American edition of MapPoint, the text name will be followed by "(North America)." If you a have installed the Europe edition of MapPoint, the text name will be followed by "(Europe)." If you have both editions installed, you can select either one; they are interchangeable.

10. **Go to the Project window, right-click Connect, and then click View Code.**

11. **You now need to select and then delete all the code in the Code window because this code was designed to work with Visual Basic add-ins and you are creating an Office COM add-in.**

12. **Now add the following code in the Code window.**

```
Option Explicit

Public m_formDisplayed    As Boolean
Public obj_App            As Mappoint.Application
Dim m_frmAddIn            As New frmAddIn
```

```
Sub Hide()
    '// Hides the form and remembers its state

    On Error Resume Next
    m_formDisplayed = False
    m_frmAddIn.Hide
End Sub

Sub Show()
    '// Shows the form and remembers its state
    On Error Resume Next

    If m_frmAddIn Is Nothing Then
        Set m_frmAddIn = New frmAddIn
    End If

    Set m_frmAddIn.obj_App = obj_App
    Set m_frmAddIn.Connect = Me
    m_formDisplayed = True
    m_frmAddIn.Show vbModal
End Sub

'//---------------------------------------------------------
'// This method adds the add-in to MapPoint
'//---------------------------------------------------------
Private Sub AddinInstance_OnConnection(ByVal Application
        As Object, ByVal ConnectMode As
        AddInDesignerObjects.ext_ConnectMode, ByVal
        AddInInst As Object, custom() As Variant)
    On Error GoTo error_handler

    'Save the MapPoint instance
    Set obj_App = Application


'// The following has the name of the menu item that
is added:

    obj_App.AddCommand "MapPoint Addin...", "Show", Me
    If ConnectMode = ext_cm_AfterStartup Then
        If GetSetting(App.Title, "Settings",
        "DisplayOnConnect", _
            "0") = "1" Then
            'Set this to display the form on connect
            Me.Show
        End If
    End If
    Exit Sub

error_handler:
    MsgBox Err.Description
End Sub

'//---------------------------------------------------------
```

```
'// This method removes the add-in from MapPoint
'//----------------------------------------------------------
Private Sub AddinInstance_OnDisconnection(ByVal
        RemoveMode As
        AddInDesignerObjects.ext_DisconnectMode, custom()
        As Variant)
    On Error Resume Next

    '// Delete the commands that were added for this add-
        in

    obj_App.RemoveCommands Me
    Unload m_frmAddIn
    Set m_frmAddIn = Nothing
End Sub
```

13. **Go to the Project window, right-click the** `frmAddIn` **form, and click View Code.**

14. **Replace this code:**

```
Public VBInstance As VBIDE.VBE
```

with this code, which provides the Add-in with a reference to the proper instance of MapPoint in case more than one is running:

```
Public obj_App As Mappoint.Application
```

15. **Remove the following code that is not used by MapPoint:**

```
Private Sub OKButton_Click()

        MsgBox "AddIn operation on: " &
        VBInstance.FullName

End Sub
```

16. **Choose File⇨Save Project.**

You will be prompted to save three different files. Make sure that each has the appropriate names of `Connect.Dsr`, `frmMapPointAddIn.frm` (instead of the default of `frmAddIn.frm`) and `MyMapPointAddIn.vbp` (instead of the default of `MyAddIn.vbp`).

17. **Choose File⇨Make MyMapPointAddIn.dll to finish building the COM Add-in.**

You are now ready to add the COM Add-in to MapPoint.

18. **Start MapPoint and then click Next Choose Tools⇨MapPoint Addin.**

Your new COM Add-in is nothing more than a blank window but it's a great start!

MapPoint's support for Office VBA

Unlike other Microsoft Office family members, MapPoint 2002 does not include Visual Basic for Applications (VBA). At first, this absence may appear to be a missing link. However, much of what you will want to do with the MapPoint object model when integrating with other Office applications will be completed with the VBA incorporated in Microsoft Word, Excel, Access, and PowerPoint.

In other circumstances, you will find that using the MapPoint object model is best suited when you embed the included MapPoint ActiveX Control within your mission-critical Visual Basic Application, avoiding the need for VBA completely.

With either approach, remember that you will need a basic understanding Visual Basic programming or have a good friend that is willing to support your programming needs to make MapPoint go the extra mile.

Okay, so maybe it all appears as technical stuff in this chapter, but we want to point out the MapPoint-specific sections of the preceding code.

In the OnConnection event, the following line of code tells MapPoint to add a MapPoint Addin menu item to the Tools menu:

```
obj_App.AddCommand "MapPoint Addin...", "Show", Me
```

When that menu item is called, the method indicated in the second parameter (in this case, the Show method) is called.

The third parameter is a reference to the object (in this case, the Connect designer) that has the Show method. You can add multiple menu items with their own handlers by calling this method again.

In the OnDisconnection event, the following line of code removes any commands that have been added by this add-in:

```
obj_App.RemoveCommands Me
```

Give your project a unique name by choosing Next Choose Project⇨ MyAddInProperties. In the Project Name box, enter the name of your add-in (MyMapPointAddin). If you also change the name of the designer from Connect, remember to update the code that references it.

You can now save your project and make the COM Add-in by selecting Make MyMapPointAddIn.dll under the File menu.

The MyMapPointAddin sample is nothing more than an empty shell (see Figure 15-4) but it provides a nice starting point from which you can build more MapPoint COM Add-ins without having to start from scratch.

Figure 15-4:
The MyMap
PointAddIn
COM Add-in.

Multiple Drivetime Zones Example

So let's take your newly created shell and do something useful with it. Remember: the magic of the MapPoint object model is the ability it provides to you to extend and automate its functionality. In the following example, you will learn how to automate MapPoint so that you can create three custom drivetime zones around one of a preset list of locations. The code also automates the tasks of shape color, line width and placement behind the roads and adds a textbox that includes the three specific times you provided.

Here are the steps required to add power to your shell.

1. **Using the Windows Explore, copy the folder containing your MyMapPointAddIn project.**

   Paste a new copy and rename the folder MultiDrivetimeZones.

2. **Start Visual Basic 6.0.**

3. **Open the MyMapPointAddin project in the MultiDrivetimeZones folder.**

4. **Choose File⇨Save Project as, changing the name of the** frmMapPointAddIn.frm **to** frmMultiDrivetimeZonesAddIn.frm **and the name of the** MyMapPointAddIn.vbp **file to** MultiDrivetimeZonesAddIn.vbp.

5. **Go to the Project window, right-click Connect, and then click View Code.**

6. **Search this block of code and replace** `MapPoint Addin...` **with** `Multiple Drivetime Zones Addin...`

7. **Select the** `frmMultiDrivetimeZonesAddin` **form and change the form caption to** `MapPoint 2002 - Multiple DriveTime Zones`.

8. **Resize the form to a width of 4830 and a height of 2250 using the form's Properties window.**

9. **Add a combo box and rename it** `ComboLocation`; **also, add a label control and change the caption to** `Location:`.

10. **Add three textboxes and name them** `Zone1Minutes`, `Zone2Minutes`, **and** `Zone3Minutes`. **Change the text in them to** 30, 60, **and** 90, **respectively. Add three label controls and change their captions to read** `Zone 1 Minutes:`, `Zone 2 Minutes:`, **and** `Zone 3 Minutes:`.

11. **Add the following code to the form load window:**

```
Private Sub Form_Load()
    ComboLocation.AddItem "Atlanta, GA"
    ComboLocation.AddItem "Boston, MA"
    ComboLocation.AddItem "Dallas, TX"
    ComboLocation.AddItem "Denver, CO"
    ComboLocation.AddItem "Chicago, IL"
    ComboLocation.AddItem "Kansas City, KS"
    ComboLocation.AddItem "Los Angelos, CA"
    ComboLocation.AddItem "St. Louis, MO"
    ComboLocation.ListIndex = 0
End Sub
```

12. **Delete the OKButton and replace it with a new one named CreateButton. Insert the following code in the click code window.**

The first section of this code is used to validate the values entered by the end user to make sure that they are within the appropriate range of 1 to 999 minutes allowed for each drivetime zone. If an invalid value is found, a message box is displayed that explains what is valid, and the drivetime zones are not created.

```
Private Sub CreateButton_Click()
    Dim CityState As String

    If Val(Zone1Minutes.Text) <= 0 Then
        MsgBox " Zone 1 needs a value between 1 and 999
        minutes"
        Exit Sub
    End If

    If Val(Zone2Minutes.Text) <= 0 Then
        MsgBox " Zone 2 needs a value between 1 and 999
        minutes"
```

```
        Exit Sub
    End If

    If Val(Zone3Minutes.Text) <= O Then
        MsgBox " Zone 3 needs a value between 1 and 999
        minutes"
        Exit Sub
    End If

    Set objMap = objApp.ActiveMap

    CityState = ComboLocation.Text

    '// Get a location and zoom in
    Set objLoc =
        objMap.FindPlaceResults(CityState).Item(1)
    Set objMap.Location = objLoc

    ThreeDrivetimeZines

    Connect.Hide

End Sub
```

13. Add the following code to the end of the Form window code.

This function is used to call the function that creates the three drivetime zones as based on the values provided by the end user.

```
Function ThreeDrivetimeZones()
    Dim objMap As MapPoint.Map
    Dim objLoc As MapPoint.Location
    Dim intWidth As Integer
    Dim intHeight As Integer

    '// Create three drivetime zones
    CreateDriveTimeZone Zone1Minutes.Text
    CreateDriveTimeZone Zone2Minutes.Text
    CreateDriveTimeZone Zone3Minutes.Text

    PaintShapes 3

    intWidth = 200
    intHeight = 50

    Set objMap = objApp.ActiveMap

    Set objLoc = objMap.Location

    '// Add the textboxshape
    objMap.Shapes.AddTextbox objLoc, intWidth, intHeight

    objMap.Shapes.Item(4).Line.Weight = 1
    objMap.Shapes.Item(4).Text = Zone1Minutes.Text & ", "
```

```
& Zone2Minutes.Text & " and " & Zone3Minutes.Text & "
        Minute Drivetime Zones"

    objMap.Altitude = objMap.Altitude * 0.85

End Function
```

14. **Add the following code to the end of the Form window code.**

This function creates an individual drivetime zone.

```
Function CreateDriveTimeZone(intMinutes As Integer)
    Dim objMap As MapPoint.Map
    Dim objLoc As MapPoint.Location
    Dim objFindResults As MapPoint.FindResults
    Dim objShape As MapPoint.Shape
    Dim intMinutesDriven As Integer

On Error GoTo errhandler

    intMinutesDriven = intMinutes

    Set objMap = objApp.ActiveMap

    objMap.PlaceCategories.Visible = geoTrue

    '// Set the location of the centerpoint to center-
        point of the map
    Set objLoc = objMap.Location

    objLoc.GoTo
    objMap.Altitude = 100

    '// Calculate a drivetime zone
    Set objShape = objMap.Shapes.AddDrivetimeZone(objLoc,
        geoOneMinute * intMinutesDriven)

    Exit Function

errhandler:
    MsgBox "Error has taken place during drivetime zone
        calculation!"
    Resume Next

End Function
```

15. **Add the following code to the end of the Form window code.**

This function is used to change the fill color, line color, line weight, visible, and ZOrder properties of the newly created drivetime zones.

```
Function PaintShapes(intShapeCount As Integer)
    Dim objMap As MapPoint.Map
    Dim x As Integer
    Dim y As Integer

On Error GoTo errhandler

    Set objMap = objApp.ActiveMap
    x = 1
    y = 1 '// Used to select next forecolor...

    Do While x <= intShapeCount
        If y = 1 Then
            objMap.Shapes(x).Fill.ForeColor = &HC0FFC0
            y = y + 1
        ElseIf y = 2 Then
            objMap.Shapes(x).Fill.ForeColor = &HC0C0FF
            y = y + 1
        ElseIf y = 3 Then
            objMap.Shapes(x).Fill.ForeColor = &H80FFFF
            y = 1 '// Reset to start over again in
     Fill.Forcolor options...
        End If
        objMap.Shapes(x).Line.ForeColor = vbBlack
        objMap.Shapes(x).Line.Weight = 1
        objMap.Shapes(x).Fill.Visible = True
        objMap.Shapes(x).ZOrder geoSendBehindRoads
        objMap.Shapes(x).ZOrder geoSendToBack
        objMap.Shapes(x).SizeVisible = True

        x = x + 1
    Loop

    Exit Function

errhandler:
    MsgBox "Error painting shape.  Could be no shape is
        available."

End Function
```

16. **Save the files in the project.**

17. **Choose File⇨Make MyMapPointAddin.dll to build the .dll and rename the saved project to** `MutipleDriveTimeZonesAddin.dll`.

18. **Start MapPoint and choose Tools⇨Multiple Drivetime Zones Addin.**

    Your new COM Add-in is ready to use (see Figure 15-5)!

Figure 15-5:
The
completed
Multiple
Drivetime
Zone COM
Add-in.

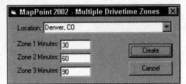

Chapter 16

Embedding MapPoint into Your Application

• •

In This Chapter

▶ Getting started with embedding the MapPoint ActiveX Control into Visual Basic

▶ Putting a MapPoint map into a Visual Basic application

▶ Making the world go 'round in code

▶ Creating the My First MapPoint Control application

• •

T he MapPoint 2002 ActiveX Control opens up a whole new world of access to the power of business mapping. You can still integrate MapPoint from within other Microsoft Office family members using their VBA, and you can build extension COM Add-ins that expand the MapPoint Office application. Additionally, you can embed key features provided by MapPoint into mission-critical Visual Basic 6.0 applications. Now you can "Control" the world!

Unlike many ActiveX Controls, you need to remember that the MapPoint ActiveX Control is not designed to be used with Microsoft Internet Explorer.

Now You Can "Control" The World!

Many users find themselves living in mission-critical applications that just so happen to not be MapPoint! Yet these applications are just ripe for the benefits that MapPoint could provide. Prior to MapPoint 2002, users could save their data in Access, Excel, or text-delimited files and open MapPoint as a separate application, and perform the tasks they needed. They could even automate and extend the features then used in MapPoint with a custom COM Add-in, but the whole process of integration with your mission-critical application was clumsier than mere normals should have to deal with.

Okay, maybe this scenario is not all that outrageous, but it's a little like going next door from your house each morning, noon, and evening to a separate building that contains your kitchen! Not a bad idea if you cook as badly as I do, but there must be a better way. The ActiveX Control provides just that approach, giving your end users complete access to everything MapPoint provides without leaving home.

Just as important, by using the MapPoint ActiveX Control you can also restrict the functionality you provide your end users so that they are more productive. Could be you don't want the end user of your mission-critical application figuring out the best route to take on their upcoming vacation. No problem. With the proper use of the control, you can provide as much or as little MapPoint functionality as desired and at the same time automate and extend your business-mapping needs.

The following samples give you a look at how easy it is to getting started with the MapPoint Control. You can feel free to pick and choose which samples you decide to play with, but we highly recommend you do them in order. These examples are just teasers but they highlight some very important basics that will serve you well later.

You can skip over the first two examples if you must, but we highly recommend that you make sure to at least review and run the My First MapPoint Control project before you go on to the next chapter. Yes, we call it the "first" even though it's the last one in this chapter, but the Generic sample is so simple it really does not qualify as a first project and the Spinning globe is cool but limited (just as spinning a basketball on your finger doesn't qualify as a real basketball game). Trust us in that you will find the My First MapPoint Control project worthy of your time.

Big Can Be Truly Beautiful!

It's extremely important to note that the MapPoint ActiveX Control is the world's fattest control, and Microsoft appears to be very proud of that fact. In a world in which thin is perceived to be better, this may appear to be undesirable; if you look closer, you will find that it is only possible to control the world if you have access to that world.

Unlike other mapping controls that you can use, the "big is beautiful" nature of MapPoint requires some room for maneuvering but provides access to the control the entire world! Check out Appendix A to get a detailed account of the size of the control and the required map files.

The sample projects in this chapter include:

- ✔ **Generic:** Just the map, please! This is not a very functional example but it's the foundation from which you will always start.

- ✔ **Spin or Goto It:** Make the world go around or go right to a specific point on the earth. This sample highlights the navigation principles within MapPoint that are important if you want to see the results of your efforts.

- ✔ **My First MapPoint:** Use this project to create your first true MapPoint Control Visual Basic sample. With this project, you can see how to import data. It also holds a nice surprise worthy of your time!

Starting with the Generic Project

This is the simplest of examples using the MapPoint ActiveX Control. All it does is display a map within a Visual Basic 6.0 form. Not a very worthy cause if that's all you do with it, but it also comes in handy when new developers need a jump start in getting a MapPoint map on a Visual Basic form. And it serves as a good launching point should you ever need to build numerous different projects using the control. Do the initial work once and then use it over and over again. That's what we did when we created each of the following samples.

You can find a completed copy of this sample code on CD1 in the code samples folder.

1. **Install MapPoint 2002 if you haven't already (see Appendix A for installation help.)**

   By default, the MapPoint ActiveX Control will also be installed at the same time and ready to use.

2. **Create a new Visual Basic 6.0 Standard.EXE project.**

3. **Choose Project⇨Components because you need to add the MapPoint Control to the Visual Basic toolbox.**

   The Components dialog box will appear (see Figure 16-1).

4. **Scroll down and check the Microsoft Mappoint Control 9.0; then click OK.**

   The MapPoint Control icon will appear in the toolbox (see Figure 16-2).

   Adding the MapPoint Control automatically provides access to the MapPoint Type Library. Chose View⇨Object Browser. You can then select the MappointCtl library, in which you can explore the MapPoint object model syntax (see Figure 16-3).

Figure 16-1:
Scroll down
the list of
components
until you
find the
Microsoft
Mappoint
Control 9.0
and click
OK.

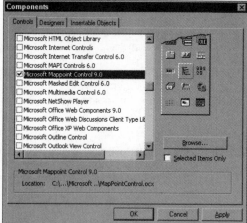

Figure 16-2:
The
MapPoint
tool button
is shaped
like a
Pushpin.

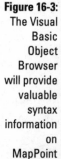

Figure 16-3:
The Visual
Basic
Object
Browser
will provide
valuable
syntax
information
on
MapPoint
Control
objects.

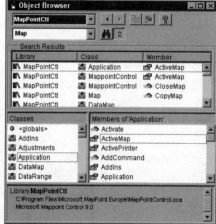

5. **Select the MapPoint Control from the toolbox and draw the control onto the form (see Figure 16-4).**

   In the Design mode, the MapPoint Control is a white rectangle with the MapPoint Pushpin icon in the center.

6. **Add code that will display a default map; to do so, use one of the following methods:**

   • If you have the North American edition of MapPoint, add the following code to the Form Load code window:

```
Sub Form_Load()
    MappointControl1.NewMap geoMapNorthAmerica
End Sub
```

   • If you have the European edition of MapPoint, add the following code to the Form Load code window:

```
Sub Form_Load()
    MappointControl1.NewMap geoMapEurope
End Sub
```

The MapPoint control works with either edition, so you can switch back and forth between European and North American maps if you have both editions installed on your PC.

You can load an existing MapPoint map (with the extension .ptm) or MapPoint template (with the extension .ptt) file by using the `MappointControl OpenMap` method.

Figure 16-4:
The MapPoint Control is a white rectangle with the Pushpin logo in the center when it is placed on a Visual basic form.

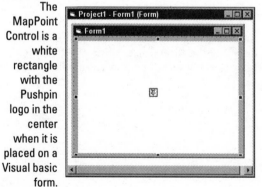

When you run the preceding project, notice that you can zoom and pan the map using the mouse or arrow keys after you have selected the map by clicking it. You also have access to the right-click pop-up menus. Any changes you make to the map's view, or through the functionality available from the pop-up menus, will cause the MapPoint Control's Activemap.Saved property to be set to False. This will cause a Map Save dialog box to appear when you close the application (see Figure 16-5). Unless you set the `Activemap.Saved` method to `True`, the MapPoint Control will always prompt end users to see whether they want to save any map that has been changed in any manner, including panning and zooming.

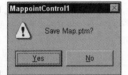

Figure 16-5:
A Map Save
dialog box.

You can avoid the generation of this dialog box by using the following code:

```
Sub Form_Unload(Cancel As Integer)
    MappointControl1.ActiveMap.Saved = True
End Sub
```

Spinning the Globe: The Spin and Goto It Project

This project sounds a little like the name of a children's board game, but taking control of the world and deciding the direction it spins and the angle of the rotation is something that the Greek god Atlas did on a regular basis.

With a flick of his hand, he could also hold the world at any distance, looking at any specific location with ease. With this simple example, you can do the same without the added weight of the entire Earth on your shoulders. At first this undertaking may seem more like play than practical work, but being able to deliberately move around within MapPoint is very important. This project also demonstrates the methods used to change the map style, font size display, and globe view versus flat map settings. If you are looking for a way to go to a specific address on the map, you will find an example in the Find Project in Chapter 17.

You can find a completed copy of this sample code on CD1 in the code samples folder.

To begin the project, follow the instructions from the Generic sample at the start of this chapter to get a MapPoint Control on a Visual Basic form. Resize the MapPoint Control to leave room for the new buttons, labels, and textboxes on the left. Then, follow these steps:

1. **Insert the following two lines of code in the general declarations section of Form1.**

   The first variable, SpinDirection, defines the direction of the spin and the KeepMoving variable toggles the rotation of the map on and off.

   ```
   Public SpinDirection As Integer
   Public KeepMoving As Boolean
   ```

2. **Add the code that follows this step's text to the Form_Load section.**

   This is where you set the KeepMoving variable to True so that the map rotates as the application opens and launches a North American map. You also set the objMap.MapStyle to the political style (geoMapStylePolitical) and the font size to the very smallest size. Feel free to change the settings on the last two to see how the map style and font size change the look of the map. The Object Browser in Visual Basic lists all the available geo constants built into the control.

Note that from here on, you will often be declaring a `MapPointCtl` map and a location object. You will use these to reference the appropriate MapPoint map (in this case, the `.ActiveMap`) and to reference the appropriate location for any action that you take. You can have multiple locations defined at any one time, so you need to make sure that you act on the correct one.

```
Private Sub Form_Load()
    Dim objMap As MapPointCtl.Map
    Dim objLoc As MapPointCtl.Location

    KeepMoving = True

    '// Open a North American map

    Me.MappointControl1.NewMap geoMapNorthAmerica

    '// Set the map object to the current map

    Set objMap = MappointControl1.ActiveMap

    '// Set the location to Latitude 15.0000,
    '// Longitude 0.0000 & Altitude 35,000 miles.
    '// This is roughly somewhere along the
    '// southern border of Mali, Africa and only
    '// significant in that it makes the rotating
    '// globe look more natural to those in
    '// the northern hemisphere.

    Set objLoc = objMap.GetLocation(15, 0, 35000)

    '// Move the location settings

    objLoc.GoTo

    '// Set the projection so that you will
    '// see a globe instead of a flat
    '// map at higher altitudes

    objMap.Projection = geoGlobeViewWhenZoomedOut

    '// Change the map style to the Political style

    objMap.MapStyle = geoMapStylePolitical

    '// Set the font to the smallest size

    objMap.MapFont = geoMapFontSmallest

    '// Set the starting spin direction to the west.

    SpinDirection = geoWest
End Sub
```

3. **Set the MapPoint Control's Activemap.Saved value to True to avoid presenting a Map Save dialog box to your end users when they close the application.**

In the real world, you may not do this because you may want to prompt users to save any changes they make to the map, but in this sample we don't care to save the world. You can just create a new one the next time you use the project. Acting as Atlas comes with much power.

```
Private Sub Form_Unload(Cancel As Integer)
    MappointControl1.ActiveMap.Saved = True
End Sub
```

4. **Draw a Visual Basic timer control onto the form. It does not matter where you place the timer control because it will be invisible at runtime.**

You will use this timer to control the movement and speed of the globe.

Level its name set to the default `Timer1` so that it will match the following code sample. Add code that will pan the map in the direction specified in the `SpinDirection` variable if the `KeepMoving` variable is set to true. The 0.01 setting is an optional `Double` expressed as a fraction of the screen width or height for each pan step. In this example, the world moves too fast if you do not provide this optional value.

```
Private Sub Timer1_Timer()
    Dim objMap As MapPointCtl.Map
    Set objMap = MappointControl1.ActiveMap

    If KeepMoving = True Then

    '// Pan(AKA, spin) the map in the
    '// direction specified and in steps
    '// expressed as a fraction of the
    '// screen width or height.

        objMap.Pan SpinDirection, 0.01
    End If

    MappointControl1.ActiveMap.Saved = True
End Sub
```

5. **Create the buttons that you will use to set the value of the SpinDirection variable and adjust the direction of the spin.**

With the following code, you're adding the four buttons: Command1, Command2, Command3, and Command4. The completed form should look like the one in Figure 16-6. The code also changes the caption value to `West`, `East`, `North`, and `South`, respectively. We find it best to change the name and add the code directly after we add each new button instead of waiting until we have them all on the form.

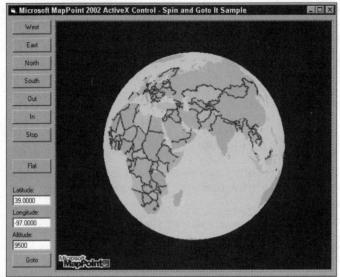

Figure 16-6:
The Spin
and Goto It
Project
Form1; leave
room for the
buttons on
the left.

```
Private Sub Command1_Click()

    '// Spin to the West

    SpinDirection = geoWest
End Sub

Private Sub Command2_Click()

    '// Spin to the East

    SpinDirection = geoEast
End Sub

Private Sub Command3_Click()

    '// Go North to the top of the earth. Once you go all
    '// the way to the North Pole it will stop.

    SpinDirection = geoNorth

End Sub

Private Sub Command4_Click()

    '// Go South to the bottom of the earth
    '// Once you go all the way to the
    '// South Pole it will stop.

    SpinDirection = geoSouth
End Sub
```

6. **Add buttons Command5 and Command6 and add the code that you will use to adjust the viewing altitude of the map.**

   This code changes the viewing altitude up and down 500 miles at a time.

   ```
   Private Sub Command5_Click()

       '// Move out from the earth

       Dim objMap As MapPointCtl.Map
       Set objMap = MappointControl1.ActiveMap
       objMap.Altitude = objMap.Altitude + 500
   End Sub

   Private Sub Command6_Click()

       '// Move in to the earth

       Dim objMap As MapPointCtl.Map
       Set objMap = MappointControl1.ActiveMap
       objMap.Altitude = objMap.Altitude - 500
   End Sub
   ```

7. **Enter the following code to add the Command7 button and change its caption to Stop.**

   You do this so that end users have a way of stopping the world should they want to get off!

   This code toggles the `KeepMoving` variable between `True` and `False` and renames the caption so that users will know what action it will perform when they next select it. This is the last line of code needed to support the spin concept of their project. Go ahead and run the project and give it a try before you move on to the Goto feature.

   ```
   Private Sub Command7_Click()
       If KeepMoving = True Then
           KeepMoving = False
           Command7.Caption = "Rotate"
       Else
           KeepMoving = True
           Command7.Caption = "Stop"
       End If
   End Sub
   ```

8. **Add the Command8 button to the form and change its caption to Stop.**

   In addition to declaring the `objMap` and `objLoc` objects, you also need to declare variables for the longitude, latitude, and altitude of the location you want to "goto." Note that this code also stops the rotation by setting the `KeepMoving` variable to false.

   The code also performs simple error checking to make sure that the latitude, longitude, and altitude settings provided by the end user are within valid ranges.

```
Private Sub Command8_Click()
    Dim objMap As MapPointCtl.Map
    Dim objLoc As MapPointCtl.Location
    Dim Latitude, Longitude, Altitude As Long

    '// Stop the rotation in preparation for the goto

    KeepMoving = False
    Command7.Caption = "Rotate"

    '// Set the map object to the current map

    Set objMap = MappointControl1.ActiveMap

    '// Set the location Latitude,
    '// Longitude & Altitude to values
    '// entered in Text1, Text2 & Text2

    Latitude = Val(Text1.Text)
    Longitude = Val(Text2.Text)
    Altitude = Val(Text3.Text)

    '// Check to make sure the Latitude is
    '// within allowable range

    If Latitude < -90 Or Latitude > 90 Then
        MsgBox ("Latitude outside of allowable range!")
        Exit Sub
    End If

    '// Check to make sure the Longitude is
    '// within allowable range

    If Longitude < -180 Or Longitude > 180 Then
        MsgBox ("Longitude outside of allowable range!")
        Exit Sub
    End If

    '// Check to make sure the Altitude is
    '// within allowable range

    If Altitude < 1 Or Altitude > 50000 Then
        MsgBox ("Altitude outside of allowable range!")
        Exit Sub
    End If

    Set objLoc = objMap.GetLocation(Latitude, Longitude,
        Altitude)

    '// Move the location settings

    objLoc.GoTo
End Sub
```

9. Add the Command9 button to the form and change its caption property to Flat.

Add the following code to set the projection of the map. In simple terms this means the world is either flat or round. It's sort of a modern-day, politically correct approach that accommodates both Columbus and those who believe the world is really flat.

The action and name of this button changes depending on what action is last performed by the end user.

```
Private Sub Command9_Click()
    Dim objMap As MapPointCtl.Map

    '// Set the map object to the current map
    Set objMap = MappointControl1.ActiveMap

    If Command9.Caption = "Flat" Then

    '// Set the projection so that you will
    '// see a globe instead of a flat map
    '// at higher altitudes

        objMap.Projection = geoFlatViewWhenZoomedOut
        Command9.Caption = "Globe"
    Else

    '// Set the projection so that you will
    '// see a globe instead of a flat map
    '//  at higher altitudes

        objMap.Projection = geoGlobeViewWhenZoomedOut
        Command9.Caption = "Flat"
    End If
End Sub
```

Depending on the speed of your PC, you will experience different rates of speed in the panning results with this project. Slower PCs spin the map slower and can resemble an old family movie with a choppy stutter. MapPoint undertakes an enormous volume of work as you request a new view of the earth. In the lion's share of real projects you will build, this should not be a problem. Even then, it goes to show that acting like the Greek god Atlas is a lot more work than any mere normal would normally undertake.

My First MapPoint Project

So here we are ready to create your first true MapPoint application! We promise that the outcome will be informative and full of insight. Getting a MapPoint map to display in Visual Basic and then getting the world to spin around can hardly be considered real applications. In the tradition of any new programming language or environment, you now have the opportunity to build My First MapPoint application.

You can find a completed copy of this sample code on CD1 in the code samples folder.

The task at hand is to take a simple Excel file (a copy of the required Excel file named RandomDataPoints.xls can be found on CD1 in the code samples folder) with random latitude and longitude pairs and plot them onto a map (see Figure 16-7 for a view of the application before the random data is plotted). Not too complicated, as you will see. Remember that the reason for doing this is to see what type of insight you can gain from data that has geographic references. Open the Excel file and take a look at the first selection of rows of data in the spreadsheet and see whether you can gain any insight. When we first looked at it, we did not even know what general region the points would plot on the globe. It's important for cartographers to remember that positive is North and to the East and negative is South and to the West, but it may be hard to know what the data is showing. Let's get on with plotting it and see what happens.

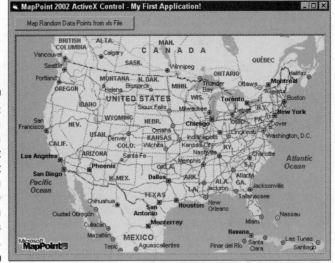

Figure 16-7: This is a view of the My First MapPoint Application before the random data is plotted.

1. **Follow the instructions from the Generic sample to get a MapPoint Control on a Visual Basic form.**

2. **Resize the MapPoint Control on the form, this time leaving room for the one new button at the top of the form:**

```
Private Sub Form_Load()
    '// Creates a new map. You must specify
    '// either the map region (geoMapEurope or
    '// geoMapNorthAmerica) to open the default
    '// template for that region or a file name of
    '// a template to use for the new map.

    Me.MappointControl1.NewMap geoMapNorthAmerica
End Sub
```

3. **Add the Command1 button and add the following code to the Command1_Click code window.**

We like to declare a string variable to store the path and filename of the source Excel file. You can extend the functionality of this code to use the common dialog box, but we save doing that for the next chapter.

This code also declares `Map`, `DataSet`, and `Pushpin` objects.

The powerful portion of this code is the `.ImportData` method, through which you import the data on the map object.

Just to make it look cleaner, you're also changing the Pushpin symbol from the default black-and-white Pushpin to a red circle. You then move the map to see the data by using the `.ZoomTo` method on the `DataSet` object. Here is a way to navigate around the world to get a view of just what you want.

```
Private Sub Command1_Click()
    Dim FilePathAndName As String
    Dim objMap As MapPointCtl.Map
    Dim objDataSet As MapPointCtl.DataSet
    Dim objPushPin As MapPointCtl.Pushpin

    '// Define the path and file of the data source
    '// In this instance we are opening an Excel file
    '// and reading the data from Sheet1.

    FilePathAndName = App.Path & _
        "\RandomDataPoints.xls!Sheet1"

    '// Returns the Map object that is visible
    '// from the MapPoint Control

    Set objMap = MappointControl1.ActiveMap

    '// Import data into a dataset
    '// Similar to the Import Data Wizard

    Set objDataSet =
```

```
objMap.DataSets.ImportData(FilePathAndName)

    '// Set the Pushpin symbol for the Pushpin set
    '// 25 is a large red circle

    objDataSet.Symbol = 25

    '// Zooms to the best map view of the
    '// specified DataSet object

    objDataSet.ZoomTo

End Sub
```

4. **Enter the following code to set the MapPoint Control's Activemap.Saved value to True to avoid presenting a Map Save dialog box to your end users when they close the application.**

In the real world, you may not do this because you may want to prompt users to save any changes they make to the map.

```
Private Sub Form_Unload(Cancel As Integer)

    '// Any changes, including zooming and panning,
    '// made to the map causes this the ActiveMap.Saved
    '// to be set to false and the end user will be
    '// prompted by the MapPoint engine to see if they
    '// want to save the changed map. Setting it to
    '// true will eliminate this prompt but the map
    '// file will not contain any of the changes made.

    MappointControl1.ActiveMap.Saved = True

End Sub
```

Now, run the project and see what you get! Just think of the amount of time it would have taken to do this same task with a paper map and those little red Pushpins. And, really, would it have been as rewarding and insightful as the My First MapPoint Control application?

The MapPoint Control and Visual Studio .NET

One of the extremely cool aspects of Visual Studio .NET is the new Common Langauge Runtime (CLR). This foundation sits under all the programming languages and will allow the flexibility of not only using the MapPoint Control with Visual Basic .NET but also allowing you to pick and choose any language that works within the Visual Studio Framework. The obvious choice would include C++ and the new C# (pronounced C Sharp). And, although, we have yet to try it, there appears to be no reason that you can't use the control with SmallTalk, FORTRAN, or COBAL or any of the other 30-plus langauges supported by CLR! You can check out our Web site to view some samples that go beyond Visual Basic. Who knows, if we have any luck and can find an aging programmer who can talk human, we may even have a COBAL example!

Chapter 17

More Embedding MapPoint into Your Application

So, now you long for more control! Controlling the world is a very addictive activity. In Chapter 16, we provide you with samples that show you how to get started. In this chapter, you can see how to do something real.

We designed the four projects in this chapter to give you control of the working end of the MapPoint object model. These projects prepare you to launch out and explore the remaining 90 percent of the power you have yet to tap into! Don't let that scare you. Gain an understanding of these four areas and you can go anywhere you want with complete control and with very little effort.

The following list provides a brief overview of the sample projects in this chapter:

✔ **Route Project:** A quick three-point routing sample that shows how easy it is to figure out how to get around the country.

✔ **Import Project:** Simple project that imports Microsoft Excel and Microsoft Access datasets.

✔ **Query Project:** Basic example that shows how to create drawing shapes and how to query them to find out what datasets and data records are within the shapes.

✔ **Find Project:** The secrets to finding anything in the world! A custom Find dialog box example that mimics the MapPoint Find dialog box.

Creating a Route with the Route Project

The Route Project example in this section demonstrates the creation and calculation of a simple route that contains a start, stop, and end (see Figure 17-1).

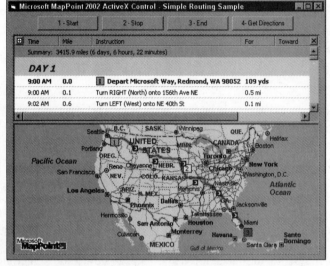

Figure 17-1:
The Route Project enables you to create a simple route that has a start, a stop, and an end.

This example is completely functional with predictable results if you click the buttons you will create in order (button 1, 2, 3, and then 4), but it's not very robust in terms of the power of routing within MapPoint and the MapPoint ActiveX Control.

The Route Project lacks error checking and declares the start, stop, and end of the route in the order that each button is pressed. The code supporting the Get Directions button will also fail if a user doesn't select two points in a route at minimum. Even so, this sample is more powerful than the "free" online routes you can get from numerous Web sites. These Web sites will offer you the option of declaring a start and an end (Point A and Point B) to any journey. If the route you want to take share a common location for the start and the end (for example, getting back home at the end of the day), you will have already used up your point A/B allocation. This sample includes a point A, B, and C, with C being a stop-off point along the way. With very little work, you will be able to extend the functionality of this project to include any number of stop-off points and then return to your A or B point.

Follow these steps to create your Route Project.

1. **Follow the instructions from the Generic sample in Chapter 16 (also located on CD1 in the code samples folder) to get the MapPoint control on a Visual Basic form.**

2. **Add four buttons to the form.**

   Leave the default names of Command1, Command2, Command3, and Command4. Modify the caption of each to read as displayed below.

3. **Type the following code in the Command1_Click code window.**

```
Private Sub Command1_Click()
    Dim objMap As MapPointCtl.Map
    Dim objLoc As MapPointCtl.Location

    '// Set the map object to the current map

    Set objMap = Me.MappointControl1.ActiveMap

    '// Find a specific location

    Set objLoc = objMap.FindResults("One Microsoft Way,
        Redmond, WA").Item(1)

    '// Add the location to the route

    objMap.ActiveRoute.Waypoints.Add objLoc

    '// Move the best map view for this
    '// location object

    objLoc.GoTo

End Sub
```

You're using the .FindResults method to locate and identify the addresses that you want to use for the route. The Item(1) perimeter at the end of this method forces a selection to the best match found by MapPoint.

Note that the lines of code that start with the '// represent comments in the sample code. You don't need them for this code to work but we include them as samples of how to document your code for later reference.

4. **Type the following code in the Command2_Click code window.**

```
Private Sub Command2_Click()
    Dim objMap As MapPointCtl.Map
    Dim objLoc As MapPointCtl.Location

    '// Set the map object to the current map

    Set objMap = Me.MappointControl1.ActiveMap

    '// Find a specific location

    Set objLoc = objMap.FindResults("603 Fulton Street,
```

```
           Remsen, IA").Item(1)

    '// Add the location to the route

    objMap.ActiveRoute.Waypoints.Add objLoc

    '// Move the best map view for this
    '// location object

    objLoc.GoTo

End Sub
```

5. Type the following code in the Command3_Click code window.

```
Private Sub Command3_Click()
    Dim objMap As MapPointCtl.Map
    Dim objLoc As MapPointCtl.Location

    '// Set the map object to the current map

    Set objMap = Me.MappointControl1.ActiveMap

    '// Find a specific location

    Set objLoc = objMap.FindResults("1901 Convention
        Center Dr, Miami Beach, FL  33139").Item(1)

    '// Add the location to the route

    objMap.ActiveRoute.Waypoints.Add objLoc

    '// Move the best map view for this
    '// location object

    objLoc.GoTo

End Sub
```

6. Type the following code in the Command4_Click code window.

```
Private Sub Command4_Click()
    Dim objMap As MapPointCtl.Map

    Set objMap = Me.MappointControl1.ActiveMap

    '//Calculate the route

    objMap.ActiveRoute.Calculate

End Sub
```

This is all the magic code that you need to cause the control to run around on all 6.4 million miles of routable streets and roads and return with a route map and the turn-by-turn directions.

So now you know how far it is across the country from the northwest to the southeast with a stop in the heartlands. Not sure why anybody would want to stop off in Remsen, Iowa (birthplace of one of your authors!)? Just for fun, try changing the addresses to places that make sense to you. You may discover that the FindResults method does not always give you an exact match for what you expect. This is because the method returns a list of possible matches for the address or place that you provide, but the Item.(1) at the end of the method is MapPoint's way of forcing it to select the very first one in the list. By design, this one is the location that MapPoint believes is the best fit. MapPoint is not always as intuitive as humans, and from time to time its first choice is not what you would pick. Later, in the Find Project at the end of this chapter, we explore ways to show the entire list of results and allow you to pick the one that you like best.

Importing Data with the Import Project

See the previous section to find out how to create your first real application and gain the power to avoid that dreaded task of having to stop and ask for directions. In this section, you can see how the power of MapPoint and the MapPoint ActiveX control goes much deeper.

This example demonstrates how easy it is to import data from Microsoft Excel and Access files. The My First MapPoint Project sample in Chapter 16 does a little data importing. When you import the sample files that we included on the CD, you will see a window like the one in Figure 17-2.

Again, you can follow the instructions from the Generic sample to get a MapPoint control on a Visual Basic form. Resize the MapPoint control and this time leave room for the two new buttons at the top of the form. (If you used the Generic sample in the previous section, you can just copy it over to a new folder, rename it, and save yourself the time of retyping it.) The Generic sample is the first step in all the samples.

1. **Add two new buttons to the form.**

   Leave the default names of Command1 and Command2. Modify the caption of each to read as displayed below.

2. **Type the following code in the Form_Load code window.**

```
Private Sub Form_Load()
    '// Creates a new North American map.

    Me.MappointControl1.NewMap geoMapNorthAmerica
End Sub
```

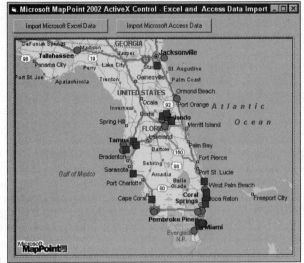

Figure 17-2:
Importing
data from
Microsoft
Access and
Excel.

3. **Type the following code in the Command1_Click code window.**

At the risk of repeating ourselves, we repeat ourselves: The code is almost identical to the My First MapPoint Control application code for the Command1_Click code, so you can cut and paste from that application to save time.

```
Private Sub Command1_Click()
    Dim objDataSet As MapPointCtl.DataSet
    Dim objMap As MapPointCtl.Map
    Dim objPushPin As MapPointCtl.Pushpin
    Dim FileName as String
    Dim FilePathAndName As String

    '// Define the path and file of the data source
    '// Note that in this instance we are opening an
    '// Excel file and reading the data from Sheet1.

    FileName      = "\FloridaAddresses.xls!Sheet1"
    FilePathAndName = App.Path & FileName

    '// Returns the Map object that is visible
    '// from the MapPoint Control

    Set objMap = MappointControl1.ActiveMap

    '// Change the mousepointer

    Screen.MousePointer = vbHourglass

    '// Import data into a dataset.
```

```
'// This is similar to the Import Data Wizard

Set objDataSet =
    objMap.DataSets.ImportData(FilePathAndName)

'// Set the Pushpin symbol for the Pushpin set
'// 25 is a large red circle

objDataSet.Symbol = 25

'// Zooms to the best map view of the
'// specified DataSet object

objDataSet.ZoomTo

'// Change the mousepointer
Screen.MousePointer = vbNormal

End Sub
```

4. Set the MapPoint control's Activemap.Saved value to False by typing the following code.

```
Private Sub Form_Unload(Cancel As Integer)
    '// Any changes, including zooming and panning,
    '// made to the map causes this the ActiveMap.Saved
    '// to be set to false and the end user will be
    '// prompted by the MapPoint engine to see if they
    '// want to save the changed map. Setting it to
    '// true will eliminate this prompt but the map
    '// file will also not contain any of the changes
    '// made.

    MappointControl1.ActiveMap.Saved = True
End Sub
```

You do this to avoid presenting a map save dialog box to your end users when they close the application. In the real world, you can't do this because you may want to prompt them to save any changes they make to the map, but in this sample, we don't want to save the map because we can just create a new one next time we use the project.

5. Add the following code to the Command2_Click code window.

This code is very much like the code for Command1_Click, but now you are importing data from Access rather than Excel. You can simplify your work here by cutting and pasting the Command1 form (that you filled out for the Route Project earlier in this chapter, if you created that project). Then do the following: Change the value in the FileName variable to point to the Access .MDB file; update the .ImportData method to include the geoImportAccessTable parameter; and just for fun, change the Pushpin symbol variable to equal 44 for large blue squares.

```
Private Sub Command2_Click()
    Dim objDatasets As MapPointCtl.DataSets
    Dim objDataSet As MapPointCtl.DataSet
    Dim objMap As MapPointCtl.Map
    Dim objPushPin As MapPointCtl.Pushpin
    Dim FileName as String
    Dim FilePathAndName As String

    '// Define the path and file of the data source
    '// Note that in this instance we are opening an
    '// Access file and reading the data from the
    '// Customers table.

    FileName = "\FloridaAddresses.mdb!Customers"
    FilePathAndName = App.Path & FileName

    '// Returns the Map object that is visible from
    '// the MapPoint Control

    Set objMap = MappointControl1.ActiveMap

    '// Get the DataSets collection

    Set objDatasets = objMap.DataSets

    '// Change the mousepointer

    Screen.MousePointer = vbHourglass

    '// Import data into a dataset
    '// Similar to the Import Data Wizard

    Set objDataSet =
        objDatasets.ImportData(FilePathAndName, ,
        geoCountryUnitedStates, , geoImportAccessTable)

    '// Set the Pushpin symbol for the Pushpin set
    '// 44 is a large blue square.

    objDataSet.Symbol = 44

    '// Zooms to the best map view of the specified
        DataSet object

    objDataSet.ZoomTo

    '// Change the mousepointer

    Screen.MousePointer = vbNormal
End Sub
```

With very little effort, you can also extend this example to import data from a text-delimited file, your Microsoft Outlook contact address file, or you can even create a Microsoft Universal data link and tap into Microsoft SQL Server. Check out the MapPoint online help for more details.

Querying Closed Shapes: The Query Project

The previous project shows how to import data from Microsoft Excel and Access. You can also place layers on a map for the demographics data provided with MapPoint. After you place this data on a map, you can look at it to gain insight. Getting to some subset of the data that is geographically specified would also be very handy, however. Within MapPoint the application, you can export the data contained in any closed drawing shape to Excel. The Query Project provides an example of the power to create and then query ovals, rectangles, and polygons in code (see Figure 17-3 below). With a little extra coding, the results can be written out into a .cvs file that can be opened in Excel. Here, we display it in a standard Visual Basic grid control.

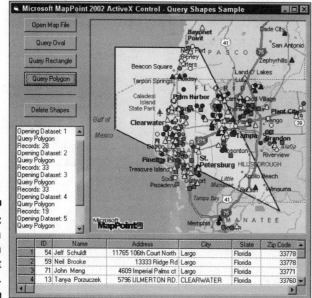

Figure 17-3:
Query data
from within
a MapPoint
file.

You can use the `FloridaAddresses.ptm` that can be found on CD1 in the code sample folder with this sample code to see the power of this feature. Follow these steps to find the wealth within.

1. **Follow the instructions from the Generic sample to get a MapPoint control on a Visual Basic form, but leave room for the other controls that you will be placing on the form.**

2. **Type the following code to declare a new North American map and also call the PrepareGrid function:**

```
Private Sub Form_Load()
    Me.MappointControl1.NewMap geoMapNorthAmerica
    PrepareGrid
End Sub
```

3. **Type the following code in the General Declarations code window of the form.**

The `PrepareGrid` function is a simple way to format the MSFlexGrid control so that the data from the `FloridaAddresses.ptm` file will look good.

```
Function PrepareGrid()

    '// Formatting of the grid to make it
    '// look good. Nothing special here.

    MSFlexGrid1.Cols = 9
    MSFlexGrid1.Rows = 12
    MSFlexGrid1.Row = 0
    MSFlexGrid1.Col = 0
    MSFlexGrid1.ColWidth(0) = 500
    MSFlexGrid1.CellAlignment = flexAlignCenterCenter
    MSFlexGrid1.Text = ""
    MSFlexGrid1.Col = 1
    MSFlexGrid1.ColWidth(1) = 500
    MSFlexGrid1.CellAlignment = flexAlignCenterCenter
    MSFlexGrid1.Text = "ID"
    MSFlexGrid1.Col = 2
    MSFlexGrid1.ColWidth(2) = 1500
    MSFlexGrid1.CellAlignment = flexAlignCenterCenter
    MSFlexGrid1.Text = "Name"
    MSFlexGrid1.Col = 3
    MSFlexGrid1.ColWidth(3) = 2000
    MSFlexGrid1.CellAlignment = flexAlignCenterCenter
    MSFlexGrid1.Text = "Address"
    MSFlexGrid1.Col = 4
    MSFlexGrid1.ColWidth(4) = 1450
    MSFlexGrid1.CellAlignment = flexAlignCenterCenter
    MSFlexGrid1.Text = "City"
    MSFlexGrid1.Col = 5
    MSFlexGrid1.ColWidth(5) = 800
    MSFlexGrid1.CellAlignment = flexAlignCenterCenter
```

```
MSFlexGrid1.Text = "State"
MSFlexGrid1.Col = 6
MSFlexGrid1.ColWidth(6) = 1000
MSFlexGrid1.CellAlignment = flexAlignCenterCenter
MSFlexGrid1.Text = "Zip Code"
MSFlexGrid1.Col = 7
MSFlexGrid1.ColWidth(7) = 1500
MSFlexGrid1.CellAlignment = flexAlignCenterCenter
MSFlexGrid1.Text = "Phone"
MSFlexGrid1.Col = 8
MSFlexGrid1.ColWidth(8) = 1000
MSFlexGrid1.CellAlignment = flexAlignCenterCenter
MSFlexGrid1.Text = "Region"

End Function
```

4. **Add a new button to the form and rename it CommandOpenMapFile, and then change its caption property to Open Map File.**

If you went through the previous examples, you know that the example had you declare in code the path and filename of the files that you used. This example takes a little more advanced approach and uses the common dialog box that comes with Visual Basic so that you can perform simple navigation around your computer to find and open the files you want to use. This example adds some basic error handling to this code to keep the application from crashing should you attempt to open a file that is not a real MapPoint file but one that shares the .PTM filename extension.

```
Private Sub CommandOpenMapFile_Click ()
    Dim objMap As MapPointCtl.Map

On Error GoTo errhandler

    '// Set up the common dialog control so
    '// that if the cancel button is pressed, it
    '// generates a runtime error that can be caught.

    CommonDialog1.CancelError = True

    '// Load the open dialog box and return
    '// the selected file path into the
    '// variable strCurrentMPPathandFile

    CommonDialog1.Filter = _
    "MapPoint Maps (*.ptm)|*.ptm*|MapPoint Templates
        (*.ptt)|*.ptt*"
    CommonDialog1.ShowOpen
    strCurrentMPPathandFile = CommonDialog1.FileName

    '// Open the map or template file into
```

```
'// the MapPoint Control

Me.MappointControl1.OpenMap strCurrentMPPathandFile

'// Always need to point to the active
'// map before changing any settings.

Set objMap = MappointControl1.ActiveMap
intCurrentFont = objMap.MapFont
intCurrentMapStyle = objMap.MapStyle

'// Any change to setting, including panning
'// and zooming, made to the active map will cause
'// it to appear as dirt and in need of being
'// saved. Because this is a first time viewing of
'// this map template I know it is really clean so
'// I force the saved setting to avoid having the
'// ActiveX Control prompt me to save the dirty map
'// upon either the loading of a new map or the
'// closing of the application.

Me.MappointControl1.ActiveMap.Saved = True

Exit Sub

errhandler:
    MsgBox "Error in opening map file. Could be you are
        attempting to open " & _
        "a map of Europe without having the Europe
        version of MapPoint or " & _
            "a map of North America without having the
        North American version of MapPoint"

End Sub
```

5. **Add three buttons to the window and rename the CommandQueryOval, CommandQueryPolygon, and CommandQueryRectangle.**

Change the caption property of each one to read Query Oval, Query Polygon, and Query Rectangle, respectively. When clicked, each of these buttons will call the QueryDataSet function and pass a perimeter that indicates what type of query passed on the type of shape is to be performed. You will find this code already created on CD1 in the sample code folder.

```
Private Sub CommandQueryOval_Click()
    QueryDataset "mpOval"
End Sub
Private Sub CommandQueryPolygon_Click()
    QueryDataset "mpPolygon"
End Sub
Private Sub CommandQueryRectangle_Click()
    QueryDataset "mpRectangle"
End Sub
```

6. **Add the following code to the project, making sure to correctly declare each of the objects listed below.**

By now you may be familiar with the Map and DataSet objects and the methods we use with them. We also use the Recordset, Location, and Field objects.

```
Function QueryDataset(ShapeType As String)
    Dim objMap As MapPointCtl.Map
    Dim objRecordset As MapPointCtl.Recordset
    Dim objDataSet As MapPointCtl.DataSet
    Dim objLoc As MapPointCtl.Location
    Dim objLocs(1 To 5) As MapPointCtl.Location
    Dim objField As MapPointCtl.Field
    Dim intRadius As Integer
    Dim intRecWidth As Integer
    Dim intRecHeight As Integer
    Dim val As String
    Dim vals(1 To 20) As String
    Dim intFieldCount As Integer
    Dim strRowText As String
    Dim i As Integer
    Dim j As Integer
    Dim x As Integer
    Dim iTotalRecordCount As Integer
    Dim shapeCreated As Boolean

On Error GoTo errhandler

    Me.MappointControl1.MousePointer = vbHourglass

    Me.MSFlexGrid1.Clear
    PrepareGrid
    Refresh

    Set objMap = Me.MappointControl1.ActiveMap

    iTotalRecordCount = 0
    i = 1
    shapeCreated = False

    'Empty the flexgrid control before filling it with
        new rows.
    MSFlexGrid1.Redraw = False
    KillAllRowsButFirst
    Text1.Text = ""

    Do While i <=
        Me.MappointControl1.ActiveMap.DataSets.Count

        Set objDataSet =
```

```
        Me.MappointControl1.ActiveMap.DataSets(i)

        Select Case ShapeType

        Case "mpOval" ' Oval Shape

'// In this section of the code we will:
'// 1. Set the radius of a circle
'//    (although it could be an oval)
'// 2. Raise the altitude of the map view
'//    to better display the circle
'// 3. Draw the circle on the map.
'// 4. Name the shape we just drew
'// 5. Change the line color of the circle
'// 6. Change the fill color of the circle
'//    and make it visible
'// 7. Move the circle behind the roads
'// 8. Set the recordset to those records
'//    from the current dataset that are
'//    within the circle

        Text1.Text = Text1.Text & vbCrLf & "Opening
        Dataset: " & i & vbCrLf & "Query Oval"
            Refresh
            Beep

            If shapeCreated = False Then

'// Set the radius for the circle

                intRadius = 100

'// Select the center of the map as the
'// objLoc location

                Set objLoc = objMap.Location

'// Set Altitude to a height that displays
'// the complete query oval.
'// The 2.75 is a fudge factor needed to get
'// high enough to see the circle.

                objMap.Altitude = intRadius * 2.75

'// Add the oval(9)shape

                objMap.Shapes.AddShape 9, objLoc,
            intRadius, intRadius

        objMap.Shapes.Item(objMap.Shapes.Count).Name =
```

```
                "Oval1"

        objMap.Shapes.Item(objMap.Shapes.Count).Line.Weig
        ht = 2

        objMap.Shapes.Item(objMap.Shapes.Count).Line.Fore
        Color = mpBlack

        objMap.Shapes.Item(objMap.Shapes.Count).Fill.Visi
        ble = True

        objMap.Shapes.Item(objMap.Shapes.Count).Fill.Fore
        Color = mpLightTurquoise

        objMap.Shapes.Item(objMap.Shapes.Count).ZOrder
        geoSendBehindRoads

                shapeCreated = True
            End If

'// Retrieve all records in a defined radius
'// for the defined datasets(i)

        Set objRecordset =
        objDataSet.QueryCircle(objLoc, intRadius)

        Case "mpRectangle"  'Rectangle shape

'// In this section of the code we will:
'// 1. Set the width and height of the
'//    rectangle
'// 2. Raise the altitude of the map view
'//    to better display the rectangle
'// 3. Draw the rectangle on the map.
'// 4. Name the shape we just drew
'// 5. Change the line color of the rectangle
'// 6. Change the fill color of the rectangle
'//    and make it visible
'// 7. Move the rectangle behind the roads
'// 8. Set the recordset to those records from
'//    the current dataset that are within
'//    the rectangle

        Text1.Text = Text1.Text & vbCrLf & "Opening
        Dataset: " & i & vbCrLf & "Query Rectangle"
        Refresh
        Beep

        If shapeCreated = False Then

'// Set height and width of rectangle

                intRecWidth = 40
```

```
                intRecHeight = 40

                '// Note: Find a specific location for
        the defined point
                Set objLoc = objMap.Location

'// Set Altitude to a height that displays the
'// complete query rectangle.
'// The 2.75 is a guess at the factor
'// needed to get high enough.

                If intRecWidth > intRecHeight Then
                    objMap.Altitude = intRecWidth * 2.75
                Else
                    objMap.Altitude = intRecHeight *
        2.75
                End If

'// Add the rectangle(1)shape
                objMap.Shapes.AddShape 1, objLoc,
        intRecWidth, intRecHeight

        objMap.Shapes.Item(objMap.Shapes.Count).Name =
        "Rectangle1"

        objMap.Shapes.Item(objMap.Shapes.Count).Line.Weig
        ht = 2

        objMap.Shapes.Item(objMap.Shapes.Count).Line.Fore
        Color = mpBlueGray

        objMap.Shapes.Item(objMap.Shapes.Count).Fill.Visi
        ble = True

        objMap.Shapes.Item(objMap.Shapes.Count).Fill.Fore
        Color = mpTan

        objMap.Shapes.Item(objMap.Shapes.Count).ZOrder
        geoSendBehindRoads

                shapeCreated = True
            End If

'// Retrieve all records in a defined rectangle
'// for the defined datasets(i)

            Set objRecordset =
        objDataSet.QueryShape(objMap.Shapes(1))

        Case "mpPolygon" ' Polygon shape

'// In this section of the code we will:
```

```
'// 1. Set the points for the polygon.
'// 2. Raise the altitude of the map view
'//    to better display the polygon
'// 3. Draw the polygon on the map.
'// 4. Name the shape we just drew
'// 5. Change the line color of the polygon
'// 6. Change the fill color of the polygon
'//    and make it visible
'// 7. Move the polygon behind the roads
'// 8. Set the recordset to those records
'//    from the current dataset that
'//    are within the polygon

        Text1.Text = Text1.Text & vbCrLf & "Opening
    Dataset: " & i & vbCrLf & "Query Polygon"
        Refresh
        Beep

        If shapeCreated = False Then

'// Create a "polygon" of locations
'// in the middle of the map
'// The first and last point are the same
'// so that the shape is closed.
'// Any number of point can be used
'// in a polygon.

            Set objLocs(1) = objMap.XYToLocation(0,
    0)
            Set objLocs(2) =
    objMap.XYToLocation(objMap.Width / 2, 0)
            Set objLocs(3) =
    objMap.XYToLocation(objMap.Width, objMap.Height)
            Set objLocs(4) = objMap.XYToLocation(0,
    objMap.Height / 2)
            Set objLocs(5) = objMap.XYToLocation(0,
    0)

'// Identify the best map view location
'// for the defined point

            Set objLoc = objMap.Union(objLocs)

'// Go to the best map view of the location

            objLoc.GoTo

'// Set Altitude to a height that displays
'// the complete query polygon.
```

```
'// The 1.25 is a guess at the factor
'// needed to get high enough.

           objMap.Altitude = objMap.Altitude * 1.25

'// Add the polyline using the array of locations

           objMap.Shapes.AddPolyline objLocs

    objMap.Shapes.Item(objMap.Shapes.Count).Name =
    "Polygon1"

    objMap.Shapes.Item(objMap.Shapes.Count).Line.Weig
    ht = 2

    objMap.Shapes.Item(objMap.Shapes.Count).Line.Fore
    Color = mpBlack

    objMap.Shapes.Item(objMap.Shapes.Count).Fill.Visi
    ble = True

    objMap.Shapes.Item(objMap.Shapes.Count).Fill.Fore
    Color = mpYellow

    objMap.Shapes.Item(objMap.Shapes.Count).ZOrder
    geoSendBehindRoads
           shapeCreated = True
       End If

'// Retrieve all records in a defined polygon
'// for the defined datasets(i)
       Set objRecordset =
       objDataSet.QueryPolygon(objLocs)

    End Select

    x = 1
    objRecordset.MoveFirst

    intFieldCount = objRecordset.Fields.Count

'// Get the values for each field
'// in each record and place them in grid.

    Do Until objRecordset.EOF
        For Each objField In objRecordset.Fields
            val = val & CStr(objField.Value) & vbTab
        Next objField
        val = val & vbCrLf

'// Load a string with the field information
```

```
'// separated by tabs then add it to the table.

                j = 1
                Do While j <= intFieldCount
                        strRowText = strRowText & vbTab &
        objRecordset.Fields.Item(j)
                        j = j + 1
                Loop

            MSFlexGrid1.AddItem x & strRowText

            strRowText = ""
            x = x + 1

            iTotalRecordCount = iTotalRecordCount + 1

            objRecordset.MoveNext

        Loop
        i = i + 1
        Text1.Text = Text1.Text & vbCrLf & "Records: " &
        x - 1
        Refresh
    Loop

    If iTotalRecordCount > 0 Then
    '// Note: We wait to kill this here because it can
    '// only be killed if there is more than one row in
'//  the grid.

        KillFirstRow
    End If

    MSFlexGrid1.Redraw = True

    Me.MappointControl1.MousePointer = vbDefault

    MsgBox "Total Record Count = " & iTotalRecordCount

    Exit Function

errhandler:
    Me.MappointControl1.MousePointer = vbDefault
    MsgBox "Problem doing query." & vbCrLf & _
    "Cannot Query shape without a dataset present."

End Function
```

7. **Use this code to delete the first row of the MSFlexGrid control.**

```
Sub KillFirstRow()

On Error GoTo errhandler

    '// We wait to kill this here because it can only
    '// be killed if there is more than one row in the
    '// grid.

    MSFlexGrid1.RemoveItem (1)
    MSFlexGrid1.Redraw = True
    Exit Sub

errhandler:
    Me.MappointControl1.MousePointer = vbDefault
    'MsgBox "No First Row to delete."
End Sub
```

8. **Add the following code to complete the cleanup of the MSFlexGrid control.**

```
Sub KillAllRowsButFirst()
    Dim intRowCount As Integer
    Dim x As Integer

On Error GoTo errhandler

    intRowCount = MSFlexGrid1.Rows

    x = intRowCount
    Do While x >= 1
        MSFlexGrid1.RemoveItem (x)
        x = x - 1
    Loop

    Exit Sub

errhandler:
    'MsgBox "No more rows to delete"
    Exit Sub
End Sub
```

9. **Add another button to the form and rename it CommandDeleteShapes; change the caption property to read DeleteShapes.**

   The code uses the `.Shapes.Item.Count` call to find out how many shapes are currently drawn on the map. You will then delete them one by one.

```
Private Sub CommandDeleteShapes_Click()
    Dim objMap As MapPointCtl.Map
    Dim intShapeCount As Integer
    Dim i As Integer

    '// Always need to point to the active map before
        changing any settings.

    Set objMap = Me.MappointControl1.ActiveMap

    '// Count the number of shapes on the map.

    intShapeCount = objMap.Shapes.Count

    i = 1

    Do While i <= intShapeCount
        '// Note: Delete each shape one at a time
        objMap.Shapes.Item(1).Delete
        i = i + 1
    Loop
End Sub
```

Use the completed sample to see how it works. You will find a copy of the completed project on CD1 in the sample code folder if you did not make one yourself. To run this sample, open a map that contains, at a minimum, one dataset of Pushpins or other mapping types. To begin the project, click Open⇨File and then navigate to the desktop. Then follow these steps:

1. Set the dimensions of the shape.

2. Raise the altitude of the map view to better display the shape.

3. Draw the shape on the map.

4. Name the shape you just drew.

5. Change the line color of the shape.

6. Change the fill color of the shape and make it visible.

7. Move the shape behind the roads.

8. Set the recordset to those records from the current dataset that are within the shape.

Finding a Location with the Find Project

Finding an address, place, or point by latitude/longitude on a map is the fundamental building block for almost any worthwhile activity when using a map. This project creates a Visual Basic version of the MapPoint Find dialog box. We see this as the most important example you can work with in this book. Understand the concepts for finding locations on a map and you will have the foundation for many new and exciting features as you control the world.

This is the first example for which the majority of the code is in a second form, not attached to the form where the Mappoint Control is placed. Start with a new form named Form1 and place the Mappoint Control on it using the instructions we use in each example in this part of the book. If you skipped them, refer to the first example in Chapter 16 and follow the instructions for the Generic map example. Then, follow these steps to create this Find sample.

1. **Choose the Add Form option on the Project menu to add a new form to the project.**

   The default selection is a form.

2. **Click the Open button in the Add Form dialog box and change the Name property to DialogFind.**

   Each of the three tabs on the dialog box will look like Figures 17-4, 17-5, and 17-6 when the dialog box is completed.

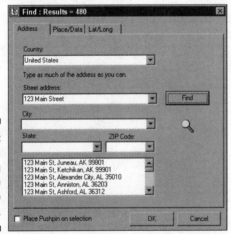

Figure 17-4:
Visual Basic Find dialog box with the Address tab selected.

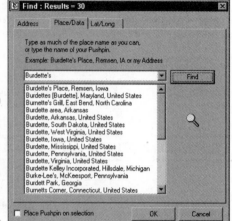

Figure 17-5:
Visual Basic
Find dialog
box with the
Place/Data
tab
selected.

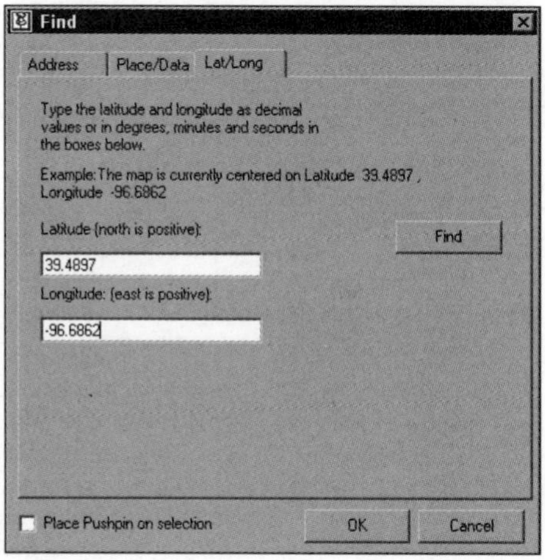

Figure 17-6:
Visual Basic
Find dialog
box with the
Latitude/
Longitude
tab
selected.

3. Add numerous standard VB controls to the form.

Table 17-1 provides the details for each of the controls. We strongly recommend that you add them in this order. Also make sure that they have
the indicated name. Place each of them within the indicated container
so that the code that follows will work correctly. To place a control
within the container, you first select the container. For example, select
Frame1 before you place the appropriate controls onto it. You will find
that placing the controls on the three Frame controls requires you to

change the Z order of them so that the correct one is on the top. You can move controls forward and backward by selecting the Order item under the Format menu. You can select Bring to Front or Send to Back.

You should change the caption property of each of the labels to reflect the table below.

If you are inclined to save time, you can copy the form over from the CD1 in the code samples folder.

Table 17-1		Controls to Add to DialogFind.frm	
Control	*Name*	*Container*	*Caption Text*
TabStrip	TabStrip1	DialogFind.frm	-
Button	OKButton	DialogFind.frm	OK
Button	CancelButton	DialogFind.frm	Cancel
CheckBox	CheckPushpin	DialogFind.frm	-
Frame	Frame1	TabStrip1	-
Button	cmdFindAddress	Frame1	-
ComboBox	ComboCountry	Frame1	-
ComboBox	ComboAddress	Frame1	-
ComboBox	ComboCity	Frame1	-
ComboBox	ComboState	Frame1	-
ComboBox	ComboZIPCode	Frame1	-
ListBox	ListFindAddress Results	Frame1	-
Label	Label1	Frame1	Country:
Label	Label2	Frame1	Type as much of the address as you can.
Label	Label3	Frame1	Street address:
Label	Label4	Frame1	City:
Label	Label5	Frame1	State:
Label	Label6	Frame1	ZIP Code:

Control	Name	Container	Caption Text
Frame	Frame2	TabStrip1	-
Button	cmdFindPlace	Frame2	-
Combo Box	ComboPlace	Frame2	-
ListBox	ListFindPlaces Results	Frame2	-
Label	Label7	Frame2	Type as much of the place name as youcan, or type the name of your Pushpin
Label	Label8	Frame2	Example: Burdette's Place, Remsen, A or my Address
Frame	Frame3	TabStrip1	-
Button	cmdFindLatLong	Frame3	-
TextBox	TextLatitude	Frame3	-
TextBox	TextLongitude	Frame3	-
Label	Label9	Frame3	Type the latitude and longitude as decimal values or in degrees, minutes, and seconds in the boxes below.
Label	Label10	Frame3	Example: the map is currently cen tered on Latitude 39.4897, Longitude −96.6862
Label	Label11	Frame3	Latitude (north is positive):
Label	Label12	Frame3	Longitude: (east is positive):

4. Select the cmdFindAddress, cmdFindPlace, and cmdFindLatlong buttons and change the .enabled value to false.

5. Change the properties on the TabStrip.

This control is special in that it has a Property Page dialog box that you open by right-clicking the control and selecting the Properties option. The following dialog box appears (see Figure 17-7)

Select the Tabs tab (make sure that the Index value is 1) and type **Address** into the Caption field. Proceed by using the arrows at the left of the Index field to move to Index 2 and type **Place/Data** in the Caption field. Then advance the Index to 3 and type **Lat/long** in the Caption field. After you have made these three changes, click the OK button to close the dialog box.

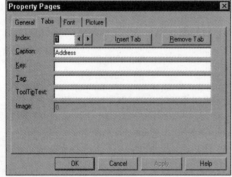

Figure 17-7:
TabStrip
Property
Pages.

6. Type the following code to declare two variables to be used throughout the project for passing the text description for the current location and to identify the active tab on the dialog box.

```
Option Explicit

Public strLocationText As String
Public intTab As Integer
```

7. Type the following code to declare and use the Map object in the DialogFind.frm Form_Load code window.

You need to do this even though the MapPoint control is located on Form1. You also need to populate the ComboCountry and ComboState combo boxes, as shown in the following code. You will use the selected values in these combo boxes when you use the FindResults method later.

```
Private Sub Form_Load()
    Dim objMap As MapPointCtl.Map

    Set objMap = Form1.MappointControl1.ActiveMap

    ComboCountry.AddItem "Canada"
```

```
ComboCountry.AddItem "United States"
ComboCountry.ListIndex = 1

ComboState.AddItem "-ANY-"
ComboState.AddItem "AL-Alabama"
ComboState.AddItem "AK-Alaska"
ComboState.AddItem "AZ-Arizona"
ComboState.AddItem "AR-Arkansas"
ComboState.AddItem "CA-California"
ComboState.AddItem "CO-Colorado"
ComboState.AddItem "CT-Connecticut"
ComboState.AddItem "DE-Delaware"
ComboState.AddItem "DC-Dist. of Columbia"
ComboState.AddItem "FL-Florida"
ComboState.AddItem "GA-Georgia"
ComboState.AddItem "HI-Hawaii"
ComboState.AddItem "ID-Idaho"
ComboState.AddItem "IL-Illinois"
ComboState.AddItem "IN-Indiana"
ComboState.AddItem "IA-Iowa"
ComboState.AddItem "KS-Kansas"
ComboState.AddItem "KY-Kentucky"
ComboState.AddItem "LA-Louisiana"
ComboState.AddItem "ME-Maine"
ComboState.AddItem "MD-Maryland"
ComboState.AddItem "MA-Massachusetts"
ComboState.AddItem "MI-Michigan"
ComboState.AddItem "MN-Minnesota"
ComboState.AddItem "MS-Mississippi"
ComboState.AddItem "MO-Missouri"
ComboState.AddItem "MT-Montana"
ComboState.AddItem "NE-Nebraska"
ComboState.AddItem "NV-Nevada"
ComboState.AddItem "NH-New Hampshire"
ComboState.AddItem "NJ-New Jersey"
ComboState.AddItem "NM-New Mexico"
ComboState.AddItem "NY-New York"
ComboState.AddItem "NC-North Carolina"
ComboState.AddItem "ND-North Dakota"
ComboState.AddItem "OH-Ohio"
ComboState.AddItem "OK-Oklahoma"
ComboState.AddItem "OR-Oregon"
ComboState.AddItem "PA-Pennsylvania"
ComboState.AddItem "RI-Rhode Island"
ComboState.AddItem "SC-South Carolina"
ComboState.AddItem "SD-South Dakota"
ComboState.AddItem "TN-Tennessee"
ComboState.AddItem "TX-Texas"
ComboState.AddItem "UT-Utah"
ComboState.AddItem "VT-Vermont"
ComboState.AddItem "VA-Virginia"
```

```
ComboState.AddItem "WA-Washington"
ComboState.AddItem "WV-West Virginia"
ComboState.AddItem "WI-Wisconsin"
ComboState.AddItem "WY-Wyoming"

Frame1.Visible = True
Frame2.Visible = False
Frame3.Visible = False
intTab = 1
End Sub
```

8. **Add the following code to the CancelButton_Click window to cancel a search and close the DialogFind dialog box when you are finished using it to find a place, address, or latitude/longitude point.**

```
Private Sub CancelButton_Click()
    Unload DialogFind
End Sub
```

9. **Add this code to the cmdFindAddress_Click window.**

When the end user clicks this button, you collect the text entered into the combo boxes that represent the parts that make up an address, and you pass them as one of the two parameters needed by the FindQuery function (discussed in Step 13).

```
Private Sub cmdFindAddress_Click()
    Dim strAddressText As String
    strAddressText = ComboAddress.Text & ", " & _
                     ComboCity.Text & ", " & _
                     ComboState.Text & ", " & _
                     ComboZIPCode.Text & ", " & _
                     ComboCountry.Text

    FindQuery 1, strAddressText, ""
End Sub
```

10. **Add this code to the cmdFindPlace button.**

When the end user clicks this button, it collects the text entered into the ComboPlace combo box and passes it as one of the two parameters needed by the FindQuery function (discussed in Step 13).

```
Private Sub cmdFindPlace_Click()
    Dim strPlaceText As String
    strPlaceText = ComboPlace

    FindQuery 2, strPlaceText, ""
End Sub
```

11. **Add this code to the cmdFindLatLong_Click code window.**

When the end user clicks this button, the text entered into the TextLatitude and TextLongitude functions is collected and passed as one of the two parameters needed by the FindQuery function (discussed in step 13). The code then displays the TextLatitude.text and

Text Longitude.text values in a message box. You also create a new Pushpin and display the Pushpin balloon by setting the Balloon.State to true with the geoBalloonState constant value.

We complete the activity by setting the .Symbol to 26, highlighting the Pushpin, and setting the Note value to "This is the place you selected!"

```
Private Sub cmdFindLatLong_Click()
    Dim objMap As MapPointCtl.Map
    Dim objLoc As MapPointCtl.Location
    Dim objPushPin As MapPointCtl.Pushpin

    FindQuery 3, TextLatitude, TextLongitude

    If CheckPushpin.Value = 1 Then
        strLocationText = ListFindPlaceResults.Text

        MsgBox TextLatitude & vbCrLf & TextLongitude

        Set objLoc = objMap.Location.Location

        '// Create a new pushpin
        Set objPushPin = objMap.AddPushpin(objLoc,
        TextLatitude & "|" & TextLongitude)

    '// Display the pushpin's balloon

        objPushPin.BalloonState = geoDisplayBalloon

    '// Change pushpin symbol to one of the
    '// standard symbols

        objPushPin.Symbol = 26

        objPushPin.Highlight = True
        objPushPin.Note = "This is the place you
        selected!"
    End If
End Sub
```

12. **Type the following code to set the .enabled value for each of the three find action buttons in the DialogFind dialog box to false.**

You do this to make the action mimic the Find dialog box in MapPoint. The following code changes the enabled values to true when the end user types in any alphanumeric text.

```
Private Sub ComboAddress_Change()
    '// Enable the find button when a field contains
    '// some alpha-numeric data

    cmdFindAddress.Enabled = True
End Sub
Private Sub ComboCity_Change()
    '// Enable the find button when a field contains
```

```
    '// some alpha-numeric data.

    cmdFindAddress.Enabled = True
End Sub
Private Sub ComboPlace_Change()
    '// Enable the find button when a field contains
    '// some alpha-numeric data.

    cmdFindPlace.Enabled = True
End Sub
Private Sub ComboState_Change()
    '// Enable the find button when a field contains
    '// some alpha-numeric data

    cmdFindAddress.Enabled = True
End Sub
Private Sub ComboZIPCode_Change()
    '// Enable the find button when a field contains
    '// some alpha-numeric data

    cmdFindAddress.Enabled = True
End Sub
Private Sub TextLatitude_Change()
    '// Enable the find button when a field contains
    '// some alpha-numeric data

    cmdFindLatLong.Enabled = True
End Sub
Private Sub TextLongitude_Change()
    '// Enable the find button when a field contains
    '// some alpha-numeric data

    cmdFindLatLong.Enabled = True
End Sub
```

13. **Everything else was simple preparation; this function is the main
    work horse of the example.**

    When you call the `FindQuery` function, you need to pass it two separate
    parameters. The first parameter defines the type of find (such as
    Address, Place/Data, Latitude/Longitude). The second parameter is the
    string that contains the location text that we want to find.

    We could have broken this code up and placed it in each of the individual Find subroutines, but having it on one place will allow you to compare the different methods.

    Although the MapPoint object model contains the `FindAddressResults`
    method, the `FindResults` method appears to more closely return the
    results found in the real MapPoint Find dialog box. This is why we use it
    for addresses.

As each possible match for the Address or Place/Data searches is found, the code places it in the `ListFindAddressResults` and `ListFindPlaceResults` list boxes. If you're searching for a Latitude/Longitude point, you go directly to the location.

The same code below also contains error checking and error handling.

```
Function FindQuery(FindType As Integer, FindString As
        String, FindString2 As String)
    Dim objMap As MapPointCtl.Map
    Dim objLoc As MapPointCtl.Location
    Dim objFindResults As MapPointCtl.FindResults
    Dim x As Integer

On Error GoTo errhandler

    MsgBox FindString & vbCrLf & FindString2

    Set objMap = Form1.MappointControl1.ActiveMap

    '// Syntax is objmap.FindAddressResults([Street],
'// [City],[OtherCity],[Region],[PostalCode],[Country])

    Select Case FindType
        Case Is = 1
            Set objFindResults =
        objMap.FindResults(FindString)
            ListFindAddressResults.Clear
            x = 1
            Do While x <= objFindResults.Count
                Set objLoc = objFindResults.Item(x)
                ListFindAddressResults.AddItem
        objLoc.Name
                x = x + 1
            Loop
        Case Is = 2
            Set objFindResults =
        objMap.FindPlaceResults(FindString)
            ListFindPlaceResults.Clear
            x = 1
            Do While x <= objFindResults.Count
                Set objLoc = objFindResults.Item(x)
                ListFindPlaceResults.AddItem objLoc.Name
                x = x + 1
            Loop
        Case Is = 3
            Set objLoc = objMap.GetLocation(FindString,
        FindString2)
            objLoc.GoTo
```

```
    End Select

    Me.Caption = " Find : Results = " & x - 1

    Exit Sub

errhandler:
    MsgBox "Problem in Find."
End Sub
```

After you place the list of possible addresses found by the FindQuery function, you can use this list box to provide a means for your end users to select the one they want to go to.

14. **Place the following code in the ListFindAddressResults_Click code window in the DialogFind dialog box.**

```
Private Sub ListFindAddressResults_Click()
    Dim objMap As MapPointCtl.Map
    Dim objLoc As MapPointCtl.Location
    Dim objPushPin As MapPointCtl.Pushpin

    Set objMap = Form1.MappointControl1.ActiveMap
    Set objLoc =
        objMap.FindResults(ListFindAddressResults.Text)(1
        )
    objLoc.GoTo

    If CheckPushpin.Value = 1 Then
        strLocationText = ListFindAddressResults.Text
        MsgBox strLocationText

    '// Create a new pushpin

        Set objPushPin = objMap.AddPushpin(objLoc,
        strLocationText)

    '// Display the balloon

        objPushPin.BalloonState = geoDisplayBalloon

    '// Change pushpin symbol to one of the standard
    '// symbols. 26 is a yellow circle

        objPushPin.Symbol = 26

        objPushPin.Highlight = True
        objPushPin.Note = "This is the address you
        selected!"
    End If
End Function
```

After you place the list of possible places found by the FindQuery function, you can use this list box to provide a means for your end users to select the one they want to go to.

15. **Place the following code in the ListFindPlaceResults_Click code window.**

```
Private Sub ListFindPlaceResults_Click()
    Dim objMap As MapPointCtl.Map
    Dim objLoc As MapPointCtl.Location
    Dim objPushPin As MapPointCtl.Pushpin

    Set objMap = Form1.MappointControl1.ActiveMap
    Set objLoc =
        objMap.FindPlaceResults(ListFindPlaceResults.Text
        )(1)
    objLoc.GoTo

    If CheckPushpin.Value = 1 Then
        strLocationText = ListFindPlaceResults.Text

        MsgBox strLocationText

    '// Create a new pushpin

        Set objPushPin = objMap.AddPushpin(objLoc,
        strLocationText)

    '// Display the balloon

        objPushPin.BalloonState = geoDisplayBalloon

    '// Change pushpin symbol to one of the standard
    '// symbols. 26 is a yellow circle

        objPushPin.Symbol = 26

        objPushPin.Highlight = True
        objPushPin.Note = "This is the place you
        selected!"
    End If
End Sub
```

16. **Place the following code in the TabStrip1 Click code window. It's used to hide and display the appropriate Frame depending on what tab is selected.**

```
Private Sub TabStrip1_Click()
    If TabStrip1.SelectedItem = "Address" Then
        Frame1.Visible = True
        Frame2.Visible = False
        Frame3.Visible = False
        intTab = 1
    ElseIf TabStrip1.SelectedItem = "Place/Data" Then
        Frame1.Visible = False
        Frame2.Visible = True
```

```
        Frame3.Visible = False
intTab = 2
    Else 'Lat/Long
        Frame1.Visible = False
        Frame2.Visible = False
        Frame3.Visible = True
        intTab = 3
    End If
    Me.Caption = "Find"
End Sub
```

17. **Place the following code in the OKButton_Click code window in the DialogFind dialog box.**

This code unloads and closes your Find dialog box.

```
Private Sub OKButton_Click()
    Unload DialogFind
End Sub
```

You may not be a MapPoint expert just by going through these examples, but you can see how easy it is to tap into the power of MapPoint.

Chapter 18

MapPoint and the World of Geographic Information Systems

Geographic Information Systems (known as GIS to the cartographers of North America and as SIG to many Europeans) have been around for some time. Many companies have whole departments full of people who spend their entire working lives mucking around in the world of spatial data. Other companies are dedicated 100 percent to doing GIS work on the behalf of their customers.

Understanding GIS

If you are a trained cartographer or even if you are only somewhat familiar with others who live in that world, the question always seems to come up as to whether MapPoint is a GIS system. The question seems to arise from the desire to know whether MapPoint has power enough to play with the big boys or is rather just a cool toy that isn't capable of real analysis or providing real spatial insight. The best way to decide whether MapPoint has GIS power is to compare MapPoint functionality to that of GIS applications with a magical GIS translator!

MapPoint to GIS Translator

Although MapPoint has a heritage within Microsoft filled with such mapping relatives as Microsoft Streets and Trips, AutoRoute, and Encarta Interactive Atlas, the latest version of MapPoint appears to be the first release that provides the functionality previously available only with high-end GIS applications. Professional GIS folks can share many stories about why they need the greater power of GIS.

MapPoint is not all things to all people in that by design it does not allow you to perform spatial data capture and manipulation. For some "real" cartographers, this is a limitation that makes them turn away. Interestingly, the "data capture" feature of the traditional GIS is made more or less obsolete because MapPoint comes with the highest-quality spatial maps available today. The combination of MapPoint the application and MapPoint the spatial maps, along with the included demographic data, gives even a GIS professional access to functions such as the following examples. (If these terms are foreign to you, don't worry. It just goes to show that you can use MapPoint without being a cartographer or even understanding that profession's lingo!)

- **Point-in-Poly:** A seemingly simple but actually complex calculation that identifies all points that fall within the boundaries of a specified polygon. In MapPoint terminology, this is as simple as the Export to Excel functionality.

- **Advanced Routing:** The ability to do multiple stop routes with the flexibility built in to accommodate driving speeds, road type preferences, and stop-over times while obeying all legal turn and one-way restrictions. Advanced routing also includes detailed turn-by-turn text driving directions. All this is standard in MapPoint and optional in GIS systems for an additional price.

- **Thematic Mapping (data mapping):** The act of shading different areas with gradient colors indicating degrees of lower to higher values. Known as Shaded Area Maps in MapPoint.

- **Geocoding (mapping data to locations):** The act of taking a street address, city, state, and ZIP code and identifying the exact location on a map.

With MapPoint, these functions are available without the added investment of time, money, formal education in cartography, and the corresponding headaches of having to "hunt down and skin" your own maps.

Further functionality is made possible by the MapPoint ActiveX Control and expanded Object Model, which provide GIS and Visual Basic developers access to GIS functions that they can embed in their own solutions. This added functionality also proves a simple means for extending MapPoint so that you can import MapInfo MIF files and ESRI SHAPE files on top of MapPoint maps as annotation layer objects. We explore this specific example in greater detail at the end of this chapter.

Playing in Harmony with GIS Files

The ability of MapPoint to work in harmony with spatial data sets created in GIS applications is a feature that many enterprise customers desire. What you will quickly discover is that this is not native functionality supported in MapPoint.

MapPoint isn't designed to be a SHAPE or MIF file viewer. Many situations exist, however, in which users want to take legacy GIS data and bring it into MapPoint to share it with non-GIS-savvy users and to combine its functionality that is available only either in the GIS system or in MapPoint.

But remember that MapPoint has an extensive object model that you can use to add functionality. On CD1 in the code samples folder, you will find a MapPoint COM Add-in and the supporting source code that will allow you to import ESRI SHAPE files and MapInfo MIF files into a MapPoint map. The Spatial Data Import sample COM Add-in demonstrates how easily you can create this functionality either as a COM Add-in or with through a Visual Basic application using the new MapPoint ActiveX control.

Nonprogramming end users can use the compiled sample, or MapPoint VB developers can extend the code freely as desired.

The sample uses Visual Basic and the new extended MapPoint object model methods to take the native source GIS point data sets and import them as MapPoint Pushpin sets along with any native attribution associated with each point (such as name, address, latitude/longitude). You can import the native GIS polygons and lines to create a layer of MapPoint drawing objects and display them within a MapPoint map. Through the code, you can set the line color and size and the shape fill color, and you can move the polygons and lines behind the MapPoint road network.

Importing some GIS file feature types can be problematic. If you have polygons that contain holes, you will quickly discover that the MapPoint drawing objects cannot make donut holes. Other GIS data objects may also not work with this code sample.

After you've imported the polygons into MapPoint, you can use them for visualization and to perform spatial queries (that is, point-in-poly queries in VB code and through the Export to Excel command using the MapPoint application user interface) of any MapPoint data layers contained in the MapPoint map. These can include queries of MapPoint Pushpin sets or demographic or end-user data displayed in a MapPoint shaded area, shaded circle, sized circle, multiple symbol, pie chart, sized pie chart, column chart, or series column chart data sets. The queries can include multiple layers of information simultaneously.

This sample also does not provide functionality for exporting from MapPoint the GIS layers that were imported. Writing such a feature should be possible but the coding required might be extensive. This sample also does not support using imported boundaries with the MapPoint data mapping wizard.

By design, you can't replace the MapPoint maps with your own maps using this import feature or any other method — doing so would negate one of the key benefits that MapPoint provides. Extensive research shows that an overwhelming majority of users want to *use* maps, not acquire, create, and maintain them. Given the broad extent of coverage provided by the North American and European MapPoint editions, no better maps are available today, so the problems related to "rolling" your own maps go away.

It's a little-known fact that Microsoft has been building maps for almost 10 years. Users of MapPoint benefit from having a team of Microsoft cartographers, testers, and program managers who worry about the details of mapmaking.

Remember that MapPoint comes with very extensive integrated maps that include political and administrative boundaries (census tracts, postal codes, counties, metropolitan areas, states, countries, and more) and an extensive transportation network. The North American edition includes more than 6.4 million routable streets and roads. The European editions include more than 4.8 million routable streets and roads. The road networks in both editions contain attribution for turn and one-way, and they specify five different speed classifications. Although this GIS import example demonstrates how to import GIS lines, it's important to note that they can't be added to the MapPoint transportation layer and won't be routable. The maps also include an extensive collection of populated places and points of interest (POI).

MapPoint is designed for everyday business mapping and it leaves the very technical and complex GIS problems to the GIS applications. If you want to create and modify your own spatial data sets, we recommend using GIS applications such as those from ESRI and MapInfo.

If you want to integrate the benefits of your spatial data sets with the power of MapPoint, you will like the code sample mentioned previously in the chapter.

Part VI
The Part of Tens

The 5th Wave — By Rich Tennant

As I recall, you were the one who said we didn't really need MapPoint installed.

In this part . . .

Actually, in the following two chapters of ten parts each (more or less), you have the opportunity to learn something about how you can use MapPoint in ways that will take you farther than you might first have thought.

You will learn about cool approaches to getting the most out of the application that didn't fit well in earlier chapters of this book, and you will also get some insight into the many types of business uses that can benefit from the power of MapPoint.

Chapter 19

(Almost) Ten Ways to Maximize Your MapPoint Experience

*Y*ou can travel many roads as you explore and experience MapPoint. Over the last three years we have watched users as they dive into the application from many different angles. Sometimes they have taken the road most traveled. At other times they have remained stuck in the revolving world of click and type, never quite realizing that working smart is just as important as working hard. This chapter shows you numerous shortcuts and approaches that can increase your gas mileage to triple digits.

As you use MapPoint, you may well find many more creative ways to get more out of the application. We would love to hear from you and obtain your permission to pass on the ideas to the MapPoint newsgroups and Web sites that support MapPoint discussion. You can reach us at bjholt@microsoft.com and JFreeze@justPC.com.

Update Your Source Data

MapPoint 2002 maps represent relatively current and accurate data. Microsoft stitches spatial data together from multiple spatial data vendors to provide one of the best maps available at any price. Sometimes these are missing a street or an address range, but you usually can work around that problem.

The main secret to success in locating what you need to find is simple: make sure that your source addresses are real, up-to-date, and as detailed as possible. Clean up the old ZIP codes, incomplete or empty fields, and just plan junk. Use the following list as a guide to optimize the results of your searches:

- **Wrong or missing North/South and East/West designation:** So how far away from each other are "123 East Main Street" and "123 West Main Street" in Marlborough, MA 01752? Did you know there is also a "123 Main Street" in the same city? The postal carrier might know the people that live at one or the other but MapPoint needs your help.

- **Post Office Box:** P.O. Boxes live side-by-side in a Post Office and in most instances are blocks or even miles away from the owners' real physical addresses. Not even a mail carrier visits the real location. If your addresses contain a postal code field, you can successfully map to the Post Office, which may or may not be what you want.

- **Rural Route:** The initials RR have meant both railroad and rural route. Many states have dispensed with this type of designation, however, so an address such as RR1 Box 98 may now be 15403 Marble Ave.

- **Incorrect streets classifications:** So is it Street, Avenue, Place, or Road? You'd be amazed at how many cities have "123 Pine" as more than one, and many times they are not even close to each other. If your data is missing this descriptor, your results may not be accurate.

- **Bad postal codes:** Postal codes are one of the greatest indexing systems that touch us each day. Get one wrong and MapPoint will do its best to help you out but you're sending mixed signals to an engine that is looking for a single correct address, not two or more at once. "XXXXX" is not a valid U.S. postal code and "ABC 123" is not assigned to anywhere, Canada. You will also discover that some U.S. ZIP codes are not real places but rather are references to military addresses around the world.

- **Bad states/provinces:** We've seen databases for which the human operators decided to invent the state of "XX" or the states of BLANK and NULLS. Both will result in a state of confusion and less than desirable success rates.

✔ **Missing fields and slang names:** So you live in Philadelphia and have an Excel file that contains all of your customer's addresses. You know that they are all in Philadelphia and you would expect MapPoint to be smart enough to read your mind. Maybe you have a city field and you decide that "Philly" or "Vegas" are understandable names that anybody would know. MapPoint will try its best but proper names will always get better results.

Just as bad as wrong addresses are the dreaded "non-addresses!"

✔ **End of First Street:** Another real world example. So which end is the end when you have a North and South First street? Simple geometry says there are three possible points that could be 10 miles from each other.

✔ **Highway 56:** Do you know how long Highway 56 is?

✔ **Smith and Weston:** In Texas, these are fighting words. In MapPoint, you will end up at one of four restaurants and two auto repair establishments and all have names that sound only somewhat like the gun.

When you're in doubt, MapPoint helps you out

When it all is said and done MapPoint goes out of its way to be forgiving and to guide you along. Remember that any address or place that it cannot uniquely identify will be offered to you in a list of "Best guesses." MapPoint even attempts to correct spelling If you enter an address in the Find field on the toolbar with or without commas separating the street address, city, state and ZIP code, MapPoint attempts to correct the spelling and to make quality guesses as to which word or group of words reference the different parts of an address. If what you enter appears to be a place rather than an address, MapPoint will even attempt to find that place.

Address Checker to the rescue!

One very cool tool to use with MapPoint is the free Address Checker COM Add-in included on CD1 in the samples code folder. This COM Add-in reads any Access, Excel, or text-delimited file and checks to see whether it contains legitimate MapPoint address and places. It generates a "scrubbed" copy of your source file, allowing you to clean up your act once and never have to be reminded of your sins again going forward. This sample COM Add-in is currently designed to read files with a specific required list of fields (Excel and Access sample included), but we included the source code so that you can modify it as you desire.

Locate Missing Locations

So what do you do when MapPoint is missing a street or MapPoint decided to place 123 Main Street two houses or two blocks down the street from where you know the location really is? From time to time this will happen but it is the exception and not the rule.

Here's one solution that might satisfy your need for exactness. MapPoint Pushpins can be moved on the map by simply selecting them and dragging them to any location. After you have moved the Pushpin, it will remain in the new location within the current MapPoint file. You can also search by name of the Pushpin or use the What's Nearby functionality and MapPoint will go to the new location. Save the MapPoint file and then, when you reopen it, the Pushpin will still be in the new location!

If a place or location is missing from the map entirely, you can create a Pushpin and place it at the appropriate location. It will also be searchable and you can use the What's Nearby feature.

In both instances (relocated or newly created), you will also be able to include the location as the start, at a stop, or at the end of the route. The text itinerary will include instructions referring to travel ending with the text ". . . onto local road(s)".

Doing a new search or data import or link will display results for the inaccurate results originally encountered. Saving the map as a MapPoint template file containing the corrected locations and using it as the starting point for future maps may help.

It is also possible that the last few direction instructions will be incorrect and arrive at the location from a wrong direction.

Make Use of Templates

Think of a template file as a combination of a style sheet and the base data that you can use repeatedly without recreating it as long as the information it contains has not changed.

Templates are useful for mapping data on a map by territories. If the territory boundaries are static, you don't have to rebuild territory maps each time you need to use them. Although you can save a territory map as a MapPoint map (.PTM) just as easily as in a MapPoint template file (.PTT), you can save them as templates to help avoid the problems created by overwriting an earlier map that you still want to keep around.

A practical use for this approach might be the creation of a template that contains the locations of all your stores and even the locations of your competitors. If these locations are accurate and up-to-date, you can then map regularly updated customer lists onto this template, saving you the time required to map the static locations. Another good use for template files comes into play when you have to anticipate a reoccurring use of any drawing objects that you place on a map. These drawing objects can be ones that you have manually created or those that you have imported using the approach outlined in Chapter 18.

Mine MapPoint for Lists of Boundaries

Have you ever wished that you could get a list of all the ZIP codes in a specific county, state, or the entire United States? How about a list of counties or even census tracts for a specific area? These lists would be handy for many uses, including figuring out how accurate your source data matches the spatial data in MapPoint.

So how do you mine MapPoint for these goodies? Follow these simple steps:

1. **Open the Data Mapping Wizard by clicking Data⇨Data Mapping Wizard from the menu bar, or click the Data Mapping Wizard on MapPoint's Standard toolbar.**

2. **Click the Next button while leaving the data selection to the default Add Demographics to the Map selection.**

3. **Select the Demographics data source and map any value to the geographic boundaries (such as census tracts, postal codes, counties, states, countries) that you want to mine back out of the maps.**

4. **On the generated map, choose View⇨Zoom⇨Out to zoom out to a high altitude where you can see the entire geographic area you want to mine.**

   Switch the flat map view if you are mining data at the country level by making sure that the View⇨Globe View when Zoomed Out is not checked. Note that the smaller boundary areas such as census tracts and postal codes may appear to disappear at high altitudes, but the data you are going to mine is still there and available.

5. **Drag a rectangle over the area you want to mine and perform an Export to Excel action.**

   You do this by placing the mouse point at the upper-left corner of the area you want to surround and dragging the pointer to the lower-left corner while holding the mouse button down. When you release the button a selection rectangle will appear. Right-click in the rectangle and choose Export to Excel from the pop-up menu.

6. **Open the resulting Excel file.**

7. **Delete the Square Miles column.**

You now have a complete listing of the geometry contained within the base MapPoint map. You can sort the data in the Excel worksheet in whatever order you decide.

If you look on CD1 included at the back of this book you will find a collection of boundaries that we have already created for you in the Sample Boundary Data folder. You can then use the boundaries as the master list that you can use to clean up your own source data.

In some instances and for some uses, you may be sitting and scratching your head wondering how in the world you will decide which list of boundaries are the most accurate. MapPoint lists are very clean and in many instances cleaner than most source data address references. Be warned that these lists and any addresses found in MapPoint are not necessarily related to any postal service address cleaning applications.

Link to Your Source Data for Periodic Use

Linking to your source data is a very wise approach if you have data sources that remain the same as far as layout but change only in the measures that you want to display on the map.

Create Excel files that show daily sales by ZIP code. After you have updated the sales figures, click Data⇨ Update Linked Records. You can also use the UpdateLink method in the object model to incorporate the updates into your customized COM Add-ins or ActiveX control projects.

Remember that linking to data sources also has a downside. Should you want to share your MapPoint file with other MapPoint users, they will also need access to the linked data source. This could be good or it could create a problem if you don't want to share access to the source files.

Edit the Legend for Just the Right Look

Although MapPoint allows you to create very clean and professional-looking maps, one of the areas that falls short is the ability to modify and tweak the ordering of datasets within the legend. This simple thing can at times be very annoying, but there is a way to get the look you want.

The approach to getting the order the way you desire is simple after you figure out that MapPoint will always take the last data set you worked with and place it at the top of the list, moving the next to the last one down to the second place in the list.

To get the order you want:

1. **Decide the order from top to bottom for each of the datasets.**

2. **Make sure the Legend pane is visible; if it is not, toggle the Legend and Overview item under the View menu.**

3. **Right-click the text in the legend and select the Properties menu item to select the data set at the bottom and then make a change to one of its properties.**

   If you already are satisfied with the Name and Symbol of the data set, you need to select another symbol, close the Properties dialog box, and then reopen it and change back to your preferred selection. This sequence of events might appear strange but all you are doing is forcing MapPoint to move the data set listing to the top of the list.

4. **Select the data set that you want to place second from the bottom and repeat the process.**

5. **Continue up the list until you have made changes to all the data sets in the Legend.**

Although this process also works from non-Pushpin datasets, it affects only the ordering in the legend. This is not a way to move different data mapped layers forward or backward as they are displayed on the map. If you have two data sets plotted on the map as shaded area maps and they are for coverage of geometry that overlaps, controlling the order of display is impossible. Show one set and the other will be covered. The best way to solve this problem is to either create two separate maps or map files, or use sized or shaded circles for one data set to overlay the shaded area data set.

Scan the MapPoint News Groups and Web Sites

The online communities related to MapPoint have grown tremendously and provide many insightful resources, ideas, and sample code. If you have problems figuring out how to make the object model or MapPoint do specific tasks or you just want to get some good ideas as to how you can get more out of the application, make it a regular practice to drop in and check things out.

Here is a list of the online places where you can learn more about MapPoint:

- ✔ http://www.microsoft.com/mappoint
- ✔ http://msdn.microsoft.com/mappoint
- ✔ http://www.mp2kmag.com
- ✔ http://www.navglobe.com
- ✔ http://spatialnews.geocomm.com/community/lists/
  info_mappoint.html

Chapter 20

Ten Business Uses for MapPoint

- -

In This Chapter

▶ Planning services and deliveries

▶ Using targeted mailings and order fulfillment

▶ Benefiting Real Estate sales

▶ Mapping locations for police and fire departments

▶ Selecting store and sales representative locations

▶ Managing customer relationships (CRM)

▶ Creating political maps

▶ Analyzing sales and territories

▶ Planning and analyzing insurance

▶ Tracking assets

- -

The business uses for MapPoint 2002 and the MapPoint 2002 ActiveX Control are almost endless. The following ten categories present just some of the many uses for MapPoint. You can put many of these tips to use manually but you should also think about how you might automate some of these ideas by creating a COM add-in or incorporating them into a MapPoint ActiveX Control project. If you have any stories of cool and valuable uses, please drop us an e-mail (bjholt@microsoft.com) and we'll share with others.

Service and Delivery Planning

The use of mapping applications by companies big and small for planning and tracking service and delivery activities was at best an expensive and time-consuming undertaking until recent years. Whether you are dispatching drivers, delivering merchandise, or trying to navigate around for sales and services, having good-quality routes with detailed information about how long journeys take will save time and money. Some ways to use MapPoint to deliver on time include mapping out a list of customers by address and optimizing the stops and scheduling time for stops to determine whether the route can be accomplished without false promises.

Use demographics or key business data on existing routes to determine exits and stops for likely new users of your services to make sure that you can deliver efficiently. You can impress your clients or your boss by determining the best route between houses that you plan to show to your real estate customers. Or plan the optimized route for your next business trip and overlay it with Pushpin sets of other current customers or key prospects.

Targeted Mailing Lists and Order Fulfillment

The first three rules of retail are Location, Location, Location!

In Chapter 11, we outline the MapMerge feature that would help any retail or mail order company. But now for the rest of the story! Before you start mailing to every Tom, Dick, and Mary, you may first want to make sure that customers don't ignore your expensive mailing because your retail location or locations are just too far away or would require the customer to travel by many of your competitors en route. These may not be concerns when someone is shopping for an expensive item such as an automobile but is very important when you are selling dry-cleaning, car washes, vacuums, take-out pizza, or other merchandise readily available by many merchants.

The factors you use to estimate the distance or time that a customer or prospect will travel varies by your situation and experience, but sending an offer for discount flood insurance to nearby prospects when they are outside the coverage area is a waste of money. Targeting a geographic area to promote check-cashing services in areas where average household income is high is also likely to be a waste of money.

In other instances you might find it more efficient to fulfill the delivery of an order for one store or location that is really closer in drivetime distance.

Ways to reduce your waste include:

- ✔ **Create a drivetime zone or radius circles.** Create a Pushpin map showing all your current customers. Add to the map a separate Pushpin set of addresses of potential customers from the lists that you're already using. You can create different drivetime zones from each of your store locations and visually make a judgment as to what zone best represents current customers. You can also use simpler radius objects to cover an area within n miles or kilometers of a point. Perform an Export to Excel command and send mailings only to the customers and prospects that fall within the desired zone.

✔ **Create freeform objects that incorporate domain knowledge.** Drivetime zones are calculated freeform drawing shapes based on minutes. You can use the MapPoint freeform tool to create zones based on other qualifiers. These may include political barriers such as county borders or just general knowledge you have about areas that you want or don't want to do business in. In some instances, you may want to identify non-administrative or political boundaries that cover a franchise area ending on one side of a freeway in one direction, or in the middle of a river in another direction. After you create these boundaries, you may want to save them as a template and import your customer and prospect lists and perform an Export to Excel command to target your audience.

✔ **Be proactive with requirements.** Create demographic or sales data maps by ZIP code and discover where you are most likely to get success. Use the Export to Excel command to export the data, sort it by priority, and provide it to your mass-mailing vendor and with instructions to target prospects only in those areas.

Intelligent Real Estate Sales

Location, Location, Location! Many home purchases are made by people moving into new neighborhoods, communities, or states. Using MapPoint as a tool can make a Realtor more efficient and improve the customer relationship tremendously. Use MapPoint to display available properties that meet the buyer's desires and overlay the map with demographics important to the buyer. You can perform a What's Nearby search to show neighboring restaurants, banks, schools, and public transportation locations, and plot recently sold properties including sales prices. Help homebuyers see routes they can take for places of work, leisure, school, and so on. For households with more than one wage earner, you can create two drivetime zones of equal times that overlap each other to some degree or that represent the wishes of the buyers. Plot the available properties that meet any other criteria they have or maybe drivetime zones for favorite shopping areas or cultural activities.

Creating a shaded area map that demonstrates the household income, education, or average ages by ZIP code or census tract can be very valuable in helping a homebuyer discover that a too-cheap-to-be-true house may really be too cheap to be true. Plotting out crime data is also a valuable benefit. Finally, map the real estate tax adjustment of a community and using this information as a foundation for a map of available houses can be quite revealing and valuable.

Police and Fire Departments

The use of maps by police forces and fire departments has been a very costly undertaking to date because of the cost and expertise involved with typical GIS solutions. Using MapPoint to map the locations of everything from different types of crimes to the locations of different types of automobile accidents or fires or hazardous or toxic waste sites can be very valuable. Mapping the sites of auto thefts and the sites where the cars are recovered can be very revealing. Adding to this map the home, work, and hang-out addresses of identified auto thieves can help solve problems. You can perform similar analyses with any type of criminal activity.

Another use of MapPoint is to create a shaped area map by ZIP code of violent crimes and to plot Pushpin sets of known criminals. For fire departments, plotting the location of historic fires or crime scenes and doing drivetime zones from fire or police stations can highlight holes in response-time coverage.

Store and Sales Representative Location Site Selection

The art of picking sites for stores or deciding where to geographically add a sales representative to your sales force can benefit from MapPoint analysis. Whether you're in the large retail coffee shop business or a thriving small business that plans to expand your online or mail-order business with new stores or local sales representatives, a map can guide your decision.

You can, for example, create Pushpin sets of customers and qualified prospects along with Pushpin sets of your current store locations and those of your competition. Create drivetime zones around your stores and look for opportunities in the gaps. Also, you may sometimes want your stores to be located as far away from the competition as possible but there are also types of business that will want to be close to the competition or possible other businesses that can feed your sales. Map out all your locations and those of the competition and feeder locations, and you might find that being close to your competitor has its advantages.

Customer Relationship Management

Customer Relationship Management (CRM) applications are being used by all sizes of companies today. Knowing where your customers are in the sales process and knowing where they are located go hand-in-hand. CRM systems come in all sizes. Larger companies may have complex layered systems in which smaller companies and individual sales representative use simpler applications such as ACT and GoldMine.

You can use MapPoint with CRM applications to export your customers and prospects import them onto a MapPoint map, and then use these locations to plan your sales visits. Also, you may want to export a snapshot of your customers and prospects, including any detailed sales history and pipeline or funnel stages in your sales process. Map your customers onto MapPoint using the multiple-symbol Pushpins, using up to eight different symbols to show the status of each customer in the sales process. Use this mapping to plan visits that are relativity close together when you need to close a number of deals prior to the end of a sales period.

Political Uses of MapPoint

Who in the world will forget the maps used to display the results of the 2000 U.S. presidential election? Maps have been used extensively for planning and reporting in politics for a very long time. Use MapPoint to create pushpin maps of the registered members of your party and use drivetime zones or drawing objects representing voting districts to perform an Export to Excel command for target marketing.

Another use is to create a map with MapPoint's demographics to better target the audiences that will best support your cause. Yet another idea is to create a shaded area map of the United States and color-code each state based on the number of votes won by each candidate. Spend two extra months in passionate debate all the way to the U.S. Supreme Court using the maps as evidence of vote fraud and mismanagement.

Sales and Territory Analysis

Understanding how successful you are in sales in relationship to the size and customer make-up of your territories can be very insightful. Balancing the number of accounts within like geographic coverages (such as same number of ZIP codes, counties, and so on) works sometimes but other times doesn't. Seeing territory size and layouts on a map and analyzing the information can help tune your sales force for higher performance.

You can use MapPoint to create sales territories and numerous data maps, such as shaded area maps for actual sales dollar volume, number of units sold, the percentage increase over last period, and projected growth in percent and actual dollars. You can include a layer of sized or shaded circles for each customer location showing specific numbers. A county may look very good at first, but you may find that all the sales are coming from one account! Another use for MapPoint is to recreate some of the maps with adjusted territory sizes. In some instances, it may be good to make things equal; in others, you may want to put your best sales person on key accounts.

Insurance Planning and Analysis

Insurance is a game of numbers and the geographic dimensions plays a big part in helping to manage the risk involved. MapPoint can benefit sales and adjustment agents and the folks who calculate the rates. For example, knowing how close a fire station is from a property can be very valuable. Knowing how long it takes to drive there is even more valuable. Another example is the strong correlation between car theft/vandalism and the demographic profile of areas. The same can be said for many other classifications of insurance. Flood insurance is obviously not all that valuable in a desert but it may be risky business in an area where claims have historically been high. You can map the history and see where the risk is located. Insurance companies are constantly monitored by the government and others to ensure they don't use racial profiling to discriminate against minorities. MapPoint can be used for compliance analysis and reporting

Asset Tracking

Knowing where your trucks, valuable equipment, or merchandise is at any point in time can help improve efficiency and minimize loss and theft. Many large companies have systems that allow them to track their assets in real time as they move around the map. Using MapPoint or the MapPoint ActiveX control to build an inexpensive viewer of this information can expand its availability to many others who need to know. Even being able to track and identify the historic locations of assets can be valuable. Mapping inventory at different sites at different points in time can help you plan. Add to this the calculations from upstream suppliers and customers and information about spoilage, theft, and other losses, and you may gain even more insight.

Appendix A

Installing MapPoint

• •

• •

*Y*ou may think that installing MapPoint would have little room for variation, but the MapPoint installation gives you a few valuable options that
are worth considering. It's important to look at MapPoint from a global perspective, remembering that MapPoint, unlike other Microsoft Office family
members, is more than just the application and some templates. With
MapPoint you have this one minor thing, namely the "world," that you need
to have around for the the application to work!

Likewise, if you're a system administrator and want to install MapPoint on
numerous PCs, you'll be pleased to know that MapPoint 2002 can also be
deployed within your enterprise over a network. Moving many copies of the
world around from PC to PC could be a real challenge.

You also need to give some consideration to the installation of Pocket Streets
on your PocketPC and the MapPoint ActiveX Control.

Installing MapPoint on Your PC or Laptop

Both the North American and the Europe versions of MapPoint 2002 come as
two CD sets. The two versions are sold separately but share all the same
installation features. The installation is simple, but you should first do a little
homework to help guide you through the journey.

Early in the installation process, you will be prompted to choose between a standard and a full install. Although not earth shattering, this decision effects where the Earth lives. In grade school, you were taught that Earth is the third planet from the sun — but in MapPoint terms, you can place it in one of three different locations.

The MapPoint map files are collectively known as the MAD files. MAD stands for Map Application Database, but rumor has it that it really stands for the state of mind of the original Microsoft programmer who invented the compression technology that crams the entire planet into relatively small files that fit on a CD. The MapPoint North America map files represent more than 65 gigabytes of spatial data compressed almost 100:1. When you use the application, the files never need to be permanently uncompressed, but even at their reduced size the weight of the world is not insignificant.

Standard install: Run it from the CD

If your computer has minimum hard drive space available, you will find the standard install appropriate. This choice spares you hard drive space to the tune of about 750 megabytes in the North American edition and around 650 megabytes in any of the European editions. Each time you use MapPoint, you need to make sure that you have the MapPoint "Run" CD in the CD drive. If you need to use both editions, keep both "Run" CDs handy. We consider this to be somewhat of a hassle, considering the descending price of CD drives and our difficulty in keeping track of CDs, but it just goes to show that you can travel the world on a budget if you need to.

Full install: I've got the whole world on my drive!

A full install is identical to the standard install except for the fact that the MapPoint maps files are copied over to your hard drive. In some instances, this fact may result in faster performance; in all instances, it eliminates the need to dig through your junk drawer for the precious key to the world.

Deploying MapPoint over a Network

Back in the days of MapPoint 2001, organizations that wanted to automatically deploy MapPoint as they were accustomed to doing with other Office family members found themselves at a dead-end. MapPoint 2002 has corrected this missing link.

If you are the controller of your domain, better known as a system administrator, you can now use standard command-line options or the Office Custom Installation Wizard to share the world with your team. Documentation for the Office Custom Installation Wizard is located in the online Microsoft Office Resource Kit that can be found at: `fhttp://msdn.microsoft.com/library/default.asp?url=/library/en-us/off2krk/html/45t2_2.asp`.

Before you deploy MapPoint over a network, you must have a licensed copy of MapPoint for every computer on which you want to run it.

To create an administrative installation location, follow these steps:

1. **Place the MapPoint Setup disc in your CD-ROM drive.**

2. **Open a command prompt window and enter the following:**

   `msiexec /a X:\msmap\data.msi`

   where *X* is your disc drive location.

   The Administrative Installation Wizard starts.

3. **Click Next.**

4. **Choose a network location for the administrative installation location, for example, `\\machine\share\MapPoint\`.**

5. **Follow the Administrative Installation Wizard on-screen instructions.**

   When you're finished creating the administrative installation location, users can install MapPoint either through an advertisement or by browsing to the location and double-clicking `setup.exe`.

After you create an administrative installation location, you can make MapPoint available through Advertising. Advertising is a Windows installer method for making a program available to the user without installing it. When the user attempts to use the program, the program is installed and run.

To make MapPoint available on the network through advertising, follow these steps:

1. **On a user's computer, open a command prompt window.**

2. **Type the following command:**

   `msiexec /jm \\machine\share\MapPoint\msmap\data.msi`

   where `\\machine\share\MapPoint` is the administrative installation location.

   A shortcut is placed on the user's Start menu. When the user clicks this shortcut, the MapPoint setup is launched automatically.

Installing the ActiveX Control

Every time you install MapPoint 2002, you automatically install the MapPoint ActiveX Control! This is really way too easy.

Of course, an IT department or a developer will sometimes want to create a unique installation that installs only the MapPoint ActiveX Control and intentionally disables the MapPoint user interface. This is a little trickier but not by much.

Start by making sure that each computer on which your application is installed has a full MapPoint license or a MapPoint runtime license; otherwise, your application's calls to MapPoint will fail. To install the ActiveX Control, follow these steps:

1. **Purchase runtime licenses for MapPoint for recipients of your application.**

2. **Create your application and compile it.**

3. **Create the Setup file for your compiled application, making sure that it calls the MapPoint** `setup.exe`.

4. **Copy all files, including subfolders, from the MapPoint Setup disc to a folder (*<New Folder>*) on your computer. You can leave the name of the folder *New Folder* or give the new folder a name that you will remember.**

5. **Delete the following files from *<New Folder>*:**

   - `autorun.inf`
   - `cd1run.exe`
   - `mp.ico`
   - `setup.ini`

6. **Rename the following files in *<New Folder>*:**

   - `readme.wri` to `mpcreadme.wri`
   - `setup.exe` to `mpcsetup.exe`

7. **Copy** `setup.ini` **from the Runtime folder to *<New Folder>*; then rename** `setup.ini` **to** `mpcsetup.ini`.

8. **Replace** `<New Folder>\MSMap\data.msi` **with the file of the same name from the Runtime folder.**

9. **Remove the following folders, along with the files and subfolders within them:**

   - Runtime
   - PStreets

10. **Copy your application Setup files to** *<New Folder>*, **including at least** `setup.exe`, `setup.1st`, **and your project's CAB file created by the Package and Deployment Wizard.**

11. **Copy any other application files, such as** `autorun.inf`, **icons, executable, data, or other utilities or files that you want to include.**

12. **Create your application installation disc (such as a CD or DVD) with** *<New Folder>* **as the root folder of the disc.**

    The root folder must include your application `setup.exe` and the MapPoint `mpcsetup.exe`.

13. **Distribute a copy of the MapPoint Run disc along with your installation disc, keeping the same volume name and file structure.**

    The MapPoint Run disc contains data that is necessary for installation or at runtime, depending on the installation option selected.

Pocket Streets

You can install Pocket Streets separately from MapPoint, as outlined in Chapter 13, but you can also automatically install it at the same time that you install MapPoint by checking the Install Pocket Streets check box in the MapPoint installation dialog box.

Appendix B

About the CDs

· ·

In This Appendix

▶ System requirements

▶ Using the CD with Windows

▶ What you'll find on the CD

▶ Troubleshooting

· ·

System Requirements

Make sure that your computer meets the minimum system requirements shown in the following list. If your computer doesn't match up to most of these requirements, you may have problems using the software and files on the CD. For the latest and greatest information, please refer to the ReadMe file located at the root of the CD-ROM.

- ✔ PC with a Pentium processor running at 133 Mhz or faster; Pentium III recommended

- ✔ At least 64 MB of RAM recommended; other applications running simultaneously may require additional memory

- ✔ 300 MB of available hard-disk space (910 MB for full configuration); Windows Me, or Office 2000 SR-1 or later require an extra 50 MB for System Files Update (hard-drive usage will vary depending on configuration)

- ✔ CD-ROM drive

- ✔ Super VGA (800 X 600) or higher-resolution monitor with 256 colors or higher

Additional items or services required to use certain features:

- ✔ 128 MB of RAM recommended for optimal Territories performance

- ✔ Visual Basic 6.0 or later required for MapPoint ActiveX Control

- ✔ Microsoft Exchange, Internet SMTP/POP3, IMAP4, or MAPI-compliant messaging software required to use e-mail

✔ GPS functionality requires a GPS device that supports NMEA 2.0 or later

✔ Some Internet functionality may require Internet access and payment of a separate fee to a service provider; local and/or long-distance telephone toll charges may apply

✔ 14,400 or higher-baud modem

✔ Microsoft ActiveSync(r) 3.1 required for installation of Pocket Streets

✔ Pocket Streets can be installed on Pocket PCs, Pam-sized PCs running Windows CE 2.11 or later, and HPCs running Windows CE 2.0 or later.

If you need more information on the basics, check out these books published by Hungry Minds, Inc.: *PCs For Dummies,* by Dan Gookin; *Macs For Dummies,* by David Pogue; *iMacs For Dummies* by David Pogue; *Windows 95 For Dummies, Windows 98 For Dummies, Windows 2000 Professional For Dummies, Microsoft Windows ME Millennium Edition For Dummies,* all by Andy Rathbone.

Using the CD with Microsoft Windows

1. **Insert CD1 (Setup) into your CD-ROM drive. Installation will automatically begin. If it does not, double-click My Computer and then double-click your CD-ROM drive icon. Choose setup.exe.**

2. **From the setup screen, click Next and follow the instructions.**

3. **Insert CD2 (Run) into your CD-ROM drive before launching the MapPoint 2002 Trial Program.**

4. **Click Start, click Programs, and then double-click MapPoint 2002 to launch the program. For an overview of the product and feature instructions, click MapPoint Tutorial on the Help menu.**

To edit copies of the code samples, you need to first move the appropriate folders and all the files contained within over to your hard drive.

1. **Insert CD 1 (Setup). Open the Code Samples folder. Open Windows Explorer, navigate to the code sample folder and copy the entire subfolder or subfolders that contain the samples you want to move onto your hard drive.**

2. **Files copied from a CD are attributed as read only. Before you start using them, you need to change their attribution to read-write. To do this, right click the folder that you have copied to your hard drive to display the Properties dialog box.**

3. **Uncheck the Read-only box at the bottom in the Attributes section.**

4. **Select the Apply Changes to the Folder, Subfolders and Files radio button and press OK.**

You can now open the sample code files in Visual Basic or open the Excel and Access files and make any desired changes.

What You'll Find on the CD

The CD-ROM contains source code examples and applications. Following is a summary of the contents of the CD-ROM arranged by category.

Samples

Every program in any listing in the book is on CD1 in subfolders contained in the folder named Samples.

Application

The following application is on the set of two CD-ROMs:

Microsoft® MapPoint 2002 Trial Version - 60-day Trial

Troubleshooting

If you have difficulty installing or using the CD-ROM programs, try the following solutions:

- ✓ **Turn off any anti-virus software that you may have running.** Installers sometimes mimic virus activity and can make your computer incorrectly believe that it is being infected by a virus. (Be sure to turn the anti-virus software back on later.)

- ✓ **Close all running programs.** The more programs you're running, the less memory is available to other programs. Installers also typically update files and programs; if you keep other programs running, installation may not work properly.

If you still have trouble with the CD, please call the Hungry Minds Customer Service phone number: (800) 762-2974. Outside the United States, call (317) 572-3994. Hungry Minds will provide technical support only for installation and other general quality control items; for technical support on the applications themselves, consult the program's vendor or author.

Index

Pushpin *(continued)*
balloon text, editing, 61–62
coloring, 116
creating, 13–14, 61
data set, 144
drawing by hand, 103–104
drivetime zones, creating, 94–96
enclosing set, 116
finding missing locations, 322
highlighting, 105
hyperlinks, 18, 62–63
manipulating, 64–65
Pocket Streets, 229, 233, 234–236
programming, 243, 244, 248
routes, basing on, 80
sets, 67–68
symbols, customizing, 17
symbols, designing, 68–70
uses, 61
Visual Basic control, 303
Pushpin Maps, 169, 178

• Q •

quality option, printing maps, 132
Query Analyzer
defined, 192
rows, selecting, 194–198
starting, 193–194
summarizing data, 198–201
views, creating, 201–203
Query Project, 287–299
querying, closed shapes with ActiveX
control, 287–299
quotation mark ('), 196

• R •

radius circles, 112–113, 292, 328
railroad tracks, 41
ranges
demographic, 181
values, selecting from database, 196, 198
real estate sales, 102, 329

rebate, MapPoint for Microsoft Office
users, 18
records, resolving incomplete, 145
Recordset object, 244, 291
Rectangle tool, 112
Redo button, 24, 27–28
relational database
accessing, 186–189
compatibility issues, 19
Data Mapping Wizard, using tables in,
173, 189–191
as data source, 142
linking versus importing, 185–186
Query Analyzer, 193–203
summarizing data, 191–192
renaming
Pushpin balloons, 64
territories, 159
reserves, legends, 42
reshaping drawings
Freeform tool, 118–119
Scribble tool, 118–119
rest stops, 87, 88–89, 92–93
restaurants. *See* Points of Interest (POIs)
Road and Data Map, 33–34
road construction, avoiding, 81–83
Road Map, 32–33
roads
distinguishing among, 41
object model, 243
route planning, 77–78
speed limits, default, 84
Route menu, 23
Route object, 243
route planning
ActiveX control, 280–283
avoiding areas, 74
benefits, 327–328
described, 16, 23
directions, deciphering, 74–75
drivetime zones, setting, 94–98
driving day, modifying average, 85–87
driving speeds, setting average, 83–84
fixed routes, 80–81
fuel settings, 91–93

Geographic Information Systems
(GIS), 314
Global Positioning System (GPS), 221–222
highlighting, 105–106
less expensive Microsoft software, 11
object model, 243
optimize route, 80, 81
point-to-point driving instructions, 71–74
printing, 129
road construction, avoiding, 81–83
road type, setting preference for, 77–78
shortest, 75–77
starting, 24
stops, 78–80, 88–91
rows, SQL Server
counting, 198
selecting, 192, 194–198
rural routes (RR), 320

• S •

sales
analyzing, 331–332
summarizing in database before
importing, 191–192
territories. *See* territories
tracking customers through process,
330–331
sales territories
adding geographical areas, 158
analyzing, 331–332
building manually, 154–157
button, 24
colors, changing appearance, 159–160
creating, 169
defined, 148
defining, 14, 17, 23, 330
deleting, 158–160
distances, setting appropriate. *See*
drivetime zones (DTZ)
generating automatically, 149–153
importing versus linking, 150
irreversibility, 28
mapping data source to, 144
marking, 14–15, 330
renaming, 159

Save button, 24, 27, 74
saved Web pages, viewing, 138
SavedWebPage object, 244
SaveMap method, 246
saving
maps as Web page, 135–138
maps with marked addresses, 53
planned routes, 74
scale, adding or removing from map, 25
scheduled stops, 89–90
Scribble tool
described, 107–108
enclosing pushpin sets, 116
reshaping drawings, 118–119
Search the Web button, 25
searches
Pushpins, 64
widening, 60
without address, 55–56
security, accessing database files, 187–189
Select statement
defined, 192
rows, choosing, 194–198
summarizing data, 198–201
views, creating, 201–203
Select tool, 126, 133, 228
SelectedArea object, 243
selecting which appear
choosing areas on map, 30
Points of Interest (POIs), 45–46
Series Column Chart Maps, 167–168
services, planning routes. *See* route
planning
sets, pushpins, 67–68
Shaded Area Maps
demographic data, 177
described, 162–163, 176
Shaded Circle Maps, 163, 164
SHAPE files, 315
Shape object, 243, 292
shapes
described, 111–112
enclosing, 116
moving, 117–118
querying data in enclosed, 287–299
set, 108–110

Notes